Statistical Tables
for Economic, Business and Social Studies

Second Edition

Z.W. Kmietowicz
and Y. Yannoulis

Longman
Scientific &
Technical

Copublished in the United States with
John Wiley & Sons, Inc., New York

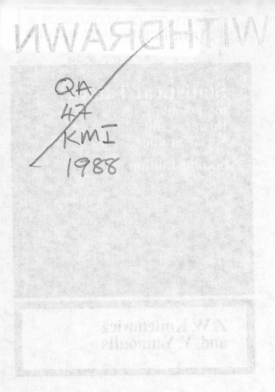

Longman Scientific & Technical,
Longman Group UK Limited,
Longman House, Burnt Mill, Harlow,
Essex CM20 2JE, England
and Associated Companies throughout the world.

This edition published 1988

This is a new edition based on the authors'
*Mathematical, Statistical and Financial Tables for the
Social Sciences*, which was first published in 1976.
(Translated into German 1982.)

British Library Cataloguing in Publication Data

Kmietowicz, Z. W.
  Statistical tables for economic, business
  and social studies.—2nd ed.
  1. Mathematics—Tables, etc.
  I. Title II. Yannoulis, Yannis
  510'.212   QA47

ISBN 0582 44070 X

Produced by Longman Singapore Publishers (Pte) Ltd.
Printed in Singapore.

Useful data

$e = 2.71828$; $e^2 = 7.38906$; $1/e = 0.36788$; $\sqrt{e} = 1.64872$

$\pi = 3.14159$; $\pi^2 = 9.8696$; $1/\pi = 0.31831$; $\sqrt{\pi} = 1.77245$

$\sqrt{10} = 3.16228$; $\sqrt[3]{10} = 2.15443$; $\sqrt[3]{100} = 4.64159$; $\sqrt{2} = 1.41473$

$\log_{10}e = 0.43429$; $\log_e 10 = 2.30259$; $\log_{10}\pi = 0.49715$; $\log_e\pi = 1.14473$; $\log_e x = \log_e 10 . \log_{10}x$; $\log_{10}x = \log_{10}e . \log_e x$; $\log_e 10 = 1/\log_{10}e$.

Area under Normal curve between: $\mu \pm \sigma = 0.68268$; $\mu \pm 2\sigma = 0.95450$; $\mu \pm 3\sigma = 0.99730$; $\mu \pm 1.6449\sigma = 0.9$; $\mu \pm 1.9600\sigma = 0.95$; $\mu \pm 2.5758\sigma = 0.99$.

Circle: $\pi = \dfrac{C}{D} = \dfrac{C}{2r}$ (r = radius; D = diameter; C = circumference), $C = D\pi = 2r\pi$.

Area of: square = l^2 (l = length of one side); rectangle = base × height; parallelogram = base × perpendicular height; triangle = $\frac{1}{2}$ base × height; circle = πr^2; sphere = $4\pi r^2$; curved surface of cylinder = $2\pi r b$ (b = height); trapezium = height × average length of parallel sides.

Volume of: cube = l^3; sphere = $\frac{4}{3}\pi r^3$; cylinder = $\pi r^2 b$; cone = $\frac{1}{3}\pi r^2 b$; pyramid = $\frac{1}{3}$ area of base × height.

Metric measures

Length

1000 micrometres	= 1 millimetre (mm)
10 millimetres	= 1 centimetre (cm)
10 centimetres	= 1 decimetre (dm)
10 decimetres	= 1 metre (m)
10 metres	= 1 decametre (dam)
10 decametres	= 1 hectometre (hm)
10 hectometres	= 1 kilometre (km)

Weight

1000 microgrammes	= 1 milligramme (mg)
10 milligrammes	= 1 centigramme (cg)
10 centigrammes	= 1 decigramme (dg)
10 decigrammes	= 1 gramme (g)
10 grammes	= 1 decagramme (dag)
10 decagrammes	= 1 hectogramme (hg)
10 hectogrammes	= 1 kilogramme (kg)
1000 kilogrammes	= 1 tonne

Volume and capacity

10 millilitres (ml)	= 1 centilitre (cl)
10 centilitres	= 1 decilitre (dl)
10 decilitres	= 1 litre (l)
10 litres	= 1 decalitre (dal)
10 decalitres	= 1 hectolitre (hl)
10 hectolitres	= 1 kilolitre (kl)

Area

1 are	= 100 square metres (m^2)
1 decare	= 10 ares
1 hectare	= 100 ares
1 deciare	= 1/10 of an are
1 centiare	= 1/100 of an are
	= 1 square metre (m^2)

Conversion (metric to British and British to metric)

Length

1 cm	=	0.39370 in
1 m	=	39.37011 in
	=	3.28084 ft
	=	1.09361 yd
1 km	=	0.62137 mile
1 in	=	2.54000 cm
1 yd	=	0.91440 m
1 mile	=	1.60934 km

Weight

1 g	=	0.03527 oz
1 kg	=	2.20462 lb
1 tonne	=	0.98421 ton
1 oz	=	28.34953 g
1 lb	=	0.45359 kg
1 ton	=	1.01605 tonne

Volume and capacity

1 cubic cm	= 0.06102 cubic in (in^3)
1 cubic m	= 1.30795 cubic yd (yd^3)
1 litre	= 1.75980 pints
	= 0.21998 gallon
1 cubic in	= 16.38702 cubic cm (cm^3)
1 cubic yd	= 0.76455 cubic m (m^3)
1 pint	= 0.56825 litre
1 gallon	= 4.54596 litres

Area

1 cm^2	= 0.15500 in^2
1 m^2	= 1.19599 yd^2
1 km^2	= 0.38610 m^2
1 hectare (ha)	= 2.47106 acres

1 in^2	= 6.45159 cm^2
1 yd^2	= 0.83613 m^2
1 m^2	2.58998 km^2
1 acre	= 0.40469 hectare (ha)

Basic data about
probability distributions

Distribution	$f(x)$	$\bar{x} = E(x) = \mu_1'$	$\sigma^2 = \mathrm{var}(x) = \mu_2$	Moment coefficient of skewness $(\mu_3/\mu_2^{3/2})$	Moment generating function
Discrete 1. Uniform	$\dfrac{1}{n}$ $x = k + b, k + 2b, \ldots k + nb$	$k + \tfrac{1}{2}b(n + 1)$	$\dfrac{1}{12} b^2(n^2 - 1)$	0	$\dfrac{e^{(k+b)t}(1 - e^{nbt})}{n(1 - e^{bt})}$
2. Binomial $(p + q = 1)$	${}^nC_x p^x q^{n-x}$ $x = 0, 1, 2, \ldots n$	np	npq	$(q - p)/\sqrt{npq}$	$(q + pe^t)^n$
3. Poisson	$e^{-m}\dfrac{m^x}{x!}$ $x = 0, 1, 2, \ldots$	m	m	$1/\sqrt{m}$	$\exp[m(e^t - 1)]$
4. Geometric $(p + q = 1)$	pq^{x-1} $x = 1, 2, 3, \ldots$	$\dfrac{1}{p}$	$\dfrac{q}{p^2}$	$\dfrac{1 + q}{\sqrt{q}}$	$\dfrac{pe^t}{1 - qe^t}$
5. Negative Binomial $(p + q = 1)$	${}^{r+x-1}C_x p^r q^x$ $x = 0, 1, 2, \ldots$	$\dfrac{rq}{p}$	$\dfrac{rq}{p^2}$	$\dfrac{1 + q}{\sqrt{rq}}$	$\left(\dfrac{p}{1 - qe^t}\right)^r$
Continuous 6. Rectangular (Uniform)	$\dfrac{1}{b - a}$ $a \leqslant x \leqslant b$	$\tfrac{1}{2}(a + b)$	$\dfrac{(b - a)^2}{12}$	0	$\dfrac{e^{bt} - e^{at}}{t(b - a)}$
7. Negative Exponential	$\theta e^{-\theta x}$ $x > 0$	$\dfrac{1}{\theta}$	$\dfrac{1}{\theta^2}$	2	$\dfrac{\theta}{\theta - t}$
8. Normal	$\dfrac{1}{\sigma\sqrt{2\pi}} \exp\left\{-\tfrac{1}{2}\left(\dfrac{x - \mu}{\sigma}\right)^2\right\}$ $-\infty < x < +\infty$	μ	σ^2	0	$\exp[\mu t + \tfrac{1}{2}\sigma^2 t^2]$
9. Gamma $\alpha > 0, \beta > 0$	$\dfrac{1}{\beta^\alpha \Gamma(\alpha)} x^{\alpha - 1} e^{-x/\beta}$ $x > 0$	$\alpha\beta$	$\alpha\beta^2$	$2/\sqrt{\alpha}$	$(1 - \beta t)^{-\alpha}$
10. χ^2 (Chi-squared)	$\dfrac{1}{2^{\nu/2}\Gamma\left(\frac{\nu}{2}\right)} x^{\left(\frac{\nu}{2} - 1\right)} e^{-x/2}$ $x > 0$	ν	2ν	$2\sqrt{\dfrac{2}{\nu}}$	$(1 - 2t)^{-\nu/2}$

Basic data about **probability distributions** – *continued*
Probability distributions not possessing a useful moment-generating function.

Distribution	$f(x)$	$\bar{x} = E(x) = \mu_1'$	$\sigma^2 = \mathrm{var}(x) = \mu_2$	Moment coefficient of skewness $(\mu_3/\mu_2^{3/2})$
Discrete 11. Hypergeometric $A = Np,\ B = Nq$ $N = A + B$	$\dfrac{^{Np}C_x\,^{Nq}C_{n-x}}{^{N}C_n}$ $x = 0, 1, 2, \ldots n$	np	$npq\left(\dfrac{N-n}{N-1}\right)$	$\dfrac{(q-p)(N-2n)\sqrt{N-1}}{(N-2)\sqrt{npq(N-n)}}$
Continuous 12. Pareto $\alpha > 0,\ \beta > 0$	$\alpha\beta^\alpha x^{-(\alpha+1)}$ $x > \beta$	$\dfrac{\alpha\beta}{\alpha-1}$	$\dfrac{\alpha\beta^2}{(\alpha-2)(\alpha-1)^2}$	$\dfrac{2(\alpha+1)\sqrt{\alpha-2}}{\sqrt{\alpha}(\alpha-3)}$
13. Lognormal	$\dfrac{1}{x\sigma\sqrt{2\pi}}\exp\left\{-\dfrac{1}{2\sigma^2}(\log_e x - \mu)^2\right\}$ $x > 0$	$e^{\mu + \frac{1}{2}\sigma^2}$	$e^{2\mu + \sigma^2}(e^{\sigma^2}-1)$	$(e^{3\sigma^2}-1)/(e^{\sigma^2}-1)^{3/2}$
14. Beta $\alpha > 0,\ \beta > 0$	$\dfrac{\Gamma(\alpha+\beta)}{\Gamma(\alpha)\Gamma(\beta)}x^{\alpha-1}(1-x)^{\beta-1}$ $0 < x < 1$	$\dfrac{\alpha}{\alpha+\beta}$	$\dfrac{\alpha\beta}{(\alpha+\beta)^2(\alpha+\beta+1)}$	$\dfrac{2(\beta-\alpha)\sqrt{\alpha+\beta+1}}{(\alpha+\beta+2)\sqrt{\alpha\beta}}$
15. t	$\dfrac{\Gamma\left(\dfrac{\nu+1}{2}\right)\left(1+\dfrac{x^2}{\nu}\right)^{-\left(\frac{\nu+1}{2}\right)}}{\sqrt{\nu\pi}\,\Gamma(\nu/2)}$ $-\infty < x < +\infty$	0	$\dfrac{\nu}{\nu-2}$ $\nu > 2$	0
16. F	$\dfrac{\Gamma\left(\dfrac{\nu_1+\nu_2}{2}\right)\nu_1^{\frac{\nu_1}{2}}\nu_2^{\frac{\nu_2}{2}}x^{\left(\frac{\nu_1-2}{2}\right)}}{\Gamma\left(\dfrac{\nu_1}{2}\right)\Gamma\left(\dfrac{\nu_2}{2}\right)(\nu_2+\nu_1 x)^{\left(\frac{\nu_1+\nu_2}{2}\right)}}$ $x > 0$	$\dfrac{\nu_2}{\nu_2-2}$ $\nu_2 > 2$	$\dfrac{2\nu_2^2(\nu_1+\nu_2-2)}{\nu_1(\nu_2-2)^2(\nu_2-4)}$ $\nu_2 > 4$	$\dfrac{2(2\nu_1+\nu_2-2)\sqrt{2(\nu_2-4)}}{(\nu_2-6)\sqrt{\nu_1(\nu_1+\nu_2-2)}}$ $\nu_2 > 6$

Contents

Acknowledgements

During the preparation of this publication we obtained assistance from a number of colleagues engaged in teaching quantitative methods to Social Science students and we would like to mention their contribution.

Our greatest debt is to D. Harkess, Research Officer, School of Economic Studies, University of Leeds, and to A. J. MacLeod, Research Officer, Department of Economics, Queen's University, Belfast, for invaluable help with computing problems arising from compilation of most of the tables presented in this booklet. We would also like to thank for their helpful comments and suggestions concerning the contents Professor C. E. V. Leser, A. D. Pearman, E. G. Drettakis, R. A. Hart, A. G. Witts, F. W. A. Zanker and D. G. Slattery (Economics), E. Graham (Business Studies), A. B. Royse (Sociology), J. Hartley (Education) and H. McAllister (Psychology). We also want to express our thanks to Professor D. F. Kerridge for permission to use his computer programs of the t and F distributions, and Professor K. V. Mardia and P. J. Zemroch for letting us use their computer program to obtain values of F-distribution for large numbers of degrees of freedom. Finally, we would like to thank the secretarial staff of our departments for their help with the preparation and typing of the manuscript, particularly Mrs M. M. Seddon, Mrs T. E. Brier, Mrs A. Williams and Mrs M. Gilmore.

Acknowledgements to the Second Edition
I should like to thank K. N. Field, B. P. M. McCabe, T. C. Mills, A. D. Pearman, A. G. Witts, D. M. Wood and F. W. A. Zanker (University of Leeds), Professor G. D. A. Phillips (University of Manchester) and M. J. Harrison (University of Dublin) for helpful comments and suggestions. My thanks are also due to Mrs P. Dix and R. Whitehead for computing assistance. My greatest debt is to Mrs P. Hatton who typed the manuscript and checked the tables.

Publisher's Acknowledgements to the Second Edition
We are grateful to the following for permission to reproduce copyright material:

American Cyanamid Co. for table 21 (Wilcoxon & Wilcox, adapted); American Statistical Association for tables 18 (Miller, adapted) & 24 (Kruskal & Wallis, adapted); American Psychological Association for part of table 19 (Goodman) copyright 1954 by the American Psychological Association; Biometrika Trustees for table 12 (Glasser & Winter); the author, R. W. Farebrother for table 15 (adapted); Institute of Educational Research for table 23 (Aube, adapted); Institute of Mathematical Statistics for part of table 19 (Massey), tables 20 (Swed & Eisenhart, adapted) & 22 (Mann & Whitney); the author, J. Koerts for table 14 (Koerts & Abrahamse); Unwin Hyman Ltd. for tables 30 & 31 (Neave).

Preface to the Second Edition

The aim of the new edition is to update the tables which appeared in 1976 and were reprinted three times. The second edition differs considerably from the first. Fifteen of the tables in this edition are new or extensively revised. A few have been dropped or amalgamated. As a result of these changes, the number of tables has increased from 33 to 40. The new accounting, quality control and decision-making tables should increase the usefulness of the publication for management and business studies. The new and revised tables of probability distributions, regression and correlation analysis, and non-parametric statistics should improve the attractiveness of the tables for all the social sciences.

The publication presents within one cover a set of statistical, accounting and logarithmic tables used most widely in the social sciences, i.e. economics, management, business studies, sociology, politics, psychology, geography and education. The tables which are usually scattered over a number of books and articles, and which are not always in the form required by the general user, are brought together here and presented in a convenient form.

The tables are primarily designed for teaching and research purposes in universities, polytechnics, colleges and schools, but social scientists working outside the field of education should find them equally useful for their professional work. They should be particularly valuable to students and teachers of quantitative methods in tutorials and classes, and are ideally suited for examination purposes as they provide all the tables likely to be needed.

Although it is assumed that users will be familiar with the tables, diagrams, explanatory notes and examples are provided to make reference easier.

The tables are arranged in three sections. Section 1, which constitutes the core of the publication, contains most frequently used statistical tables. They are grouped for convenience into four subsections. Subsection (a) presents basic probability distributions, and includes one new table, i.e. the Hypergeometric distribution. The tables of the χ^2 and F distributions are considerably extended. Subsection (b) contains tables needed for tests of significance in regression and correlation analysis. It includes two new tables: Significance of the rank correlation coefficient and the von Neumann ratio. The table of the Durbin–Watson d-statistic is replaced by a more accurate one. The tables in Subsection (c) are used in non-parametric tests. They include two new tables: Confidence intervals for the median and Number of runs test. The table used for the Sign test is replaced by a more accurate one. Subsection (d) contains miscellaneous statistical tables. It includes three new tables: Unit Normal loss integral, Control chart for the mean, and Control charts for the range and standard deviation.

Section 2 contains the basic accounting tables used in financial decision making and investment appraisal. It includes two new tables dealing with continuous compounding and continuous discounting.

Section 3 contains logarithmic tables.

Z. W. Kmietowicz.

Section 1

Statistical tables

(a) Probability distributions

Table 1. Binomial distribution

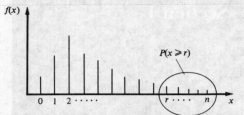

Cumulative probabilities in the right-hand tail, i.e. $P(x \geqslant r) = \sum_{x=r}^{n} {}^{n}C_x p^x (1-p)^{n-x}$, for different values of n, r and p.

Example: For $p = 0.2$ and $n = 5$, $P(x \geqslant 3) = 0.0579$, and $P(x = 3) = P(x \geqslant 3) - P(x \geqslant 4) = 0.0579 - 0.0067 = 0.0512$. If $p > 0.5$, $P(x \geqslant r) = 1 - P(x \geqslant n - r + 1)$ when p and $(1-p)$ are interchanged, e.g. for $p = 0.8$ and $n = 5$, $P(x \geqslant 2) = 1 - P(x \geqslant 5 - 2 + 1 = 4)$ when $p = 0.2$ and $n = 5$, i.e. $1 - 0.0067 = 0.9933$.

n	r	0.05	0.10	0.15	0.20	0.25	0.30	0.35	0.40	0.45	0.50
2	0	1.0000	1.0000	1.0000	1.0000	1.0000	1.0000	1.0000	1.0000	1.0000	1.0000
	1	0.0975	0.1900	0.2775	0.3600	0.4375	0.5100	0.5775	0.6400	0.6975	0.7500
	2	0.0025	0.0100	0.0225	0.0400	0.0625	0.0900	0.1225	0.1600	0.2025	0.2500
3	0	1.0000	1.0000	1.0000	1.0000	1.0000	1.0000	1.0000	1.0000	1.0000	1.0000
	1	0.1426	0.2710	0.3859	0.4880	0.5781	0.6570	0.7254	0.7840	0.8336	0.8750
	2	0.0073	0.0280	0.0608	0.1040	0.1562	0.2160	0.2818	0.3520	0.4253	0.5000
	3	0.0001	0.0010	0.0034	0.0080	0.0156	0.0270	0.0429	0.0640	0.0911	0.1250
4	0	1.0000	1.0000	1.0000	1.0000	1.0000	1.0000	1.0000	1.0000	1.0000	1.0000
	1	0.1855	0.3439	0.4780	0.5904	0.6836	0.7599	0.8215	0.8704	0.9085	0.9375
	2	0.0140	0.0523	0.1095	0.1808	0.2617	0.3483	0.4370	0.5248	0.6090	0.6875
	3	0.0005	0.0037	0.0120	0.0272	0.0508	0.0837	0.1265	0.1792	0.2415	0.3125
	4		0.0001	0.0005	0.0016	0.0039	0.0081	0.0150	0.0256	0.0410	0.0625
5	0	1.0000	1.0000	1.0000	1.0000	1.0000	1.0000	1.0000	1.0000	1.0000	1.0000
	1	0.2262	0.4095	0.5563	0.6723	0.7627	0.8319	0.8840	0.9222	0.9497	0.9688
	2	0.0226	0.0815	0.1648	0.2627	0.3672	0.4718	0.5716	0.6630	0.7438	0.8125
	3	0.0012	0.0086	0.0266	0.0579	0.1035	0.1631	0.2352	0.3174	0.4069	0.5000
	4		0.0005	0.0022	0.0067	0.0156	0.0308	0.0540	0.0870	0.1312	0.1875
	5			0.0001	0.0003	0.0010	0.0024	0.0053	0.0102	0.0185	0.0313
6	0	1.0000	1.0000	1.0000	1.0000	1.0000	1.0000	1.0000	1.0000	1.0000	1.0000
	1	0.2649	0.4686	0.6229	0.7379	0.8220	0.8824	0.9246	0.9533	0.9723	0.9844
	2	0.0328	0.1143	0.2235	0.3446	0.4661	0.5798	0.6809	0.7667	0.8364	0.8906
	3	0.0022	0.0159	0.0473	0.0989	0.1694	0.2557	0.3529	0.4557	0.5585	0.6563
	4	0.0001	0.0013	0.0059	0.0170	0.0376	0.0705	0.1174	0.1792	0.2553	0.3438
	5		0.0001	0.0004	0.0016	0.0046	0.0109	0.0223	0.0410	0.0692	0.1094
	6				0.0001	0.0002	0.0007	0.0018	0.0041	0.0083	0.0156
7	0	1.0000	1.0000	1.0000	1.0000	1.0000	1.0000	1.0000	1.0000	1.0000	1.0000
	1	0.3017	0.5217	0.6794	0.7903	0.8665	0.9176	0.9510	0.9720	0.9848	0.9922
	2	0.0444	0.1497	0.2834	0.4233	0.5551	0.6706	0.7662	0.8414	0.8976	0.9375
	3	0.0038	0.0257	0.0738	0.1480	0.2436	0.3529	0.4677	0.5801	0.6836	0.7734
	4	0.0002	0.0027	0.0121	0.0333	0.0706	0.1260	0.1998	0.2898	0.3917	0.5000
	5		0.0002	0.0012	0.0047	0.0129	0.0288	0.0556	0.0963	0.1529	0.2266
	6			0.0001	0.0004	0.0013	0.0038	0.0090	0.0188	0.0357	0.0625
	7					0.0001	0.0002	0.0006	0.0016	0.0037	0.0078
8	0	1.0000	1.0000	1.0000	1.0000	1.0000	1.0000	1.0000	1.0000	1.0000	1.0000
	1	0.3366	0.5695	0.7275	0.8322	0.8999	0.9424	0.9681	0.9832	0.9916	0.9961
	2	0.0572	0.1869	0.3428	0.4967	0.6329	0.7447	0.8309	0.8936	0.9368	0.9648
	3	0.0058	0.0381	0.1052	0.2031	0.3215	0.4482	0.5722	0.6846	0.7799	0.8555
	4	0.0004	0.0050	0.0214	0.0563	0.1138	0.1941	0.2936	0.4059	0.5230	0.6367
	5		0.0004	0.0029	0.0104	0.0273	0.0580	0.1061	0.1737	0.2604	0.3633
	6			0.0002	0.0012	0.0042	0.0113	0.0253	0.0498	0.0885	0.1445
	7				0.0001	0.0004	0.0013	0.0036	0.0085	0.0181	0.0352
	8						0.0001	0.0002	0.0007	0.0017	0.0039

Table 1 – *continued*

n	r	0.05	0.10	0.15	0.20	0.25	0.30	0.35	0.40	0.45	0.50
9	0	1.0000	1.0000	1.0000	1.0000	1.0000	1.0000	1.0000	1.0000	1.0000	1.0000
	1	0.3698	0.6126	0.7684	0.8658	0.9249	0.9596	0.9793	0.9899	0.9954	0.9980
	2	0.0712	0.2252	0.4005	0.5638	0.6997	0.8040	0.8789	0.9295	0.9615	0.9805
	3	0.0084	0.0530	0.1409	0.2618	0.3993	0.5372	0.6627	0.7682	0.8505	0.9102
	4	0.0006	0.0083	0.0339	0.0856	0.1657	0.2703	0.3911	0.5174	0.6386	0.7461
	5		0.0009	0.0056	0.0196	0.0489	0.0988	0.1717	0.2666	0.3786	0.5000
	6		0.0001	0.0006	0.0031	0.0100	0.0253	0.0536	0.0994	0.1658	0.2539
	7				0.0003	0.0013	0.0043	0.0112	0.0250	0.0498	0.0898
	8					0.0001	0.0004	0.0014	0.0038	0.0091	0.0195
	9							0.0001	0.0003	0.0008	0.0020
10	0	1.0000	1.0000	1.0000	1.0000	1.0000	1.0000	1.0000	1.0000	1.0000	1.0000
	1	0.4013	0.6513	0.8031	0.8926	0.9437	0.9718	0.9865	0.9940	0.9975	0.9990
	2	0.0861	0.2639	0.4557	0.6242	0.7560	0.8507	0.9140	0.9536	0.9767	0.9893
	3	0.0115	0.0702	0.1798	0.3222	0.4744	0.6172	0.7384	0.8327	0.9004	0.9453
	4	0.0010	0.0128	0.0500	0.1209	0.2241	0.3504	0.4862	0.6177	0.7340	0.8281
	5	0.0001	0.0016	0.0099	0.0328	0.0781	0.1503	0.2485	0.3669	0.4956	0.6230
	6		0.0001	0.0014	0.0064	0.0197	0.0473	0.0949	0.1662	0.2616	0.3770
	7			0.0001	0.0009	0.0035	0.0106	0.0260	0.0548	0.1020	0.1719
	8				0.0001	0.0004	0.0016	0.0048	0.0123	0.0274	0.0547
	9						0.0001	0.0005	0.0017	0.0045	0.0107
	10								0.0001	0.0003	0.0010
12	0	1.0000	1.0000	1.0000	1.0000	1.0000	1.0000	1.0000	1.0000	1.0000	1.0000
	1	0.4596	0.7176	0.8578	0.9313	0.9683	0.9862	0.9943	0.9978	0.9992	0.9998
	2	0.1184	0.3410	0.5565	0.7251	0.8416	0.9150	0.9576	0.9804	0.9917	0.9968
	3	0.0196	0.1109	0.2642	0.4417	0.6093	0.7472	0.8487	0.9166	0.9579	0.9807
	4	0.0022	0.0256	0.0922	0.2054	0.3512	0.5075	0.6533	0.7747	0.8655	0.9270
	5	0.0002	0.0043	0.0239	0.0726	0.1576	0.2763	0.4167	0.5618	0.6956	0.8062
	6		0.0005	0.0046	0.0194	0.0544	0.1178	0.2127	0.3348	0.4731	0.6128
	7		0.0001	0.0007	0.0039	0.0143	0.0386	0.0846	0.1582	0.2607	0.3872
	8			0.0001	0.0006	0.0028	0.0095	0.0255	0.0573	0.1117	0.1938
	9				0.0001	0.0004	0.0017	0.0056	0.0153	0.0356	0.0730
	10						0.0002	0.0008	0.0028	0.0079	0.0193
	11							0.0001	0.0003	0.0011	0.0032
	12									0.0001	0.0002
14	0	1.0000	1.0000	1.0000	1.0000	1.0000	1.0000	1.0000	1.0000	1.0000	1.0000
	1	0.5123	0.7712	0.8972	0.9560	0.9822	0.9932	0.9976	0.9992	0.9998	0.9999
	2	0.1530	0.4154	0.6433	0.8021	0.8990	0.9525	0.9795	0.9919	0.9971	0.9991
	3	0.0301	0.1584	0.3521	0.5519	0.7189	0.8392	0.9161	0.9602	0.9830	0.9935
	4	0.0042	0.0441	0.1465	0.3018	0.4787	0.6448	0.7795	0.8757	0.9368	0.9713
	5	0.0004	0.0092	0.0467	0.1298	0.2585	0.4158	0.5773	0.7207	0.8328	0.9102
	6		0.0015	0.0115	0.0439	0.1117	0.2195	0.3595	0.5141	0.6627	0.7880
	7		0.0002	0.0022	0.0116	0.0383	0.0933	0.1836	0.3075	0.4539	0.6047
	8			0.0003	0.0024	0.0103	0.0315	0.0753	0.1501	0.2586	0.3953
	9				0.0004	0.0022	0.0083	0.0243	0.0583	0.1189	0.2120
	10					0.0003	0.0017	0.0060	0.0175	0.0426	0.0898
	11						0.0002	0.0011	0.0039	0.0114	0.0287
	12							0.0001	0.0006	0.0022	0.0065
	13								0.0001	0.0003	0.0009
	14										0.0001

Table 1 – *continued*

n	r	0.05	0.10	0.15	0.20	0.25	0.30	0.35	0.40	0.45	0.50
16	0	1.0000	1.0000	1.0000	1.0000	1.0000	1.0000	1.0000	1.0000	1.0000	1.0000
	1	0.5599	0.8147	0.9257	0.9719	0.9900	0.9967	0.9990	0.9997	0.9999	1.0000
	2	0.1892	0.4853	0.7161	0.8593	0.9365	0.9739	0.9902	0.9967	0.9990	0.9997
	3	0.0429	0.2108	0.4386	0.6482	0.8029	0.9006	0.9549	0.9817	0.9934	0.9979
	4	0.0070	0.0684	0.2101	0.4019	0.5950	0.7541	0.8661	0.9349	0.9719	0.9894
	5	0.0009	0.0170	0.0791	0.2018	0.3698	0.5501	0.7108	0.8334	0.9147	0.9616
	6	0.0001	0.0033	0.0235	0.0817	0.1897	0.3402	0.5100	0.6712	0.8024	0.8949
	7		0.0005	0.0056	0.0267	0.0796	0.1753	0.3119	0.4738	0.6340	0.7728
	8		0.0001	0.0011	0.0070	0.0271	0.0744	0.1594	0.2839	0.4371	0.5982
	9			0.0002	0.0015	0.0075	0.0257	0.0671	0.1423	0.2559	0.4018
	10				0.0002	0.0016	0.0071	0.0229	0.0583	0.1241	0.2272
	11					0.0003	0.0016	0.0062	0.0191	0.0486	0.1051
	12						0.0003	0.0013	0.0049	0.0149	0.0384
	13							0.0002	0.0009	0.0035	0.0106
	14								0.0001	0.0006	0.0021
	15									0.0001	0.0003
18	0	1.0000	1.0000	1.0000	1.0000	1.0000	1.0000	1.0000	1.0000	1.0000	1.0000
	1	0.6028	0.8499	0.9464	0.9820	0.9944	0.9984	0.9996	0.9999	1.0000	1.0000
	2	0.2265	0.5497	0.7759	0.9009	0.9605	0.9858	0.9954	0.9987	0.9997	0.9999
	3	0.0581	0.2662	0.5203	0.7287	0.8647	0.9400	0.9764	0.9918	0.9975	0.9993
	4	0.0109	0.0982	0.2798	0.4990	0.6943	0.8354	0.9217	0.9672	0.9880	0.9962
	5	0.0015	0.0282	0.1206	0.2836	0.4813	0.6673	0.8114	0.9058	0.9589	0.9846
	6	0.0002	0.0064	0.0419	0.1329	0.2825	0.4656	0.6450	0.7912	0.8923	0.9519
	7		0.0012	0.0118	0.0513	0.1390	0.2783	0.4509	0.6257	0.7742	0.8811
	8		0.0002	0.0027	0.0163	0.0569	0.1407	0.2717	0.4366	0.6085	0.7597
	9			0.0005	0.0043	0.0193	0.0596	0.1391	0.2632	0.4222	0.5927
	10			0.0001	0.0009	0.0054	0.0210	0.0597	0.1347	0.2527	0.4073
	11				0.0002	0.0012	0.0061	0.0212	0.0576	0.1280	0.2403
	12					0.0002	0.0014	0.0062	0.0203	0.0537	0.1189
	13						0.0003	0.0014	0.0058	0.0183	0.0481
	14							0.0003	0.0013	0.0049	0.0154
	15								0.0002	0.0010	0.0038
	16									0.0001	0.0007
	17										0.0001
20	0	1.0000	1.0000	1.0000	1.0000	1.0000	1.0000	1.0000	1.0000	1.0000	1.0000
	1	0.6415	0.8784	0.9612	0.9885	0.9968	0.9992	0.9998	1.0000	1.0000	1.0000
	2	0.2642	0.6083	0.8244	0.9308	0.9757	0.9924	0.9979	0.9995	0.9999	1.0000
	3	0.0755	0.3231	0.5951	0.7939	0.9087	0.9645	0.9879	0.9964	0.9991	0.9998
	4	0.0159	0.1330	0.3523	0.5886	0.7748	0.8929	0.9556	0.9840	0.9951	0.9987
	5	0.0026	0.0432	0.1702	0.3704	0.5852	0.7625	0.8818	0.9490	0.9811	0.9941
	6	0.0003	0.0113	0.0673	0.1958	0.3828	0.5836	0.7546	0.8744	0.9447	0.9793
	7		0.0024	0.0219	0.0867	0.2142	0.3920	0.5834	0.7500	0.8701	0.9423
	8		0.0004	0.0059	0.0321	0.1018	0.2277	0.3990	0.5841	0.7480	0.8684
	9		0.0001	0.0013	0.0100	0.0409	0.1133	0.2376	0.4044	0.5857	0.7483
	10			0.0002	0.0026	0.0139	0.0480	0.1218	0.2447	0.4086	0.5881
	11				0.0006	0.0039	0.0171	0.0532	0.1275	0.2493	0.4119
	12				0.0001	0.0009	0.0051	0.0196	0.0565	0.1308	0.2517
	13					0.0002	0.0013	0.0060	0.0210	0.0580	0.1316
	14						0.0003	0.0015	0.0065	0.0214	0.0577
	15							0.0003	0.0016	0.0064	0.0207
	16								0.0003	0.0015	0.0059
	17									0.0003	0.0013
	18										0.0002

Approximation: 1. When $p < 0.1$, use the Poisson distribution with $m = np$ (see Table 2).

2. Where $0.1 \leqslant p \leqslant 0.9$ and $np > 5$, use Normal distribution with $\mu = np$ and $\sigma = \sqrt{np(1-p)}$ (see Table 5).

4

Table 2. Poisson distribution

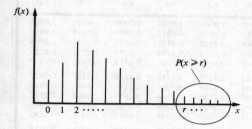

Cumulative probabilities in the right-hand tail, i.e. $P(x \geqslant r) = \sum_{x=r}^{\infty} e^{-m} \frac{m^x}{x!}$, for different values of m and r. **Example:** For m (mean) $= 2$, $P(x \geqslant r = 3) = 0.3233$ and $P(x = 3) = P(x \geqslant 3) - P(x \geqslant 4) = 0.3233 - 0.1429 = 0.1804$.

r \ m	0.1	0.2	0.3	0.4	0.5	0.6	0.7	0.8	0.9	1.0
0	1.0000	1.0000	1.0000	1.0000	1.0000	1.0000	1.0000	1.0000	1.0000	1.0000
1	0.0952	0.1813	0.2592	0.3297	0.3935	0.4512	0.5034	0.5507	0.5934	0.6321
2	0.0047	0.0175	0.0369	0.0616	0.0902	0.1219	0.1558	0.1912	0.2275	0.2642
3	0.0002	0.0011	0.0036	0.0079	0.0144	0.0231	0.0341	0.0474	0.0629	0.0803
4		0.0001	0.0003	0.0008	0.0018	0.0034	0.0058	0.0091	0.0135	0.0190
5				0.0001	0.0002	0.0004	0.0008	0.0014	0.0023	0.0037
6							0.0001	0.0002	0.0003	0.0006
7										0.0001

r \ m	1.1	1.2	1.3	1.4	1.5	1.6	1.7	1.8	1.9	2.0
0	1.0000	1.0000	1.0000	1.0000	1.0000	1.0000	1.0000	1.0000	1.0000	1.0000
1	0.6671	0.6988	0.7275	0.7534	0.7769	0.7981	0.8173	0.8347	0.8504	0.8647
2	0.3010	0.3374	0.3732	0.4082	0.4422	0.4751	0.5068	0.5372	0.5663	0.5940
3	0.0996	0.1205	0.1249	0.1665	0.1912	0.2166	0.2428	0.2694	0.2963	0.3233
4	0.0257	0.0338	0.0431	0.0537	0.0656	0.0788	0.0932	0.1087	0.1253	0.1429
5	0.0054	0.0077	0.0107	0.0143	0.0186	0.0237	0.0296	0.0364	0.0441	0.0527
6	0.0010	0.0015	0.0022	0.0032	0.0045	0.0060	0.0080	0.0104	0.0132	0.0166
7	0.0001	0.0003	0.0004	0.0006	0.0009	0.0013	0.0019	0.0026	0.0034	0.0045
8			0.0001	0.0001	0.0002	0.0003	0.0004	0.0006	0.0008	0.0011
9							0.0001	0.0001	0.0002	0.0002

r \ m	2.1	2.2	2.3	2.4	2.5	2.6	2.7	2.8	2.9	3.0
0	1.0000	1.0000	1.0000	1.0000	1.0000	1.0000	1.0000	1.0000	1.0000	1.0000
1	0.8775	0.8892	0.8997	0.9093	0.9179	0.9257	0.9328	0.9392	0.9450	0.9502
2	0.6204	0.6454	0.6691	0.6916	0.7127	0.7326	0.7513	0.7689	0.7854	0.8009
3	0.3504	0.3773	0.4040	0.4303	0.4562	0.4816	0.5064	0.5305	0.5540	0.5768
4	0.1614	0.1806	0.2007	0.2213	0.2424	0.2640	0.2859	0.3081	0.3304	0.3528
5	0.0621	0.0725	0.0838	0.0959	0.1088	0.1226	0.1371	0.1523	0.1682	0.1847
6	0.0204	0.0249	0.0300	0.0357	0.0420	0.0490	0.0567	0.0651	0.0742	0.0839
7	0.0059	0.0075	0.0094	0.0116	0.0142	0.0172	0.0206	0.0244	0.0287	0.0335
8	0.0015	0.0020	0.0026	0.0033	0.0042	0.0053	0.0066	0.0081	0.0099	0.0119
9	0.0003	0.0005	0.0006	0.0009	0.0011	0.0015	0.0019	0.0024	0.0031	0.0038
10	0.0001	0.0001	0.0001	0.0002	0.0003	0.0004	0.0005	0.0007	0.0009	0.0011
11					0.0001	0.0001	0.0001	0.0002	0.0003	0.0003
12									0.0001	0.0001

Table 2 – *continued*

r \ m	3.2	3.4	3.6	3.8	4.0	4.2	4.4	4.6	4.8	5.0
0	1.0000	1.0000	1.0000	1.0000	1.0000	1.0000	1.0000	1.0000	1.0000	1.0000
1	0.9592	0.9666	0.9727	0.9776	0.9817	0.9850	0.9877	0.9899	0.9918	0.9933
2	0.8288	0.8532	0.8743	0.8926	0.9084	0.9220	0.9337	0.9437	0.9523	0.9596
3	0.6201	0.6603	0.6973	0.7311	0.7619	0.7898	0.8149	0.8374	0.8575	0.8753
4	0.3975	0.4416	0.4848	0.5265	0.5665	0.6046	0.6406	0.6743	0.7058	0.7350
5	0.2194	0.2558	0.2936	0.3322	0.3712	0.4102	0.4488	0.4868	0.5237	0.5595
6	0.1054	0.1295	0.1559	0.1844	0.2149	0.2469	0.2801	0.3142	0.3490	0.3840
7	0.0446	0.0579	0.0733	0.0909	0.1107	0.1325	0.1564	0.1820	0.2092	0.2378
8	0.0168	0.0231	0.0308	0.0401	0.0511	0.0639	0.0786	0.0951	0.1133	0.1334
9	0.0057	0.0083	0.0117	0.0160	0.0214	0.0279	0.0358	0.0451	0.0558	0.0681
10	0.0018	0.0027	0.0040	0.0058	0.0081	0.0111	0.0149	0.0195	0.0251	0.0318
11	0.0005	0.0008	0.0013	0.0019	0.0028	0.0041	0.0057	0.0078	0.0104	0.0137
12	0.0001	0.0002	0.0004	0.0006	0.0009	0.0014	0.0020	0.0029	0.0040	0.0055
13		0.0001	0.0001	0.0002	0.0003	0.0004	0.0007	0.0010	0.0014	0.0020
14					0.0001	0.0001	0.0002	0.0003	0.0005	0.0007
15							0.0001	0.0001	0.0001	0.0002
16										0.0001

r \ m	5.5	6.0	6.5	7.0	7.5	8.0	8.5	9.0	9.5	10.0
0	1.0000	1.0000	1.0000	1.0000	1.0000	1.0000	1.0000	1.0000	1.0000	1.0000
1	0.9959	0.9975	0.9985	0.9991	0.9994	0.9997	0.9998	0.9999	0.9999	1.0000
2	0.9734	0.9826	0.9887	0.9927	0.9953	0.9970	0.9981	0.9988	0.9992	0.9995
3	0.9116	0.9380	0.9570	0.9704	0.9797	0.9862	0.9907	0.9938	0.9958	0.9972
4	0.7983	0.8488	0.8882	0.9182	0.9409	0.9576	0.9699	0.9788	0.9851	0.9897
5	0.6425	0.7149	0.7763	0.8270	0.8679	0.9004	0.9256	0.9450	0.9597	0.9707
6	0.4711	0.5543	0.6310	0.6993	0.7586	0.8088	0.8504	0.8843	0.9115	0.9329
7	0.3140	0.3937	0.4735	0.5503	0.6218	0.6866	0.7438	0.7932	0.8351	0.8699
8	0.1905	0.2560	0.3272	0.4013	0.4754	0.5470	0.6144	0.6761	0.7313	0.7798
9	0.1056	0.1528	0.2084	0.2709	0.3380	0.4075	0.4769	0.5443	0.6082	0.6672
10	0.0538	0.0839	0.1226	0.1695	0.2236	0.2834	0.3470	0.4126	0.4782	0.5421
11	0.0253	0.0426	0.0668	0.0985	0.1378	0.1841	0.2366	0.2940	0.3547	0.4170
12	0.0110	0.0201	0.0339	0.0533	0.0792	0.1119	0.1513	0.1970	0.2480	0.3032
13	0.0045	0.0088	0.0160	0.0270	0.0427	0.0638	0.0909	0.1242	0.1636	0.2084
14	0.0017	0.0036	0.0071	0.0128	0.0216	0.0342	0.0514	0.0739	0.1019	0.1355
15	0.0006	0.0014	0.0030	0.0057	0.0103	0.0173	0.0274	0.0415	0.0600	0.0835
16	0.0002	0.0005	0.0012	0.0024	0.0046	0.0082	0.0138	0.0220	0.0335	0.0487
17	0.0001	0.0002	0.0004	0.0010	0.0020	0.0037	0.0066	0.0111	0.0177	0.0270
18		0.0001	0.0002	0.0004	0.0008	0.0016	0.0030	0.0053	0.0089	0.0143
19			0.0001	0.0001	0.0003	0.0007	0.0013	0.0024	0.0043	0.0072
20					0.0001	0.0003	0.0005	0.0011	0.0020	0.0035
21						0.0001	0.0002	0.0004	0.0009	0.0016
22							0.0001	0.0002	0.0004	0.0007
23								0.0001	0.0001	0.0003
24									0.0001	0.0001

Table 3. Hypergeometric distribution

Values of $f(X) = \binom{A}{X}\binom{N-A}{n-X} \Big/ \binom{N}{n}$ for different combinations of N, A and n. **Example:** For $N = 10$, $A = 5$ and $n = 4$, $f(X = 3) = 0.2381$. For values of A and n not given, $f(X)$ may be found using the relations: $f(N, A, n, X) = f(N, n, A, X) = f(N, N - A, n, n - X)$. **Example:** $f(10, 5, 7, 3) = f(10, 7, 5, 3) = f(10, 3, 5, 2) = f(10, 5, 3, 2) = 0.4167$. Due to rounding, sometimes probabilities do not sum to one.

N	A	n	X	f(X)	N	A	n	X	f(X)	N	A	n	X	f(X)	N	A	n	X	f(X)
2	1	1	0	.5000	7	3	3	0	.1143	9	3	3	0	.2381	10	4	4	3	.1143
			1	.5000				1	.5143				1	.5357				4	.0048
3	1	1	0	.6667				2	.3429				2	.2143	10	5	1	0	.5000
			1	.3333				3	.0286				3	.0119				1	.5000
4	1	1	0	.7500	8	1	1	0	.8750	9	4	1	0	.5556	10	5	2	0	.2222
			1	.2500				1	.1250				1	.4444				1	.5556
4	2	1	0	.5000	8	2	1	0	.7500	9	4	2	0	.2778				2	.2222
			1	.5000				1	.2500				1	.5555	10	5	3	0	.0833
4	2	2	0	.1667	8	2	2	0	.5357				2	.1667				1	.4167
			1	.6667				1	.4286	9	4	3	0	.1190				2	.4167
			2	.1667				2	.0357				1	.4762				3	.0833
5	1	1	0	.8000	8	3	1	0	.6250				2	.3571	10	5	4	0	.0238
			1	.2000				1	.3750				3	.0476				1	.2381
5	2	1	0	.6000	8	3	2	0	.3571	9	4	4	0	.0397				2	.4762
			1	.4000				1	.5357				1	.3175				3	.2381
5	2	2	0	.3000				2	.1071				2	.4762				4	.0238
			1	.6000	8	3	3	0	.1786				3	.1587	10	5	5	0	.0040
			2	.1000				1	.5357				4	.0079				1	.0992
6	1	1	0	.8333				2	.2679	10	1	1	0	.9000				2	.3968
			1	.1667				3	.0179				1	.1000				3	.3968
6	2	1	0	.6667	8	4	1	0	.5000	10	2	1	0	.8000				4	.0992
			1	.3333				1	.5000				1	.2000				5	.0040
6	2	2	0	.4000	8	4	2	0	.2143	10	2	2	0	.6222	11	1	1	0	.9091
			1	.5333				1	.5714				1	.3556				1	.0909
			2	.0667				2	.2143				2	.0222	11	2	1	0	.8182
6	3	1	0	.5000	8	4	3	0	.0714	10	3	1	0	.7000				1	.1818
			1	.5000				1	.4286				1	.3000	11	2	2	0	.6545
6	3	2	0	.2000				2	.4286	10	3	2	0	.4667				1	.3273
			1	.6000				3	.0714				1	.4667				2	.0182
			2	.2000	8	4	4	0	.0143				2	.0667	11	3	1	0	.7273
6	3	3	0	.0500				1	.2286	10	3	3	0	.2917				1	.2727
			1	.4500				2	.5143				1	.5250	11	3	2	0	.5091
			2	.4500				3	.2286				2	.1750				1	.4364
			3	.0500				4	.0143				3	.0083				2	.0545
7	1	1	0	.8571	9	1	1	0	.8889	10	4	1	0	.6000	11	3	3	0	.3394
			1	.1429				1	.1111				1	.4000				1	.5091
7	2	1	0	.7143	9	2	1	0	.7778	10	4	2	0	.3333				2	.1455
			1	.2857				1	.2222				1	.5333				3	.0061
7	2	2	0	.4762	9	2	2	0	.5833				2	.1333	11	4	1	0	.6364
			1	.4762				1	.3889	10	4	3	0	.1667				1	.3636
			2	.0476				2	.0278				1	.5000	11	4	2	0	.3818
7	3	1	0	.5714	9	3	1	0	.6667				2	.3000				1	.5091
			1	.4286				1	.3333				3	.0333				2	.1091
7	3	2	0	.2857	9	3	2	0	.4167	10	4	4	0	.0714	11	4	3	0	.2121
			1	.5714				1	.5000				1	.3810				1	.5091
			2	.1429				2	.0833				2	.4286				2	.2545

Table 3 – *continued*

N	A	n	X	f(X)
11	4	3	3	.0242
11	4	4	0	.1061
			1	.4242
			2	.3818
			3	.0848
			4	.0030
11	5	1	0	.5455
			1	.4545
11	5	2	0	.2727
			1	.5455
			2	.1818
11	5	3	0	.1212
			1	.4545
			2	.3636
			3	.0606
11	5	4	0	.0455
			1	.3030
			2	.4545
			3	.1818
			4	.0152
11	5	5	0	.0130
			1	.1623
			2	.4329
			3	.3247
			4	.0649
			5	.0022
12	1	1	0	.9167
			1	.0833
12	2	1	0	.8333
			1	.1667
12	2	2	0	.6818
			1	.3030
			2	.0152
12	3	1	0	.7500
			1	.2500
12	3	2	0	.5455
			1	.4091
			2	.0455
12	3	3	0	.3818
			1	.4909
			2	.1227
			3	.0045
12	4	1	0	.6667
			1	.3333
12	4	2	0	.4242
			1	.4848
			2	.0909
12	4	3	0	.2545
			1	.5091
			2	.2182
			3	.0182
12	4	4	0	.1414
			1	.4525
			2	.3394
			3	.0646
12	4	4	4	.0020
12	5	1	0	.5833
			1	.4167
12	5	2	0	.3182
			1	.5303
			2	.1515
12	5	3	0	.1591
			1	.4773
			2	.3182
			3	.0455
12	5	4	0	.0707
			1	.3535
			2	.4242
			3	.1414
			4	.0101
12	5	5	0	.0265
			1	.2210
			2	.4419
			3	.2652
			4	.0442
			5	.0013
12	6	1	0	.5000
			1	.5000
12	6	2	0	.2273
			1	.5455
			2	.2273
12	6	3	0	.0909
			1	.4091
			2	.4091
			3	.0909
12	6	4	0	.0303
			1	.2424
			2	.4545
			3	.2424
			4	.0303
12	6	5	0	.0076
			1	.1136
			2	.3788
			3	.3788
			4	.1136
			5	.0076
12	6	6	0	.0011
			1	.0390
			2	.2435
			3	.4329
			4	.2435
			5	.0390
			6	.0011
13	1	1	0	.9231
			1	.0769
13	2	1	0	.8462
			1	.1538
13	2	2	0	.7051
			1	.2821
			2	.0128
13	3	1	0	.7692
			1	.2308
13	3	2	0	.5769
			1	.3846
			2	.0385
13	3	3	0	.4196
			1	.4720
			2	.1049
			3	.0035
13	4	1	0	.6923
			1	.3077
13	4	2	0	.4615
			1	.4615
			2	.0769
13	4	3	0	.2937
			1	.5035
			2	.1888
			3	.0140
13	4	4	0	.1762
			1	.4699
			2	.3021
			3	.0503
			4	.0014
13	5	1	0	.6154
			1	.3846
13	5	2	0	.3590
			1	.5128
			2	.1282
13	5	3	0	.1958
			1	.4895
			2	.2797
			3	.0350
13	5	4	0	.0979
			1	.3916
			2	.3916
			3	.1119
			4	.0070
13	5	5	0	.0435
			1	.2719
			2	.4351
			3	.2176
			4	.0311
			5	.0008
13	6	1	0	.5385
			1	.4615
13	6	2	0	.2692
			1	.5385
			2	.1923
13	6	3	0	.1224
			1	.4406
			2	.3671
			3	.0699
13	6	4	0	.0490
			1	.2937
			2	.4406
13	6	4	3	.1958
			4	.0210
13	6	5	0	.0163
			1	.1632
			2	.4079
			3	.3263
			4	.0816
			5	.0047
13	6	6	0	.0041
			1	.0734
			2	.3059
			3	.4079
			4	.1836
			5	.0245
			6	.0006
14	1	1	0	.9286
			1	.0714
14	2	1	0	.8571
			1	.1429
14	2	2	0	.7253
			1	.2637
			2	.0110
14	3	1	0	.7857
			1	.2143
14	3	2	0	.6044
			1	.3626
			2	.0330
14	3	3	0	.4533
			1	.4533
			2	.0907
			3	.0027
14	4	1	0	.7143
			1	.2857
14	4	2	0	.4945
			1	.4396
			2	.0659
14	4	3	0	.3297
			1	.4945
			2	.1648
			3	.0110
14	4	4	0	.2098
			1	.4795
			2	.2697
			3	.0400
			4	.0010
14	5	1	0	.6429
			1	.3571
14	5	2	0	.3956
			1	.4945
			2	.1099
14	5	3	0	.2308
			1	.4945
			2	.2473
			3	.0275
14	5	4	0	.1259

Table 3 – *continued*

N	A	n	X	f(X)	N	A	n	X	f(X)	N	A	n	X	f(X)	N	A	n	X	f(X)
14	5	4	1	.4196	14	7	5	0	.0105	15	5	1	0	.6667	15	7	2	2	.2000
			2	.3596				1	.1224				1	.3333	15	7	3	0	.1231
			3	.0899				2	.3671	15	5	2	0	.4286				1	.4308
			4	.0050				3	.3671				1	.4762				2	.3692
14	5	5	0	.0629				4	.1224				2	.0952				3	.0769
			1	.3147				5	.0105	15	5	3	0	.2637	15	7	4	0	.0513
			2	.4196	14	7	6	0	.0023				1	.4945				1	.2872
			3	.1798				1	.0490				2	.2198				2	.4308
			4	.0225				2	.2448				3	.0220				3	.2051
			5	.0005				3	.4079	15	5	4	0	.1538				4	.0256
14	6	1	0	.5714				4	.2448				1	.4396	15	7	5	0	.0186
			1	.4286				5	.0490				2	.3297				1	.1632
14	6	2	0	.3077				6	.0023				3	.0732				2	.3916
			1	.5275	14	7	7	0	.0003				4	.0037				3	.3263
			2	.1648				1	.0143	15	5	5	0	.0839				4	.0932
14	6	3	0	.1538				2	.1285				1	.3497				5	.0070
			1	.4615				3	.3569				2	.3996	15	7	6	0	.0056
			2	.3297				4	.3569				3	.1498				1	.0783
			3	.0549				5	.1285				4	.0167				2	.2937
14	6	4	0	.0699				6	.0143				5	.0003				3	.3916
			1	.3357				7	.0003	15	6	1	0	.6000				4	.1958
			2	.4196	15	1	1	0	.9333				1	.4000				5	.0336
			3	.1598				1	.0667	15	6	2	0	.3429				6	.0014
			4	.0150	15	2	1	0	.8667				1	.5143	15	7	7	0	.0012
14	6	5	0	.0280				1	.1333				2	.1429				1	.0305
			1	.2098	15	2	2	0	.7429	15	6	3	0	.1846				2	.1828
			2	.4196				1	.2476				1	.4747				3	.3807
			3	.2797				2	.0095				2	.2967				4	.3046
			4	.0599	15	3	1	0	.8000				3	.0440				5	.0914
			5	.0030				1	.2000	15	6	4	0	.0923				6	.0087
14	6	6	0	.0093	15	3	2	0	.6286				1	.3692				7	.0002
			1	.1119				1	.3429				2	.3956					
			2	.3496				2	.0286				3	.1319					
			3	.3730	15	3	3	0	.4835				4	.0110					
			4	.1399				1	.4352	15	6	5	0	.0420					
			5	.0160				2	.0791				1	.2517					
			6	.0003				3	.0022				2	.4196					
14	7	1	0	.5000	15	4	1	0	.7333				3	.2398					
			1	.5000				1	.2667				4	.0450					
14	7	2	0	.2308	15	4	2	0	.5238				5	.0020					
			1	.5385				1	.4190	15	6	6	0	.0168					
			2	.2308				2	.0571				1	.1510					
14	7	3	0	.0962	15	4	3	0	.3626				2	.3776					
			1	.4038				1	.4835				3	.3357					
			2	.4038				2	.1451				4	.1079					
			3	.0962				3	.0088				5	.0108					
14	7	4	0	.0350	15	4	4	0	.2418				6	.0002					
			1	.2448				1	.4835	15	7	1	0	.5333					
			2	.4406				2	.2418				1	.4667					
			3	.2448				3	.0322	15	7	2	0	.2667					
			4	.0350				4	.0007				1	.5333					

Approximation: For $N > 15$, use Normal distribution with mean nA/N and variance $nA(N-A)(N-n)/N^2(N-1)$, provided A and n are not very small.

Table 4. Negative exponential distribution

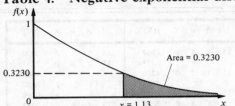

Values of $f(x) = e^{-x}$ for different values of x. **Example:** $f(x = 1.13) = e^{-1.13} = 0.3230$. Area under $f(x)$ beyond $x = 1.13$ is also given by 0.3230. Area under $f(x) = \theta e^{-\theta x}$ beyond x is given by $e^{-\theta x}$. **Example:** For $\theta = \frac{1}{5}$ area beyond $x = 12$ is given by $e^{-12/5} = e^{-2.4} = 0.0907$.

$x \rightarrow$ $\downarrow$	0.00	0.01	0.02	0.03	0.04	0.05	0.06	0.07	0.08	0.09
0	1.0000	0.9900	0.9802	0.9704	0.9608	0.9512	0.9418	0.9324	0.9231	0.9139
0.1	0.9048	0.8958	0.8869	0.8781	0.8694	0.8607	0.8521	0.8437	0.8353	0.8270
0.2	0.8187	0.8106	0.8025	0.7945	0.7866	0.7788	0.7711	0.7634	0.7558	0.7483
0.3	0.7408	0.7334	0.7261	0.7189	0.7118	0.7047	0.6977	0.6907	0.6839	0.6771
0.4	0.6703	0.6637	0.6570	0.6505	0.6440	0.6376	0.6313	0.6250	0.6188	0.6126
0.5	0.6065	0.6005	0.5945	0.5886	0.5827	0.5769	0.5712	0.5655	0.5599	0.5543
0.6	0.5488	0.5434	0.5379	0.5326	0.5273	0.5220	0.5169	0.5117	0.5066	0.5016
0.7	0.4966	0.4916	0.4868	0.4819	0.4771	0.4724	0.4677	0.4630	0.4584	0.4538
0.8	0.4493	0.4449	0.4404	0.4360	0.4317	0.4274	0.4232	0.4190	0.4148	0.4107
0.9	0.4066	0.4025	0.3985	0.3946	0.3906	0.3867	0.3829	0.3791	0.3753	0.3716
1.0	0.3679	0.3642	0.3606	0.3570	0.3535	0.3499	0.3465	0.3430	0.3396	0.3362
1.1	0.3329	0.3296	0.3265	0.3230	0.3198	0.3166	0.3135	0.3104	0.3073	0.3042
1.2	0.3012	0.2892	0.2952	0.2923	0.2894	0.2865	0.2837	0.2808	0.2780	0.2753
1.3	0.2725	0.2698	0.2671	0.2645	0.2618	0.2592	0.2567	0.2541	0.2516	0.2491
1.4	0.2466	0.2441	0.2417	0.2393	0.2369	0.2346	0.2322	0.2299	0.2276	0.2254
1.5	0.2231	0.2209	0.2187	0.2165	0.2144	0.2122	0.2101	0.2080	0.2060	0.2039
1.6	0.2019	0.1999	0.1979	0.1959	0.1940	0.1920	0.1901	0.1882	0.1864	0.1845
1.7	0.1827	0.1809	0.1791	0.1773	0.1755	0.1738	0.1720	0.1703	0.1686	0.1670
1.8	0.1653	0.1637	0.1620	0.1604	0.1588	0.1572	0.1557	0.1541	0.1526	0.1511
1.9	0.1496	0.1481	0.1466	0.1451	0.1437	0.1423	0.1409	0.1395	0.1381	0.1367
2.0	0.1353	0.1340	0.1327	0.1313	0.1300	0.1287	0.1275	0.1262	0.1249	0.1237
2.1	0.1225	0.1212	0.1200	0.1188	0.1177	0.1165	0.1153	0.1142	0.1130	0.1119
2.2	0.1108	0.1097	0.1086	0.1075	0.1065	0.1054	0.1044	0.1035	0.1023	0.1013
2.3	0.1003	0.0993	0.0983	0.0973	0.0963	0.0954	0.0944	0.0935	0.0926	0.0916
2.4	0.0907	0.0898	0.0889	0.0880	0.0872	0.0863	0.0854	0.0846	0.0837	0.0829
2.5	0.0821	0.0813	0.0805	0.0797	0.0789	0.0781	0.0773	0.0765	0.0758	0.0750
2.6	0.0743	0.0735	0.0728	0.0721	0.0714	0.0707	0.0699	0.0693	0.0686	0.0679
2.7	0.0672	0.0665	0.0659	0.0652	0.0646	0.0639	0.0633	0.0627	0.0620	0.0614
2.8	0.0608	0.0602	0.0596	0.0590	0.0584	0.0578	0.0573	0.0567	0.0561	0.0556
2.9	0.0550	0.0545	0.0539	0.0534	0.0529	0.0523	0.0518	0.0513	0.0508	0.0503
3.0	0.0498	0.0493	0.0488	0.0483	0.0478	0.0474	0.0469	0.0464	0.0460	0.0455
3.1	0.0450	0.0446	0.0442	0.0437	0.0433	0.0429	0.0424	0.0420	0.0416	0.0412
3.2	0.0408	0.0404	0.0400	0.0396	0.0392	0.0388	0.0384	0.0380	0.0376	0.0373
3.3	0.0369	0.0365	0.0362	0.0358	0.0354	0.0351	0.0347	0.0344	0.0340	0.0337
3.4	0.0334	0.0330	0.0327	0.0324	0.0321	0.0317	0.0314	0.0311	0.0308	0.0305
3.5	0.0302	0.0299	0.0296	0.0293	0.0290	0.0287	0.0284	0.0282	0.0279	0.0276
3.6	0.0273	0.0271	0.0268	0.0265	0.0263	0.0260	0.0257	0.0255	0.0252	0.0250
3.7	0.0247	0.0245	0.0242	0.0240	0.0238	0.0235	0.0233	0.0231	0.0228	0.0226
3.8	0.0224	0.0221	0.0219	0.0217	0.0215	0.0213	0.0211	0.0209	0.0207	0.0204
3.9	0.0202	0.0200	0.0198	0.0196	0.0194	0.0193	0.0191	0.0189	0.0187	0.0185
4.0	0.0183	0.0181	0.0180	0.0178	0.0176	0.0174	0.0172	0.0171	0.0169	0.0167
4.1	0.0166	0.0164	0.0162	0.0161	0.0159	0.0158	0.0156	0.0155	0.0153	0.0151
4.2	0.0150	0.0148	0.0147	0.0146	0.0144	0.0143	0.0141	0.0140	0.0138	0.0137
4.3	0.0136	0.0134	0.0133	0.0132	0.0130	0.0129	0.0128	0.0127	0.0125	0.0124
4.4	0.0123	0.0122	0.0120	0.0119	0.0118	0.0117	0.0116	0.0114	0.0113	0.0112
4.5	0.0111	0.0110	0.0109	0.0108	0.0107	0.0106	0.0105	0.0104	0.0103	0.0102
4.6	0.0101	0.0100	0.0099	0.0098	0.0097	0.0096	0.0095	0.0094	0.0093	0.0092
4.7	0.0091	0.0090	0.0089	0.0088	0.0087	0.0087	0.0086	0.0085	0.0084	0.0083
4.8	0.0082	0.0081	0.0081	0.0080	0.0079	0.0078	0.0078	0.0077	0.0076	0.0075
4.9	0.0074	0.0074	0.0073	0.0072	0.0072	0.0071	0.0070	0.0069	0.0069	0.0068
5.0	0.0067	0.0067	0.0066	0.0065	0.0065	0.0064	0.0063	0.0063	0.0062	0.0062

x	6.0	7.0	8.0	9.0	10.0	12.0	14.0	16.0	18.0	20.0
e^{-x}	0.0^2248	0.0^3912	0.0^3335	0.0^3123	0.0^4454	0.0^5614	0.0^6832	0.0^6113	0.0^7152	0.0^8206

Note: To find e^{-x} for $x > 5.09$, use the rule on exponents, e.g. $e^{-8.25} = e^{-8}e^{-0.25} = 0.0^2335 \times 0.7788 = 0.000335 \times 0.7788 = 0.000261$.

Table 5. Normal distribution (areas)

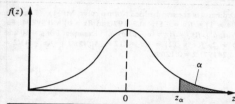

Area (α) in the tail of the standardised Normal curve, $N(0, 1)$, for different values of z. **Example:** Area beyond $z = 1.96$ (or below $z = -1.96$) is $\alpha = 0.02500$. For Normal curve with $\mu = 10$ and $\sigma = 2$, area beyond $x = 12$, say, is the same as area beyond $z = \dfrac{x - \mu}{\sigma} = \dfrac{12 - 10}{2} = 1$, i.e. $\alpha = 0.15866$.

$z \rightarrow$	0.00	0.01	0.02	0.03	0.04	0.05	0.06	0.07	0.08	0.09
0.0	.50000	.49601	.49202	.48803	.48405	.48006	.47608	.47210	.46812	.46414
0.1	.46017	.45620	.45224	.44828	.44433	.44038	.43644	.43251	.42858	.42465
0.2	.42074	.41683	.41294	.40905	.40517	.40129	.39743	.39358	.38974	.38591
0.3	.38209	.37828	.37448	.37070	.36693	.36317	.35942	.35569	.35197	.34827
0.4	.34458	.34090	.33724	.33360	.32997	.32636	.32276	.31918	.31561	.31207
0.5	.30854	.30503	.30153	.29806	.29460	.29116	.28774	.28434	.28096	.27760
0.6	.27425	.27093	.26763	.26435	.26109	.25785	.25463	.25143	.24825	.24510
0.7	.24196	.23885	.23576	.23270	.22965	.22663	.22363	.22065	.21770	.21476
0.8	.21186	.20897	.20611	.20327	.20045	.19766	.19489	.19215	.18943	.18673
0.9	.18406	.18141	.17879	.17619	.17361	.17106	.16853	.16602	.16354	.16109
1.0	.15866	.15625	.15386	.15150	.14917	.14686	.14457	.14231	.14007	.13786
1.1	.13567	.13350	.13136	.12924	.12714	.12507	.12302	.12100	.11900	.11702
1.2	.11507	.11314	.11123	.10935	.10749	.10565	.10383	.10204	.10027	.09853
1.3	.09680	.09510	.09342	.09176	.09012	.08851	.08692	.08534	.08379	.08226
1.4	.08076	.07927	.07780	.07636	.07493	.07353	.07214	.07078	.06944	.06811
1.5	.06681	.06552	.06426	.06301	.06178	.06057	.05938	.05821	.05705	.05592
1.6	.05480	.05370	.05262	.05155	.05050	.04947	.04846	.04746	.04648	.04551
1.7	.04457	.04363	.04272	.04182	.04093	.04006	.03920	.03836	.03754	.03673
1.8	.03593	.03515	.03438	.03362	.03288	.03216	.03144	.03074	.03005	.02938
1.9	.02872	.02807	.02743	.02680	.02619	.02559	.02500	.02442	.02385	.02330
2.0	.02275	.02222	.02169	.02118	.02068	.02018	.01970	.01923	.01876	.01831
2.1	.01786	.01743	.01700	.01659	.01618	.01578	.01539	.01500	.01463	.01426
2.2	.01390	.01355	.01321	.01287	.01254	.01222	.01191	.01160	.01130	.01101
2.3	.01072	.01044	.01017	.00990	.00964	.00939	.00914	.00889	.00866	.00842
2.4	.00820	.00798	.00776	.00755	.00734	.00714	.00695	.00676	.00657	.00639
2.5	.00621	.00604	.00587	.00570	.00554	.00539	.00523	.00509	.00494	.00480
2.6	.00466	.00453	.00440	.00427	.00415	.00403	.00391	.00379	.00368	.00357
2.7	.00347	.00336	.00326	.00317	.00307	.00298	.00289	.00280	.00272	.00263
2.8	.00256	.00248	.00240	.00233	.00226	.00219	.00212	.00205	.00199	.00193
2.9	.00187	.00181	.00175	.00169	.00164	.00159	.00154	.00149	.00144	.00139
3.0	.00135	.00131	.00126	.00122	.00118	.00114	.00111	.00107	.00104	.00100
3.1	.00097	.00094	.00090	.00087	.00085	.00082	.00079	.00076	.00074	.00071
3.2	.00069	.00066	.00064	.00062	.00060	.00058	.00056	.00054	.00052	.00050
3.3	.00048	.00047	.00045	.00043	.00042	.00040	.00039	.00038	.00036	.00035
3.4	.00034	.00032	.00031	.00030	.00029	.00028	.00027	.00026	.00025	.00024
3.5	.00023	.00022	.00022	.00021	.00020	.00019	.00019	.00018	.00017	.00017
3.6	.00016	.00015	.00015	.00014	.00014	.00013	.00013	.00012	.00012	.00011
3.7	.00011	.00010	.00010	.00010	.00009	.00009	.00009	.00008	.00008	.00008
3.8	.00007	.00007	.00007	.00006	.00006	.00006	.00006	.00005	.00005	.00005
3.9	.00005	.00005	.00004	.00004	.00004	.00004	.00004	.00004	.00004	.00003
4.0	.00003	.00003	.00003	.00003	.00003	.00002	.00002	.00002	.00002	.00002

α	0.4	0.25	0.2	0.15	0.1	0.05	0.025	0.01	0.005	0.001
z_α	.2533	.6745	.8416	1.0364	1.2816	1.6449	1.9600	2.3263	2.5758	3.0902

Table 6. Normal distribution (ordinates)

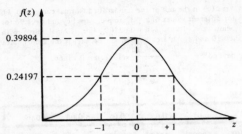

Ordinates of the standardised Normal curve, $N(0, 1)$. **Example:**
$f(z = 1) = f(z = -1) = 0.24197$ and $f(z = 0) = 0.39894$. For
$N(\mu, \sigma^2)$, $f(x) = f(z = (x - \mu)/\sigma)/\sigma$. **Example:** For $\mu = 10$ and
$\sigma = 2$, $f(x = 12) = f(z = \langle 12 - 10\rangle/2)/2 = f(z = 1)/2 = (0.24197)/2 = 0.12099$.

$z \rightarrow$ $\downarrow$	0.00	0.01	0.02	0.03	0.04	0.05	0.06	0.07	0.08	0.09
0.0	.39894	.39892	.39886	.39876	.39862	.39844	.39822	.39797	.39767	.39733
0.1	.39695	.39654	.39608	.39559	.39505	.39448	.39387	.39322	.39253	.39181
0.2	.39104	.39024	.38940	.38853	.38762	.38667	.38568	.38466	.38361	.38251
0.3	.38139	.38023	.37903	.37780	.37654	.37524	.37391	.37255	.37115	.36973
0.4	.36827	.36678	.36526	.36371	.36213	.36053	.35889	.35723	.35553	.35381
0.5	.35207	.35029	.34849	.34667	.34482	.34294	.34105	.33912	.33718	.33521
0.6	.33322	.33121	.32918	.32713	.32506	.32297	.32086	.31874	.31659	.31443
0.7	.31225	.31006	.30785	.30563	.30339	.30114	.29887	.29659	.29431	.29200
0.8	.28969	.28737	.28504	.28269	.28034	.27798	.27562	.27324	.27086	.26848
0.9	.26609	.26369	.26129	.25888	.25647	.25406	.25164	.24923	.24681	.24439
1.0	.24197	.23955	.23713	.23471	.23230	.22988	.22747	.22506	.22265	.22025
1.1	.21785	.21546	.21307	.21069	.20831	.20594	.20357	.20121	.19886	.19652
1.2	.19419	.19186	.18954	.18724	.18494	.18265	.18037	.17810	.17585	.17360
1.3	.17137	.16915	.16694	.16474	.16256	.16038	.15822	.15608	.15395	.15183
1.4	.14973	.14764	.14556	.14350	.14146	.13943	.13742	.13542	.13344	.13147
1.5	.12952	.12758	.12566	.12376	.12188	.12001	.11816	.11632	.11450	.11270
1.6	.11092	.10915	.10741	.10567	.10396	.10226	.10059	.09893	.09728	.09566
1.7	.09405	.09246	.09089	.08933	.08780	.08628	.08478	.08329	.08183	.08038
1.8	.07895	.07754	.07614	.07477	.07341	.07206	.07074	.06943	.06814	.06687
1.9	.06562	.06438	.06316	.06195	.06077	.05959	.05844	.05730	.05618	.05508
2.0	.05399	.05292	.05186	.05082	.04980	.04879	.04780	.04682	.04586	.04491
2.1	.04398	.04307	.04217	.04128	.04041	.03955	.03871	.03788	.03706	.03626
2.2	.03547	.03470	.03394	.03319	.03246	.03174	.03103	.03034	.02965	.02898
2.3	.02833	.02768	.02705	.02643	.02582	.02522	.02463	.02406	.02349	.02294
2.4	.02239	.02186	.02134	.02083	.02033	.01984	.01936	.01888	.01842	.01797
2.5	.01753	.01709	.01667	.01625	.01585	.01545	.01506	.01468	.01431	.01394
2.6	.01358	.01323	.01289	.01256	.01223	.01191	.01160	.01130	.01100	.01071
2.7	.01042	.01014	.00987	.00961	.00935	.00909	.00885	.00861	.00837	.00814
2.8	.00792	.00770	.00748	.00727	.00707	.00687	.00668	.00649	.00631	.00613
2.9	.00595	.00578	.00562	.00545	.00530	.00514	.00499	.00485	.00470	.00457
3.0	.00443	.00430	.00417	.00405	.00393	.00381	.00370	.00358	.00348	.00337
3.1	.00327	.00317	.00307	.00298	.00288	.00279	.00271	.00262	.00254	.00246
3.2	.00238	.00231	.00224	.00216	.00210	.00203	.00196	.00190	.00184	.00178
3.3	.00172	.00167	.00161	.00156	.00151	.00146	.00141	.00136	.00132	.00127
3.4	.00123	.00119	.00115	.00111	.00107	.00104	.00100	.00097	.00094	.00090
3.5	.00087	.00084	.00081	.00079	.00076	.00073	.00071	.00068	.00066	.00063
3.6	.00061	.00059	.00057	.00055	.00053	.00051	.00049	.00047	.00046	.00044
3.7	.00042	.00041	.00039	.00038	.00037	.00035	.00034	.00033	.00031	.00030
3.8	.00029	.00028	.00027	.00026	.00025	.00024	.00023	.00022	.00021	.00021
3.9	.00020	.00019	.00018	.00018	.00017	.00016	.00016	.00015	.00014	.00014
4.0	.00013	.00013	.00012	.00012	.00011	.00011	.00011	.00010	.00010	.00009

Table 7. χ^2 (Chi-squared)-distribution

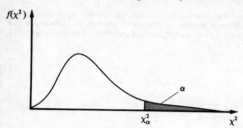

$f(\chi^2)$

Values of χ^2_α giving area (α) in the right-hand tail for different number of degrees of freedom (ν). **Example:** For $\nu = 15$ area beyond $\chi^2_{0.95} = 7.261$ is 0.950 and beyond $\chi^2_{0.10} = 22.307$ is 0.100.

α

χ^2_α χ^2

ν \ α	0.995	0.990	0.975	0.950	0.900	0.750	0.500	0.250	0.100	0.050	0.025	0.010	0.005
1	0.0^43927*	0.0^31571*	0.0^39821*	0.0^23932*	0.01579	0.1015	0.4549	1.323	2.706	3.841	5.024	6.635	7.879
2	0.01003	0.02010	0.05065	0.1026	0.2107	0.5754	1.386	2.773	4.605	5.991	7.378	9.210	10.597
3	0.07172	0.1148	0.2158	0.3518	0.5844	1.213	2.366	4.108	6.251	7.815	9.348	11.345	12.838
4	0.2070	0.2971	0.4844	0.7107	1.064	1.923	3.357	5.385	7.779	9.488	11.143	13.277	14.860
5	0.4117	0.5543	0.8312	1.145	1.610	2.675	4.351	6.626	9.236	11.070	12.833	15.086	16.750
6	0.6757	0.8721	1.237	1.635	2.204	3.455	5.348	7.841	10.645	12.592	14.449	16.812	18.548
7	0.9893	1.239	1.690	2.167	2.833	4.255	6.346	9.037	12.017	14.067	16.013	18.475	20.278
8	1.344	1.646	2.180	2.733	3.490	5.071	7.344	10.219	13.362	15.507	17.535	20.090	21.955
9	1.735	2.088	2.700	3.325	4.168	5.899	8.343	11.389	14.684	16.919	19.023	21.666	23.589
10	2.156	2.558	3.247	3.940	4.865	6.737	9.342	12.549	15.987	18.307	20.483	23.209	25.188
11	2.603	3.053	3.816	4.575	5.578	7.584	10.341	13.701	17.275	19.675	21.920	24.725	26.757
12	3.074	3.571	4.404	5.226	6.304	8.438	11.340	14.845	18.549	21.026	23.337	26.217	28.300
13	3.565	4.107	5.009	5.892	7.041	9.299	12.340	15.984	19.812	22.362	24.736	27.688	29.819
14	4.075	4.660	5.629	6.571	7.790	10.165	13.339	17.117	21.064	23.685	26.119	29.141	31.319
15	4.601	5.229	6.262	7.261	8.547	11.036	14.339	18.245	22.307	24.996	27.488	30.578	32.801
16	5.142	5.812	6.908	7.962	9.312	11.912	15.338	19.369	23.542	26.296	28.845	32.000	34.267
17	5.697	6.408	7.564	8.672	10.085	12.792	16.338	20.489	24.769	27.587	30.191	33.409	35.718
18	6.265	7.015	8.231	9.390	10.865	13.675	17.338	21.605	25.989	28.869	31.526	34.805	37.156
19	6.844	7.633	8.907	10.117	11.651	14.562	18.338	22.718	27.204	30.143	32.852	36.191	38.582
20	7.434	8.260	9.591	10.851	12.443	15.452	19.337	23.828	28.412	31.410	34.170	37.566	39.997
21	8.034	8.897	10.283	11.591	13.240	16.344	20.337	24.935	29.615	32.670	35.479	38.932	41.401
22	8.643	9.542	10.982	12.338	14.041	17.240	21.337	26.039	30.813	33.924	36.781	40.289	42.796
23	9.260	10.196	11.688	13.090	14.848	18.137	22.337	27.141	32.007	35.172	38.076	41.638	44.181
24	9.886	10.856	12.401	13.848	15.659	19.037	23.337	28.241	33.196	36.415	39.364	42.080	45.558
25	10.520	11.524	13.120	14.611	16.473	19.939	24.337	29.339	34.382	37.652	40.646	44.314	46.928
26	11.160	12.198	13.844	15.379	17.292	20.843	25.336	30.434	35.563	38.885	41.923	45.642	48.290
27	11.808	12.879	14.573	16.151	18.114	21.749	26.336	31.528	36.741	40.113	43.194	46.963	49.645
28	12.461	13.565	15.308	16.928	18.939	22.657	27.336	32.620	37.916	41.337	44.461	48.278	50.993
29	13.121	14.256	16.047	17.708	19.768	23.567	28.336	33.711	39.087	42.557	45.722	49.588	52.336
30	13.787	14.954	16.791	18.493	20.599	24.478	29.336	34.800	40.256	43.773	46.979	50.892	53.672
35	17.192	18.509	20.569	22.465	24.797	29.054	34.336	40.223	46.059	49.802	53.203	57.342	60.275
40	20.707	22.164	24.433	26.509	29.050	33.660	39.335	45.616	51.805	55.758	59.342	63.691	66.766
45	24.311	25.901	28.366	30.612	33.350	38.291	44.335	50.985	57.505	61.656	65.410	69.957	73.166
50	27.991	29.707	32.357	34.764	37.689	42.942	49.335	56.334	63.167	67.505	71.420	76.154	79.490
55	31.735	33.571	36.398	38.958	42.060	47.611	54.335	61.665	68.796	73.311	77.381	82.292	85.749
60	35.535	37.485	40.482	43.188	46.459	52.294	59.335	66.981	74.397	79.082	83.298	88.379	91.952
70	43.275	45.442	48.758	51.739	55.329	61.698	69.334	77.577	85.527	90.531	95.023	100.425	104.215
80	51.172	53.540	57.153	60.391	64.278	71.144	79.334	88.130	96.578	101.879	106.629	112.329	116.321
90	59.196	61.754	65.647	69.126	73.291	80.625	89.334	98.650	107.565	113.145	118.136	124.116	128.299
100	67.328	70.065	74.222	77.929	82.358	90.133	99.334	109.141	118.498	124.342	129.561	135.807	140.169
120	83.829	86.909	91.568	95.705	100.627	109.224	119.335	130.051	140.228	146.565	152.214	158.963	163.670
150	109.122	112.655	117.980	122.692	126.278	137.987	149.334	161.288	172.577	179.579	185.803	193.219	198.380
200	152.224	156.421	162.724	168.279	174.828	186.175	199.334	213.099	226.018	233.993	241.060	249.455	255.281
250	196.145	200.929	208.095	214.392	221.809	234.580	249.334	264.694	279.947	287.889	295.691	304.948	311.361
$z_{\frac{\alpha}{2}}$	−2.5758	−2.3263	−1.9600	−1.6449	−1.2816	−0.6745	0.0000	0.6745	1.2816	1.6449	1.9600	2.3263	2.5758

* e.g. $0.0^43927 = 0.00003927$

Interpolation: For $\nu > 100$, $\chi^2_\alpha = \frac{1}{2}(z_\alpha + \sqrt{2\nu - 1})^2$ where z_α is the standardised Normal variable shown in the bottom line of the table.

Table 8. t-distribution

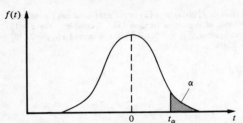

$f(t)$

0   t_α t

Critical points (t_α) for different probability levels (α) and different number of degrees of freedom (ν). Example: For $\nu = 19$, $P(t > 2.0930) = 0.025$ and $P(|t| > 2.0930) = 0.05$.

ν \ α	0.4	0.25	0.15	0.1	0.05	0.025	0.01	0.005	0.001	0.0005
1	0.3249	1.0000	1.9626	3.0777	6.3138	12.7062	31.8205	63.6567	318.3087	636.6189
2	0.2887	0.8165	1.3862	1.8856	2.9200	4.3027	6.9646	9.9248	22.3271	31.5991
3	0.2767	0.7649	1.2498	1.6377	2.3534	3.1824	4.5407	5.8409	10.2145	12.9240
4	0.2707	0.7407	1.1896	1.5332	2.1318	2.7764	3.7469	4.6041	7.1732	8.6103
5	0.2672	0.7267	1.1558	1.4759	2.0150	2.5706	3.3649	4.0321	5.8934	6.8688
6	0.2648	0.7176	1.1342	1.4398	1.9432	2.4469	3.1427	3.7074	5.2076	5.9588
7	0.2632	0.7111	1.1192	1.4149	1.8946	2.3646	2.9980	3.4995	4.7853	5.4079
8	0.2619	0.7064	1.1081	1.3968	1.8595	2.3060	2.8965	3.3554	4.5008	5.0413
9	0.2610	0.7027	1.0997	1.3830	1.8331	2.2622	2.8214	3.2498	4.2968	4.7809
10	0.2602	0.6998	1.0931	1.3722	1.8125	2.2281	2.7638	3.1693	4.1437	4.5869
11	0.2596	0.6974	1.0877	1.3634	1.7959	2.2010	2.7181	3.1058	4.0247	4.4370
12	0.2590	0.6955	1.0832	1.3562	1.7823	2.1788	2.6810	3.0545	3.9296	4.3178
13	0.2586	0.6938	1.0795	1.3502	1.7709	2.1604	2.6503	3.0123	3.8520	4.2208
14	0.2582	0.6924	1.0763	1.3450	1.7613	2.1448	2.6245	2.9768	3.7874	4.1405
15	0.2579	0.6912	1.0735	1.3406	1.7531	2.1314	2.6025	2.9467	3.7328	4.0728
16	0.2576	0.6901	1.0711	1.3368	1.7459	2.1199	2.5835	2.9208	3.6862	4.0150
17	0.2573	0.6892	1.0690	1.3334	1.7396	2.1098	2.5669	2.8982	3.6458	3.9651
18	0.2571	0.6884	1.0672	1.3304	1.7341	2.1009	2.5524	2.8784	3.6105	3.9216
19	0.2569	0.6876	1.0655	1.3277	1.7291	2.0930	2.5395	2.8609	3.5794	3.8834
20	0.2567	0.6870	1.0640	1.3253	1.7247	2.0860	2.5280	2.8453	3.5518	3.8495
21	0.2566	0.6864	1.0627	1.3232	1.7207	2.0796	2.5176	2.8314	3.5272	3.8193
22	0.2564	0.6858	1.0614	1.3212	1.7171	2.0739	2.5083	2.8188	3.5050	3.7921
23	0.2563	0.6853	1.0603	1.3195	1.7139	2.0687	2.4999	2.8073	3.4850	3.7676
24	0.2562	0.6848	1.0593	1.3178	1.7109	2.0639	2.4922	2.7969	3.4668	3.7454
25	0.2561	0.6844	1.0584	1.3163	1.7081	2.0595	2.4851	2.7874	3.4502	3.7251
26	0.2560	0.6840	1.0575	1.3150	1.7056	2.0555	2.4786	2.7787	3.4350	3.7066
27	0.2559	0.6837	1.0567	1.3137	1.7033	2.0518	2.4727	2.7707	3.4210	3.6896
28	0.2558	0.6834	1.0560	1.3125	1.7011	2.0484	2.4671	2.7633	3.4082	3.6739
29	0.2557	0.6830	1.0553	1.3114	1.6991	2.0452	2.4620	2.7564	3.3962	3.6594
30	0.2556	0.6828	1.0547	1.3104	1.6973	2.0423	2.4573	2.7500	3.3852	3.6460
35	0.2553	0.6816	1.0520	1.3062	1.6896	2.0301	2.4377	2.7238	3.3400	3.5911
40	0.2550	0.6807	1.0500	1.3031	1.6839	2.0211	2.4233	2.7045	3.3069	3.5510
45	0.2549	0.6800	1.0485	1.3006	1.6794	2.0141	2.4121	2.6896	3.2815	3.5203
50	0.2547	0.6794	1.0473	1.2987	1.6759	2.0086	2.4033	2.6778	3.2614	3.4960
60	0.2545	0.6786	1.0455	1.2958	1.6706	2.0003	2.3901	2.6603	3.2317	3.4602
70	0.2543	0.6780	1.0442	1.2938	1.6669	1.9944	2.3808	2.6479	3.2108	3.4350
80	0.2542	0.6776	1.0432	1.2922	1.6641	1.9901	2.3739	2.6387	3.1953	3.4163
90	0.2541	0.6772	1.0424	1.2910	1.6620	1.9867	2.3685	2.6316	3.1833	3.4019
100	0.2540	0.6770	1.0418	1.2901	1.6602	1.9840	2.3642	2.6259	3.1737	3.3905
120	0.2539	0.6765	1.0409	1.2886	1.6577	1.9799	2.3578	2.6174	3.1595	3.3735
150	0.2538	0.6761	1.0400	1.2872	1.6551	1.9759	2.3515	2.6090	3.1455	3.3566
200	0.2537	0.6757	1.0391	1.2858	1.6525	1.9719	2.3451	2.6006	3.1315	3.3398
300	0.2536	0.6753	1.0382	1.2844	1.6499	1.9679	2.3388	2.5923	3.1176	3.3233
∞	0.2533	0.6745	1.0364	1.2816	1.6449	1.9600	2.3263	2.5758	3.0902	3.2905

Table 9.   F-distribution

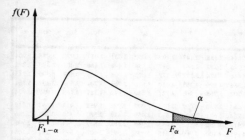

$f(F)$

Values of F_α ($\alpha = 0.1$, 0.05, 0.025, 0.01 and 0.005) for different combinations of degrees of freedom in the numerator, v_1, and denominator, v_2.   **Example:** When $v_1 = 10$ and $v_2 = 2$, area (α) to the right of $F_{0.05} = 19.40$ is 0.05. To find $F_{1-\alpha}$, leaving an area α in the left-hand tail, use the relation: $F_{1-\alpha}(v_1, v_2) = 1/F_\alpha(v_2, v_1)$.   **Example:** $F_{0.95}(2, 10) = 1/19.40 = 0.05155$.

v_2	α \ v_1	1	2	3	4	5	6	7	8	9	10	12	15	20	25	30	50	100	∞
1	0.100	39.86	49.50	53.59	55.83	57.24	58.20	58.91	59.44	59.86	60.19	60.71	61.22	61.74	62.05	62.26	62.69	63.01	63.33
	0.050	161.4	199.5	215.7	224.6	230.2	234.0	236.8	238.9	240.5	241.9	243.9	245.9	248.0	249.3	250.1	251.8	253.0	254.3
	0.025	647.8	799.5	864.2	899.0	921.8	937.1	948.2	956.7	963.3	968.6	976.7	984.9	993.1	998.1	1001	1008	1013	1018
	0.010	4052	4999	5403	5625	5764	5859	5928	5981	6022	6056	6106	6157	6209	6240	6261	6303	6334	6366
	0.005	16211	20000	21615	22500	23056	23437	23715	23925	24091	24224	24426	24630	24836	24960	25044	25211	25337	25464
2	0.100	8.526	9.000	9.162	9.243	9.293	9.362	9.349	9.367	9.381	9.392	9.408	9.425	9.441	9.451	9.458	9.471	9.481	9.491
	0.050	18.51	19.00	19.16	19.25	19.30	19.33	19.35	19.37	19.38	19.40	19.41	19.43	19.45	19.46	19.46	19.48	19.49	19.50
	0.025	38.51	39.00	39.17	39.25	39.30	39.33	39.36	39.37	39.39	39.40	39.41	39.43	39.45	39.46	39.46	39.48	39.49	39.50
	0.010	98.50	99.00	99.17	99.25	99.30	99.33	99.36	99.37	99.39	99.40	99.42	99.43	99.45	99.46	99.47	99.48	99.49	99.50
	0.005	198.5	199.0	199.2	199.2	199.3	199.3	199.4	199.4	199.4	199.4	199.4	199.4	199.4	199.5	199.5	199.5	199.5	199.5
3	0.100	5.538	5.462	5.391	5.343	5.309	5.285	5.266	5.252	5.240	5.230	5.216	5.200	5.184	5.175	5.168	5.155	5.144	5.134
	0.050	10.13	9.552	9.277	9.117	9.013	8.941	8.887	8.845	8.812	8.786	8.745	8.703	8.660	8.634	8.617	8.581	8.554	8.526
	0.025	17.44	16.04	15.44	15.10	14.88	14.73	14.62	14.54	14.47	14.42	14.34	14.25	14.17	14.12	14.08	14.01	13.96	13.90
	0.010	34.12	30.82	29.46	28.71	28.24	27.91	27.67	27.49	27.35	27.23	27.05	26.87	26.69	26.58	26.50	26.35	26.24	26.13
	0.005	55.55	49.80	47.47	46.19	45.39	44.84	44.43	44.13	43.88	43.69	43.39	43.08	42.78	42.59	42.47	42.21	42.02	41.83
4	0.100	4.545	4.325	4.191	4.107	4.051	4.010	3.979	3.955	3.936	3.920	3.896	3.870	3.844	3.828	3.817	3.795	3.778	3.761
	0.050	7.709	6.944	6.591	6.388	6.256	6.163	6.094	6.041	5.999	5.964	5.912	5.858	5.803	5.769	5.746	5.699	5.664	5.628
	0.025	12.22	10.65	9.979	9.605	9.364	9.197	9.074	8.980	8.905	8.844	8.751	8.657	8.560	8.501	8.461	8.381	8.319	8.257
	0.010	21.20	18.00	16.69	15.98	15.52	15.21	14.98	14.80	14.66	14.55	14.37	14.20	14.02	13.91	13.84	13.69	13.58	13.46
	0.005	31.33	26.28	24.26	23.15	22.46	21.97	21.62	21.35	21.14	20.97	20.70	20.44	20.17	20.00	19.89	19.67	19.50	19.32
5	0.100	4.060	3.780	3.619	3.520	3.453	3.405	3.368	3.339	3.316	3.297	3.268	3.238	3.207	3.187	3.174	3.147	3.126	3.105
	0.050	6.608	5.786	5.409	5.192	5.050	4.950	4.876	4.818	4.772	4.735	4.678	4.619	4.558	4.521	4.496	4.444	4.405	4.365
	0.025	10.01	8.434	7.764	7.388	7.146	6.978	6.853	6.757	6.681	6.619	6.525	6.428	6.329	6.268	6.227	6.144	6.080	6.015
	0.010	16.26	13.27	12.06	11.39	10.97	10.67	10.46	10.29	10.16	10.05	9.888	9.722	9.553	9.449	9.379	9.238	9.130	9.020
	0.005	22.78	18.31	16.53	15.56	14.94	14.51	14.20	13.96	13.77	13.62	13.38	13.15	12.90	12.76	12.66	12.45	12.30	12.14
6	0.100	3.776	3.463	3.289	3.181	3.108	3.055	3.014	2.983	2.958	2.937	2.905	2.871	2.836	2.815	2.800	2.770	2.746	2.722
	0.050	5.987	5.143	4.757	4.534	4.387	4.284	4.207	4.147	4.099	4.060	4.000	3.938	3.874	3.835	3.808	3.754	3.712	3.669
	0.025	8.813	7.260	6.599	6.227	5.988	5.820	5.695	5.600	5.523	5.461	5.366	5.269	5.168	5.107	5.065	4.980	4.915	4.849
	0.010	13.75	10.92	9.780	9.148	8.746	8.466	8.260	8.102	7.976	7.874	7.718	7.559	7.396	7.296	7.229	7.091	6.987	6.880
	0.005	18.63	14.54	12.92	12.03	11.46	11.07	10.79	10.57	10.39	10.25	10.03	9.814	9.589	9.451	9.358	9.170	9.026	8.879
7	0.100	3.589	3.257	3.074	2.961	2.883	2.827	2.785	2.752	2.725	2.703	2.668	2.632	2.595	2.571	2.555	2.523	2.497	2.471
	0.050	5.591	4.737	4.347	4.120	3.972	3.886	3.787	3.726	3.677	3.637	3.575	3.511	3.445	3.404	3.376	3.319	3.275	3.230
	0.025	8.073	6.542	5.890	5.523	5.285	5.119	4.995	4.899	4.823	4.761	4.666	4.568	4.467	4.405	4.362	4.276	4.210	4.142
	0.010	12.25	9.547	8.451	7.847	7.460	7.191	6.993	6.840	6.719	6.620	6.469	6.314	6.155	6.058	5.992	5.858	5.755	5.650
	0.005	16.24	12.40	10.88	10.05	9.522	9.155	8.885	8.678	8.514	8.380	8.176	7.968	7.754	7.623	7.534	7.354	7.217	7.076
8	0.100	3.458	3.113	2.924	2.806	2.726	2.668	2.624	2.589	2.561	2.538	2.502	2.464	2.425	2.400	2.383	2.348	2.321	2.293
	0.050	5.318	4.459	4.066	3.838	3.687	3.581	3.500	3.438	3.388	3.347	3.284	3.218	3.150	3.108	3.079	3.020	2.975	2.928
	0.025	7.571	6.059	5.416	5.055	4.817	4.652	4.529	4.433	4.357	4.295	4.200	4.101	3.999	3.937	3.894	3.807	3.739	3.670
	0.010	11.26	8.649	7.591	7.006	6.632	6.371	6.178	6.029	5.911	5.814	5.667	5.515	5.359	5.263	5.198	5.065	4.963	4.859
	0.005	14.69	11.04	9.596	8.805	8.302	7.952	7.694	7.496	7.339	7.211	7.015	6.814	6.608	6.482	6.396	6.222	6.088	5.951
9	0.100	3.360	3.006	2.813	2.693	2.611	2.551	2.505	2.469	2.440	2.416	2.379	2.340	2.298	2.272	2.255	2.218	2.189	2.159
	0.050	5.117	4.256	3.863	3.633	3.482	3.374	3.293	3.230	3.179	3.137	3.073	3.006	2.936	2.893	2.864	2.803	2.756	2.707
	0.025	7.209	5.715	5.078	4.718	4.484	4.320	4.197	4.102	4.026	3.964	3.868	3.769	3.667	3.604	3.560	3.472	3.403	3.333
	0.010	10.56	8.022	6.992	6.422	6.057	5.802	5.613	5.467	5.351	5.257	5.111	4.962	4.808	4.713	4.649	4.517	4.415	4.311
	0.005	13.61	10.11	8.717	7.956	7.471	7.134	6.885	6.693	6.541	6.417	6.227	6.032	5.832	5.708	5.625	5.454	5.322	5.188
10	0.100	3.285	2.924	2.728	2.605	2.522	2.461	2.414	2.377	2.347	2.323	2.284	2.244	2.201	2.174	2.155	2.117	2.087	2.055
	0.050	4.965	4.103	3.708	3.478	3.326	3.217	3.135	3.072	3.020	2.978	2.913	2.845	2.774	2.730	2.700	2.637	2.588	2.538
	0.025	6.937	5.456	4.826	4.468	4.236	4.072	3.950	3.855	3.779	3.717	3.621	3.522	3.419	3.355	3.311	3.221	3.152	3.080
	0.010	10.04	7.559	6.552	5.994	5.636	5.386	5.200	5.057	4.942	4.849	4.706	4.558	4.405	4.311	4.247	4.115	4.014	3.909
	0.005	12.83	9.427	8.081	7.343	6.872	6.545	6.302	6.116	5.968	5.847	5.661	5.471	5.274	5.153	5.071	4.902	4.772	4.639
11	0.100	3.225	2.860	2.660	2.536	2.451	2.389	2.342	2.304	2.274	2.248	2.209	2.167	2.123	2.095	2.076	2.036	2.005	1.972
	0.050	4.884	3.982	3.587	3.357	3.204	3.095	3.012	2.948	2.896	2.854	2.788	2.719	2.646	2.601	2.570	2.507	2.457	2.404
	0.025	6.724	5.256	4.630	4.275	4.044	3.881	3.759	3.664	3.588	3.526	3.430	3.330	3.226	3.162	3.118	3.027	2.956	2.883
	0.010	9.646	7.206	6.217	5.668	5.316	5.069	4.886	4.744	4.632	4.539	4.397	4.251	4.099	4.005	3.941	3.810	3.708	3.602
	0.005	12.23	8.912	7.600	6.881	6.422	6.102	5.865	5.682	5.537	5.418	5.236	5.049	4.855	4.734	4.654	4.486	4.359	4.226

15

Table 9 – *continued*

ν_2	α	1	2	3	4	5	6	7	8	9	10	12	15	20	25	30	50	100	∞
12	0.100	3.177	2.807	2.606	2.480	2.394	2.331	2.283	2.245	2.214	2.188	2.147	2.105	2.060	2.031	2.011	1.970	1.938	1.904
	0.050	4.747	3.885	3.490	3.259	3.106	2.996	2.913	2.849	2.796	2.753	2.687	2.617	2.544	2.498	2.466	2.401	2.350	2.296
	0.025	6.554	5.096	4.474	4.121	3.891	3.728	3.607	3.512	3.436	3.374	3.277	3.177	3.073	3.008	2.963	2.871	2.800	2.725
	0.010	9.330	6.927	5.953	5.412	5.064	4.821	4.640	4.499	4.388	4.296	4.155	4.010	3.858	3.765	3.701	3.569	3.467	3.361
	0.005	11.75	8.510	7.226	6.521	6.071	5.757	5.525	5.345	5.202	5.085	4.906	4.721	4.530	4.412	4.331	4.165	4.037	3.904
13	0.100	3.136	2.763	2.560	2.434	2.347	2.283	2.234	2.195	2.164	2.138	2.097	2.053	2.007	1.978	1.958	1.915	1.882	1.846
	0.050	4.667	3.806	3.411	3.179	3.025	2.915	2.832	2.767	2.714	2.671	2.604	2.533	2.459	2.412	2.380	2.314	2.261	2.206
	0.025	6.414	4.965	4.327	3.996	3.707	3.604	3.483	3.388	3.312	3.250	3.153	3.053	2.948	2.882	2.837	2.744	2.671	2.595
	0.010	9.074	6.701	5.739	5.205	4.862	4.620	4.441	4.302	4.191	4.100	3.960	3.815	3.665	3.571	3.507	3.375	3.272	3.165
	0.005	11.37	8.186	6.926	6.233	5.791	5.482	5.253	5.076	4.935	4.820	4.643	4.460	4.270	4.153	4.073	3.908	3.780	3.647
14	0.100	3.102	2.726	2.522	2.395	2.307	2.243	2.193	2.154	2.122	2.095	2.054	2.010	1.962	1.933	1.912	1.869	1.834	1.797
	0.050	4.600	3.739	3.344	3.112	2.958	2.848	2.764	2.699	2.646	2.602	2.534	2.463	2.388	2.341	2.308	2.241	2.187	2.131
	0.025	6.298	4.857	4.222	3.892	3.663	3.501	3.380	3.285	3.209	3.147	3.050	2.949	2.844	2.778	2.732	2.638	2.565	2.487
	0.010	8.862	6.515	5.564	5.035	4.695	4.456	4.278	4.140	4.030	3.939	3.800	3.656	3.505	3.412	3.348	3.215	3.112	3.004
	0.005	11.06	7.922	6.680	5.998	5.562	5.257	5.031	4.857	4.717	4.603	4.428	4.247	4.059	3.942	3.862	3.698	3.569	3.436
15	0.100	3.073	2.695	2.490	2.361	2.273	2.208	2.158	2.119	2.086	2.059	2.017	1.972	1.924	1.894	1.873	1.828	1.793	1.755
	0.050	4.543	3.682	3.287	3.056	2.901	2.790	2.707	2.641	2.588	2.544	2.475	2.403	2.328	2.280	2.247	2.178	2.123	2.066
	0.025	6.200	4.765	4.153	3.804	3.576	3.415	3.293	3.199	3.123	3.060	2.963	2.862	2.756	2.689	2.644	2.540	2.474	2.395
	0.010	8.683	6.359	5.417	4.893	4.556	4.318	4.142	4.004	3.895	3.805	3.666	3.522	3.372	3.278	3.214	3.081	2.977	2.868
	0.005	10.80	7.701	6.476	5.805	5.372	5.071	4.847	4.674	4.536	4.424	4.250	4.070	3.883	3.766	3.687	3.523	3.394	3.260
16	0.100	3.048	2.668	2.462	2.333	2.244	2.178	2.128	2.088	2.055	2.028	1.985	1.940	1.891	1.860	1.839	1.793	1.757	1.718
	0.050	4.494	3.634	3.239	3.007	2.852	2.741	2.657	2.591	2.538	2.494	2.425	2.352	2.276	2.227	2.194	2.124	2.068	2.010
	0.025	6.115	4.687	4.077	3.729	3.502	3.341	3.219	3.125	3.049	2.986	2.889	2.788	2.681	2.614	2.568	2.472	2.396	2.316
	0.010	8.531	6.226	5.292	4.773	4.437	4.202	4.026	3.890	3.780	3.691	3.553	3.409	3.259	3.165	3.101	2.967	2.863	2.753
	0.005	10.58	7.514	6.303	5.638	5.212	4.913	4.692	4.521	4.384	4.272	4.099	3.920	3.734	3.618	3.539	3.375	3.246	3.112
17	0.100	3.026	2.645	2.437	2.308	2.218	2.152	2.102	2.061	2.028	2.001	1.958	1.912	1.862	1.831	1.809	1.763	1.726	1.686
	0.050	4.451	3.592	3.197	2.965	2.810	2.699	2.614	2.548	2.494	2.450	2.381	2.308	2.230	2.181	2.148	2.077	2.020	1.960
	0.025	6.042	4.619	4.011	3.665	3.438	3.277	3.156	3.061	2.985	2.922	2.825	2.723	2.616	2.548	2.502	2.405	2.329	2.247
	0.010	8.400	6.112	5.185	4.669	4.336	4.102	3.927	3.791	3.682	3.593	3.455	3.312	3.162	3.068	3.003	2.869	2.764	2.653
	0.005	10.38	7.354	6.156	5.497	5.075	4.779	4.559	4.389	4.254	4.142	3.971	3.793	3.607	3.492	3.412	3.248	3.119	2.984
18	0.100	3.007	2.624	2.416	2.286	2.196	2.130	2.079	2.038	2.005	1.977	1.933	1.887	1.837	1.805	1.783	1.736	1.698	1.657
	0.050	4.414	3.555	3.160	2.928	2.773	2.661	2.577	2.510	2.456	2.412	2.342	2.269	2.191	2.141	2.107	2.035	1.978	1.917
	0.025	5.978	4.560	3.954	3.608	3.382	3.221	3.100	3.005	2.929	2.866	2.769	2.667	2.559	2.491	2.445	2.347	2.269	2.187
	0.010	8.285	6.013	5.092	4.579	4.248	4.015	3.841	3.705	3.597	3.508	3.371	3.227	3.077	2.983	2.919	2.784	2.678	2.566
	0.005	10.22	7.215	6.028	5.375	4.956	4.663	4.445	4.276	4.141	4.030	3.860	3.683	3.498	3.382	3.303	3.130	3.009	2.873
19	0.100	2.990	2.606	2.397	2.266	2.176	2.109	2.058	2.017	1.984	1.956	1.912	1.865	1.814	1.782	1.759	1.711	1.673	1.631
	0.050	4.381	3.522	3.127	2.895	2.740	2.628	2.544	2.477	2.423	2.378	2.308	2.234	2.155	2.106	2.071	1.999	1.940	1.878
	0.025	5.922	4.508	3.903	3.559	3.333	3.172	3.051	2.956	2.880	2.817	2.720	2.617	2.509	2.441	2.394	2.295	2.217	2.133
	0.010	8.185	5.926	5.010	4.500	4.171	3.939	3.765	3.631	3.523	3.434	3.297	3.153	3.003	2.909	2.844	2.709	2.602	2.489
	0.005	10.07	7.093	5.916	5.268	4.853	4.561	4.345	4.177	4.043	3.933	3.763	3.587	3.402	3.287	3.208	3.043	2.913	2.776
20	0.100	2.975	2.589	2.380	2.249	2.158	2.091	2.040	1.999	1.965	1.937	1.892	1.845	1.794	1.761	1.738	1.690	1.650	1.607
	0.050	4.351	3.493	3.098	2.866	2.711	2.599	2.514	2.447	2.393	2.348	2.278	2.203	2.124	2.074	2.039	1.966	1.907	1.843
	0.025	5.871	4.461	3.859	3.515	3.289	3.128	3.007	2.913	2.837	2.774	2.676	2.573	2.464	2.396	2.349	2.249	2.170	2.085
	0.010	8.096	5.849	4.938	4.431	4.103	3.871	3.699	3.564	3.457	3.368	3.231	3.088	2.938	2.843	2.778	2.643	2.535	2.421
	0.005	9.944	6.986	5.818	5.174	4.762	4.472	4.257	4.090	3.956	3.847	3.678	3.502	3.318	3.203	3.123	2.950	2.828	2.690
21	0.100	2.961	2.575	2.365	2.233	2.142	2.075	2.023	1.982	1.948	1.920	1.875	1.827	1.776	1.742	1.719	1.670	1.630	1.586
	0.050	4.325	3.467	3.072	2.840	2.685	2.573	2.488	2.420	2.366	2.321	2.250	2.176	2.096	2.045	2.010	1.936	1.876	1.812
	0.025	5.827	4.420	3.819	3.475	3.250	3.090	2.969	2.874	2.798	2.735	2.637	2.534	2.425	2.356	2.308	2.208	2.128	2.042
	0.010	8.017	5.780	4.874	4.369	4.042	3.812	3.640	3.506	3.398	3.310	3.173	3.030	2.880	2.785	2.720	2.584	2.475	2.360
	0.005	9.830	6.891	5.730	5.091	4.681	4.393	4.179	4.013	3.880	3.771	3.602	3.427	3.243	3.128	3.049	2.884	2.753	2.614
22	0.100	2.949	2.561	2.351	2.219	2.128	2.060	2.008	1.967	1.933	1.904	1.859	1.811	1.759	1.726	1.702	1.652	1.611	1.567
	0.050	4.301	3.443	3.049	2.817	2.661	2.549	2.464	2.397	2.342	2.297	2.226	2.151	2.071	2.020	1.984	1.909	1.849	1.783
	0.025	5.786	4.383	3.783	3.440	3.215	3.055	2.934	2.839	2.763	2.700	2.602	2.498	2.389	2.320	2.272	2.171	2.090	2.003
	0.010	7.945	5.719	4.817	4.313	3.988	3.758	3.587	3.453	3.346	3.258	3.121	2.978	2.827	2.733	2.667	2.531	2.422	2.305
	0.005	9.727	6.806	5.652	5.017	4.609	4.322	4.109	3.944	3.812	3.703	3.535	3.360	3.176	3.061	2.982	2.817	2.685	2.545
23	0.100	2.937	2.549	2.339	2.207	2.115	2.047	1.995	1.953	1.919	1.890	1.845	1.796	1.744	1.710	1.686	1.636	1.594	1.549
	0.050	4.279	3.422	3.028	2.796	2.640	2.528	2.442	2.375	2.320	2.275	2.204	2.128	2.048	1.996	1.961	1.885	1.823	1.757
	0.025	5.750	4.349	3.750	3.408	3.183	3.023	2.902	2.808	2.731	2.668	2.570	2.466	2.357	2.287	2.239	2.137	2.056	1.968
	0.010	7.881	5.664	4.765	4.264	3.939	3.710	3.539	3.406	3.299	3.211	3.074	2.931	2.781	2.686	2.620	2.483	2.373	2.256
	0.005	9.635	6.730	5.582	4.950	4.544	4.259	4.047	3.882	3.750	3.642	3.475	3.300	3.116	3.001	2.922	2.756	2.624	2.484
24	0.100	2.927	2.538	2.327	2.195	2.103	2.035	1.983	1.941	1.906	1.877	1.832	1.783	1.730	1.696	1.672	1.621	1.579	1.533
	0.050	4.260	3.403	3.009	2.776	2.621	2.508	2.423	2.355	2.300	2.255	2.183	2.108	2.027	1.975	1.939	1.863	1.800	1.733
	0.025	5.717	4.319	3.721	3.379	3.155	2.995	2.874	2.779	2.703	2.640	2.541	2.437	2.327	2.257	2.209	2.107	2.024	1.935
	0.010	7.823	5.614	4.718	4.218	3.895	3.667	3.496	3.363	3.256	3.168	3.032	2.889	2.738	2.643	2.577	2.440	2.329	2.211
	0.005	9.551	6.661	5.519	4.890	4.486	4.202	3.991	3.826	3.695	3.587	3.420	3.246	3.062	2.947	2.868	2.702	2.569	2.428

Table 9 – *continued*

v_2	α \ v_1	1	2	3	4	5	6	7	8	9	10	12	15	20	25	30	50	100	∞
25	0.100	2.918	2.528	2.317	2.184	2.092	2.024	1.971	1.929	1.895	1.866	1.820	1.771	1.718	1.683	1.659	1.607	1.565	1.518
	0.050	4.242	3.385	2.991	2.759	2.603	2.490	2.405	2.337	2.282	2.236	2.165	2.089	2.007	1.955	1.919	1.842	1.779	1.711
	0.025	5.686	4.291	3.694	3.353	3.129	2.969	2.848	2.753	2.677	2.613	2.515	2.411	2.300	2.230	2.182	2.070	1.996	1.906
	0.010	7.770	5.568	4.675	4.177	3.855	3.627	3.457	3.324	3.217	3.129	2.993	2.850	2.699	2.604	2.538	2.400	2.289	2.169
	0.005	9.475	6.598	5.462	4.835	4.433	4.150	3.939	3.776	3.645	3.537	3.370	3.196	3.013	2.898	2.819	2.652	2.519	2.377
26	0.100	2.909	2.519	2.307	2.174	2.082	2.014	1.961	1.919	1.884	1.855	1.809	1.760	1.706	1.671	1.647	1.594	1.551	1.504
	0.050	4.225	3.369	2.975	2.743	2.587	2.474	2.388	2.321	2.265	2.220	2.148	2.072	1.990	1.938	1.901	1.823	1.760	1.691
	0.025	5.659	4.265	3.670	3.329	3.105	2.945	2.824	2.729	2.653	2.590	2.491	2.387	2.276	2.205	2.157	2.053	1.969	1.878
	0.010	7.721	5.526	4.637	4.140	3.818	3.591	3.421	3.288	3.182	3.094	2.958	2.815	2.664	2.569	2.503	2.364	2.252	2.131
	0.005	9.406	6.541	5.409	4.785	4.384	4.103	3.893	3.730	3.599	3.492	3.325	3.151	2.968	2.853	2.774	2.607	2.473	2.330
27	0.100	2.901	2.511	2.299	2.165	2.073	2.005	1.952	1.909	1.874	1.845	1.799	1.749	1.695	1.660	1.636	1.583	1.539	1.491
	0.050	4.210	3.354	2.960	2.728	2.572	2.459	2.373	2.305	2.250	2.204	2.132	2.056	1.974	1.921	1.884	1.806	1.742	1.672
	0.025	5.633	4.242	3.647	3.307	3.083	2.923	2.802	2.707	2.631	2.568	2.469	2.364	2.253	2.183	2.133	2.028	1.945	1.853
	0.010	7.677	5.488	4.601	4.106	3.785	3.558	3.388	3.256	3.149	3.062	2.926	2.783	2.632	2.536	2.470	2.330	2.218	2.097
	0.005	9.342	6.489	5.361	4.740	4.340	4.059	3.850	3.687	3.557	3.450	3.284	3.110	2.928	2.812	2.733	2.565	2.431	2.287
28	0.100	2.894	2.503	2.291	2.157	2.064	1.996	1.943	1.900	1.865	1.836	1.790	1.740	1.685	1.650	1.625	1.572	1.528	1.478
	0.050	4.196	3.340	2.947	2.714	2.558	2.445	2.359	2.291	2.236	2.190	2.118	2.041	1.959	1.906	1.869	1.790	1.725	1.654
	0.025	5.610	4.221	3.626	3.286	3.063	2.903	2.782	2.687	2.611	2.547	2.448	2.344	2.232	2.161	2.112	2.007	1.922	1.829
	0.010	7.636	5.453	4.568	4.074	3.754	3.528	3.358	3.226	3.120	3.032	2.896	2.753	2.602	2.506	2.440	2.300	2.187	2.064
	0.005	9.284	6.440	5.317	4.698	4.300	4.020	3.811	3.649	3.519	3.412	3.246	3.073	2.890	2.775	2.695	2.527	2.392	2.247
29	0.100	2.887	2.495	2.283	2.149	2.057	1.988	1.935	1.892	1.857	1.827	1.781	1.731	1.676	1.640	1.616	1.562	1.517	1.467
	0.050	4.183	3.328	2.934	2.701	2.545	2.432	2.346	2.278	2.223	2.177	2.104	2.027	1.945	1.891	1.854	1.775	1.710	1.638
	0.025	5.588	4.201	3.607	3.267	3.044	2.884	2.763	2.669	2.592	2.529	2.430	2.325	2.213	2.142	2.092	1.987	1.901	1.807
	0.010	7.598	5.420	4.538	4.045	3.725	3.499	3.330	3.198	3.092	3.005	2.868	2.726	2.574	2.478	2.412	2.271	2.158	2.034
	0.005	9.230	6.396	5.276	4.659	4.262	3.983	3.775	3.613	3.483	3.377	3.211	3.038	2.855	2.740	2.660	2.492	2.357	2.210
30	0.100	2.881	2.489	2.276	2.142	2.049	1.980	1.927	1.884	1.849	1.819	1.773	1.722	1.667	1.632	1.606	1.552	1.507	1.456
	0.050	4.171	3.316	2.922	2.690	2.534	2.421	2.334	2.266	2.211	2.165	2.092	2.015	1.932	1.878	1.841	1.761	1.695	1.622
	0.025	5.568	4.182	3.589	3.250	3.026	2.867	2.746	2.651	2.575	2.511	2.412	2.307	2.195	2.124	2.074	1.968	1.882	1.787
	0.010	7.562	5.390	4.510	4.018	3.699	3.473	3.304	3.173	3.067	2.979	2.843	2.700	2.549	2.453	2.386	2.245	2.131	2.006
	0.005	9.180	6.355	5.239	4.623	4.228	3.949	3.742	3.580	3.450	3.344	3.179	3.006	2.823	2.708	2.628	2.459	2.323	2.176
35	0.100	2.855	2.461	2.247	2.113	2.019	1.950	1.896	1.852	1.817	1.787	1.739	1.688	1.632	1.595	1.569	1.513	1.465	1.411
	0.050	4.121	3.267	2.874	2.641	2.485	2.372	2.285	2.217	2.161	2.114	2.041	1.963	1.878	1.824	1.786	1.703	1.635	1.558
	0.025	5.485	4.106	3.517	3.179	2.956	2.796	2.676	2.581	2.504	2.440	2.341	2.235	2.122	2.049	1.999	1.890	1.801	1.702
	0.010	7.419	5.268	4.396	3.908	3.592	3.368	3.200	3.069	2.963	2.876	2.740	2.597	2.445	2.348	2.281	2.137	2.020	1.891
	0.005	8.976	6.188	5.086	4.479	4.088	3.812	3.607	3.447	3.318	3.212	3.048	2.876	2.693	2.577	2.497	2.327	2.188	2.036
40	0.100	2.835	2.440	2.226	2.091	1.997	1.927	1.873	1.829	1.793	1.763	1.715	1.662	1.605	1.568	1.541	1.483	1.434	1.377
	0.050	4.085	3.232	2.839	2.606	2.449	2.336	2.249	2.180	2.124	2.077	2.003	1.924	1.839	1.783	1.744	1.660	1.589	1.509
	0.025	5.424	4.051	3.463	3.126	2.904	2.744	2.624	2.529	2.452	2.388	2.288	2.182	2.068	1.994	1.943	1.832	1.741	1.637
	0.010	7.314	5.179	4.313	3.828	3.514	3.291	3.124	2.993	2.888	2.801	2.665	2.522	2.369	2.271	2.203	2.058	1.938	1.805
	0.005	8.828	6.066	4.976	4.374	3.986	3.713	3.509	3.350	3.222	3.117	2.953	2.781	2.598	2.482	2.401	2.230	2.088	1.932
45	0.100	2.820	2.425	2.210	2.074	1.980	1.909	1.855	1.811	1.774	1.744	1.695	1.643	1.585	1.546	1.519	1.460	1.409	1.349
	0.050	4.057	3.204	2.812	2.579	2.422	2.308	2.221	2.152	2.096	2.049	1.974	1.895	1.808	1.752	1.713	1.626	1.554	1.470
	0.025	5.377	4.009	3.422	3.086	2.864	2.705	2.584	2.489	2.412	2.348	2.248	2.141	2.026	1.952	1.900	1.788	1.694	1.586
	0.010	7.234	5.110	4.249	3.767	3.454	3.232	3.066	2.935	2.830	2.743	2.608	2.464	2.311	2.213	2.144	1.997	1.875	1.737
	0.005	8.715	5.974	4.892	4.294	3.909	3.638	3.435	3.276	3.149	3.044	2.881	2.709	2.527	2.410	2.329	2.155	2.012	1.851
50	0.100	2.809	2.412	2.197	2.061	1.966	1.895	1.840	1.796	1.760	1.729	1.680	1.627	1.568	1.529	1.502	1.441	1.388	1.327
	0.050	4.034	3.183	2.790	2.557	2.400	2.286	2.199	2.130	2.073	2.026	1.952	1.871	1.784	1.727	1.687	1.599	1.525	1.438
	0.025	5.340	3.975	3.390	3.054	2.833	2.674	2.553	2.458	2.381	2.317	2.216	2.109	1.993	1.919	1.866	1.752	1.656	1.545
	0.010	7.171	5.057	4.199	3.720	3.408	3.186	3.020	2.890	2.785	2.698	2.562	2.419	2.265	2.167	2.098	1.949	1.825	1.683
	0.005	8.626	5.902	4.826	4.232	3.849	3.579	3.376	3.219	3.092	2.988	2.825	2.653	2.470	2.353	2.272	2.097	1.951	1.786
60	0.100	2.791	2.393	2.177	2.041	1.946	1.875	1.819	1.775	1.738	1.707	1.657	1.603	1.543	1.504	1.476	1.413	1.358	1.291
	0.50	4.001	3.150	2.758	2.525	2.368	2.254	2.167	2.097	2.040	1.993	1.917	1.836	1.748	1.690	1.649	1.559	1.481	1.389
	0.025	5.286	3.925	3.343	3.008	2.786	2.627	2.507	2.412	2.334	2.270	2.169	2.061	1.944	1.869	1.815	1.690	1.599	1.482
	0.010	7.077	4.977	4.126	3.649	3.339	3.119	2.953	2.823	2.718	2.632	2.496	2.352	2.198	2.098	2.028	1.877	1.749	1.601
	0.005	8.495	5.795	4.729	4.140	3.760	3.492	3.291	3.134	3.008	2.904	2.742	2.570	2.387	2.270	2.187	2.010	1.861	1.689
70	0.100	2.779	2.380	2.164	2.027	1.931	1.860	1.804	1.760	1.723	1.691	1.641	1.587	1.526	1.486	1.457	1.392	1.335	1.265
	0.050	3.978	3.128	2.736	2.503	2.346	2.231	2.143	2.074	2.017	1.969	1.893	1.812	1.722	1.664	1.622	1.530	1.450	1.353
	0.025	5.247	3.890	3.309	2.975	2.754	2.595	2.474	2.379	2.302	2.237	2.136	2.028	1.910	1.833	1.779	1.660	1.558	1.436
	0.010	7.011	4.922	4.074	3.600	3.291	3.071	2.906	2.777	2.672	2.585	2.450	2.306	2.150	2.050	1.980	1.826	1.695	1.540
	0.005	8.403	5.720	4.661	4.076	3.698	3.431	3.232	3.076	2.950	2.846	2.684	2.513	2.329	2.211	2.128	1.940	1.797	1.618
80	0.100	2.769	2.370	2.154	2.016	1.921	1.849	1.793	1.748	1.711	1.680	1.629	1.574	1.513	1.472	1.443	1.377	1.318	1.245
	0.050	3.960	3.111	2.719	2.486	2.329	2.214	2.126	2.056	1.999	1.951	1.875	1.793	1.703	1.644	1.602	1.508	1.426	1.325
	0.025	5.218	3.864	3.284	2.950	2.730	2.571	2.450	2.355	2.277	2.213	2.111	2.003	1.884	1.807	1.752	1.632	1.527	1.400
	0.010	6.963	4.881	4.036	3.563	3.255	3.036	2.871	2.742	2.637	2.551	2.415	2.271	2.115	2.015	1.944	1.788	1.655	1.494
	0.005	8.335	5.665	4.611	4.029	3.652	3.387	3.188	3.032	2.907	2.803	2.641	2.470	2.286	2.168	2.084	1.903	1.748	1.563

Table 9 – *continued*

v_2	α	1	2	3	4	5	6	7	8	9	10	12	15	20	25	30	50	100	∞
90	0.100	2.762	2.363	2.146	2.008	1.912	1.841	1.785	1.739	1.702	1.670	1.620	1.564	1.503	1.461	1.432	1.365	1.304	1.228
	0.050	3.947	3.098	2.706	2.473	2.316	2.201	2.113	2.043	1.986	1.938	1.861	1.779	1.688	1.629	1.586	1.491	1.407	1.302
	0.025	5.196	3.844	3.265	2.932	2.711	2.552	2.432	2.336	2.259	2.194	2.092	1.983	1.864	1.787	1.731	1.610	1.503	1.371
	0.010	6.925	4.849	4.007	3.535	3.228	3.009	2.845	2.715	2.611	2.524	2.389	2.244	2.088	1.987	1.916	1.759	1.623	1.457
	0.005	8.282	5.623	4.573	3.992	3.617	3.352	3.154	2.999	2.873	2.770	2.608	2.437	2.253	2.134	2.051	1.868	1.711	1.520
100	0.100	2.756	2.356	2.139	2.002	1.906	1.834	1.778	1.732	1.695	1.663	1.612	1.557	1.494	1.453	1.423	1.355	1.293	1.214
	0.050	3.936	3.087	2.696	2.463	2.305	2.191	2.103	2.032	1.975	1.927	1.850	1.768	1.676	1.616	1.573	1.477	1.392	1.283
	0.025	5.179	3.828	3.250	2.917	2.696	2.537	2.417	2.321	2.244	2.179	2.077	1.968	1.849	1.770	1.715	1.592	1.483	1.347
	0.010	6.895	4.824	3.984	3.513	3.206	2.988	2.823	2.694	2.590	2.503	2.368	2.223	2.067	1.965	1.893	1.735	1.598	1.427
	0.005	8.241	5.589	4.542	3.963	3.589	3.325	3.127	2.972	2.847	2.744	2.583	2.411	2.227	2.108	2.024	1.840	1.681	1.485
120	0.100	2.748	2.347	2.130	1.992	1.896	1.824	1.767	1.722	1.684	1.652	1.601	1.545	1.482	1.440	1.409	1.340	1.277	1.193
	0.050	3.920	3.072	2.680	2.447	2.290	2.175	2.087	2.016	1.959	1.910	1.834	1.750	1.659	1.598	1.554	1.457	1.369	1.254
	0.025	5.152	3.805	3.227	2.894	2.674	2.515	2.395	2.299	2.222	2.157	2.055	1.945	1.825	1.746	1.690	1.565	1.454	1.310
	0.010	6.851	4.787	3.949	3.480	3.174	2.956	2.792	2.663	2.559	2.472	2.336	2.192	2.035	1.932	1.860	1.700	1.559	1.381
	0.005	8.179	5.539	4.497	3.921	3.548	3.285	3.087	2.933	2.808	2.705	2.544	2.373	2.188	2.069	1.984	1.798	1.636	1.431
150	0.100	2.739	2.338	2.121	1.983	1.886	1.814	1.757	1.712	1.674	1.642	1.590	1.533	1.470	1.427	1.396	1.325	1.259	1.169
	0.050	3.904	3.056	2.665	2.432	2.274	2.160	2.071	2.001	1.943	1.894	1.817	1.734	1.641	1.580	1.535	1.436	1.345	1.223
	0.025	5.126	3.781	3.204	2.871	2.652	2.494	2.373	2.278	2.200	2.135	2.032	1.922	1.801	1.722	1.665	1.538	1.423	1.271
	0.010	6.807	4.749	3.915	3.447	3.142	2.924	2.761	2.632	2.528	2.441	2.305	2.160	2.003	1.900	1.827	1.665	1.520	1.331
	0.005	8.118	5.490	4.453	3.878	3.508	3.245	3.048	2.894	2.770	2.667	2.506	2.335	2.150	2.030	1.944	1.756	1.590	1.374
200	0.100	2.731	2.329	2.111	1.973	1.876	1.804	1.747	1.701	1.663	1.631	1.579	1.522	1.458	1.414	1.383	1.310	1.242	1.144
	0.050	3.888	3.041	2.650	2.417	2.259	2.144	2.056	1.985	1.927	1.878	1.801	1.717	1.623	1.561	1.516	1.415	1.321	1.189
	0.025	5.100	3.758	3.182	2.850	2.630	2.472	2.351	2.256	2.178	2.113	2.010	1.900	1.778	1.698	1.640	1.511	1.393	1.229
	0.010	6.763	4.713	3.881	3.414	3.110	2.893	2.730	2.601	2.497	2.411	2.275	2.129	1.971	1.868	1.794	1.629	1.481	1.279
	0.005	8.057	5.441	4.408	3.837	3.467	3.206	3.010	2.856	2.732	2.629	2.468	2.297	2.112	1.991	1.905	1.715	1.544	1.314
500	0.100	2.716	2.313	2.095	1.956	1.859	1.786	1.729	1.683	1.644	1.612	1.559	1.501	1.435	1.391	1.358	1.282	1.209	1.087
	0.050	3.860	3.014	2.623	2.390	2.232	2.117	2.028	1.957	1.899	1.850	1.772	1.686	1.592	1.528	1.482	1.376	1.275	1.113
	0.025	5.054	3.716	3.142	2.811	2.592	2.434	2.313	2.217	2.139	2.074	1.971	1.859	1.736	1.655	1.596	1.462	1.336	1.137
	0.010	6.686	4.648	3.821	3.357	3.054	2.838	2.675	2.547	2.443	2.356	2.220	2.075	1.915	1.810	1.735	1.566	1.408	1.164
	0.005	7.950	5.355	4.330	3.763	3.396	3.137	2.941	2.789	2.665	2.562	2.402	2.230	2.044	1.922	1.835	1.640	1.460	1.184
1000	0.100	2.711	2.308	2.089	1.950	1.853	1.780	1.723	1.676	1.638	1.605	1.552	1.494	1.428	1.383	1.350	1.273	1.197	1.060
	0.050	3.851	3.005	2.614	2.381	2.223	2.108	2.019	1.948	1.889	1.840	1.762	1.676	1.581	1.517	1.471	1.363	1.260	1.078
	0.025	5.039	3.703	3.129	2.799	2.579	2.421	2.300	2.204	2.126	2.061	1.958	1.846	1.722	1.640	1.581	1.445	1.316	1.094
	0.010	6.660	4.625	3.801	3.338	3.036	2.820	2.657	2.529	2.425	2.339	2.203	2.056	1.897	1.791	1.716	1.544	1.383	1.112
	0.005	7.915	5.326	4.305	3.739	3.373	3.114	2.919	2.766	2.643	2.541	2.380	2.208	2.022	1.900	1.812	1.615	1.431	1.125
∞	0.100	2.706	2.303	2.084	1.945	1.847	1.774	1.717	1.670	1.632	1.599	1.546	1.487	1.421	1.375	1.342	1.263	1.185	1.000
	0.050	3.841	2.996	2.605	2.372	2.214	2.099	2.010	1.938	1.880	1.831	1.752	1.666	1.571	1.506	1.459	1.350	1.243	1.000
	0.025	5.024	3.689	3.116	2.786	2.567	2.408	2.288	2.192	2.114	2.048	1.945	1.833	1.708	1.626	1.566	1.428	1.296	1.000
	0.010	6.635	4.605	3.782	3.319	3.017	2.802	2.639	2.511	2.407	2.321	2.185	2.039	1.878	1.773	1.696	1.523	1.358	1.000
	0.005	7.879	5.298	4.279	3.715	3.350	3.091	2.897	2.744	2.621	2.519	2.358	2.187	2.000	1.877	1.789	1.590	1.402	1.000

(b) Regression and correlation

Table 10. Significance of correlation coefficient, when $\rho = 0$

Values of r significant at α (one-tail) and 2α (two-tail) levels for different number of degrees of freedom ($\nu = n - 2$) where n = number of observations in the sample. **Example:** If $|r| > 0.4438$ when $\nu = 18$, H_0 that $\rho = 0$ may be rejected at 5% level of significance ($2\alpha = 0.05$). When testing partial correlation coefficient, $\nu = n - k - 2$, where k = number of variables held constant, e.g. for $r_{12.3}$, $k = 1$.

ν	$\alpha = 0.25$ $2\alpha = 0.5$	$\alpha = 0.15$ $2\alpha = 0.3$	$\alpha = 0.1$ $2\alpha = 0.2$	$\alpha = 0.05$ $2\alpha = 0.1$	$\alpha = 0.025$ $2\alpha = 0.05$	$\alpha = 0.01$ $2\alpha = 0.02$	$\alpha = 0.005$ $2\alpha = 0.01$	$\alpha = 0.001$ $2\alpha = 0.002$	$\alpha = 0.0005$ $2\alpha = 0.001$
1	.7071	.8910	.9511	.9877	.9969	.9995	.9999	1.0000	1.0000
2	.5000	.7000	.8000	.9000	.9500	.9800	.9900	.9980	9990
3	.4040	.5851	.6870	.8054	.8783	.9343	.9587	.9859	.9911
4	.3473	.5112	.6084	.7293	.8114	.8822	.9172	.9633	.9741
5	.3091	.4592	.5509	.6694	.7545	.8329	.8745	.9350	.9509
6	.2811	.4202	.5067	.6215	.7067	.7887	.8343	.9049	.9249
7	.2596	.3896	.4716	.5822	.6664	.7498	.7977	.8751	.8983
8	.2423	.3648	.4428	.5494	.6319	.7155	.7646	.8467	.8721
9	.2281	.3442	.4187	.5214	.6021	.6851	.7348	.8199	.8470
10	.2161	.3267	.3981	.4973	.5760	.6581	.7079	.7950	.8233
11	.2058	.3116	.3802	.4762	.5529	.6339	.6835	.7717	.8010
12	.1968	.2984	.3646	.4575	.5324	.6120	.6614	.7501	.7800
13	.1890	.2868	.3507	.4409	.5140	.5923	.6411	.7301	.7604
14	.1820	.2764	.3383	.4259	.4973	.5742	.6226	.7114	.7419
15	.1757	.2671	.3271	.4124	.4821	.5577	.6055	.6940	.7247
16	.1700	.2587	.3170	.4000	.4683	.5425	.5897	.6777	.7084
17	.1649	.2510	.3077	.3887	.4555	.5285	.5751	.6624	.6932
18	.1602	.2439	.2992	.3783	.4438	.5155	.5614	.6481	.6788
19	.1558	.2375	.2914	.3687	.4329	.5034	.5487	.6346	.6652
20	.1518	.2315	.2841	.3598	.4227	.4921	.5368	.6219	.6524
21	.1481	.2259	.2774	.3515	.4132	.4815	.5256	.6099	.6402
22	.1447	.2207	.2711	.3438	.4044	.4716	.5151	.5986	.6287
23	.1415	.2159	.2653	.3365	.3961	.4622	.5052	.5879	.6178
24	.1384	.2113	.2598	.3297	.3882	.4534	.4958	.5776	.6074
25	.1356	.2071	.2546	.3233	.3809	.4451	.4869	.5679	.5974
26	.1330	.2031	.2497	.3172	.3739	.4372	.4785	.5587	.5880
27	.1305	.1993	.2451	.3115	.3673	.4297	.4705	.5499	.5790
28	.1281	.1957	.2407	.3061	.3610	.4226	.4629	.5415	.5703
29	.1258	.1923	.2366	.3009	.3550	.4158	.4556	.5334	.5620
30	.1237	.1891	.2327	.2960	.3494	.4093	.4487	.5257	.5541
35	.1144	.1751	.2156	.2746	.3246	.3810	.4182	.4916	.5189
40	.1070	.1638	.2018	.2573	.3044	.3578	.3932	.4633	.4896
45	.1008	.1544	.1903	.2429	.2876	.3384	.3721	.4394	.4647
50	.0956	.1465	.1806	.2306	.2732	.3218	.3542	.4188	.4432
60	.0873	.1338	.1650	.2108	.2500	.2948	.3248	.3850	.4079
70	.0808	.1238	.1528	.1954	.2319	.2737	.3017	.3583	.3798
80	.0755	.1158	.1430	.1829	.2172	.2565	.2830	.3364	.3568
90	.0712	.1092	.1348	.1726	.2050	.2422	.2673	.3181	.3375
100	.0675	.1036	.1279	.1638	.1946	.2301	.2540	.3025	.3211
120	.0616	.0946	.1168	.1496	.1779	.2104	.2324	.2771	.2943
150	.0551	.0846	.1045	.1339	.1593	.1886	.2083	.2488	.2643
200	.0477	.0733	.0905	.1161	.1381	.1636	.1809	.2162	.2298
300	.0390	.0598	.0740	.0948	.1129	.1338	.1480	.1771	.1884
500	.0302	.0463	.0573	.0735	.0875	.1038	.1149	.1376	.1464

Table 11. Significance of correlation coefficient, when $\rho \neq 0$

Values of w for different values of r in the relation $w = \frac{1}{2} \log_e \left(\frac{1 + r}{1 - r} \right)$, or values of ω for different values of ρ in the relation $\omega = \frac{1}{2} \log_e \left(\frac{1 + \rho}{1 - \rho} \right)$ where r and ρ are sample and population correlation coefficients respectively. The variable w is approximately Normally distributed with mean = ω and standard deviation = $1/\sqrt{n - 3}$, where n = sample size. Example: If $H_0 \to \rho = 0.5$, $n = 28$ and $r = 0.746$, then $\omega = 0.5493$, $w = 0.9639$, and, therefore, standardised Normal variable $z = |w - \omega|\sqrt{n - 3} = |0.9639 - 0.5493|\sqrt{28 - 3} = 2.073$. As $2.073 > 1.96$, H_0 may be rejected at 5% level of significance (two-tailed test). For negative values of r or ρ, w or ω are negative. For partial correlation coefficient, standard deviation = $1/\sqrt{n - k - 3}$ where k = number of variables held constant, e.g. for $r_{12.3}$, $k = 1$.

r or $\rho \to$	0.000	0.001	0.002	0.003	0.004	0.005	0.006	0.007	0.008	0.009
0.00	0.0000	0.0010	0.0020	0.0030	0.0040	0.0050	0.0060	0.0070	0.0080	0.0090
0.01	0.0100	0.0110	0.0120	0.0130	0.0140	0.0150	0.0160	0.0170	0.0180	0.0190
0.02	0.0200	0.0210	0.0220	0.0230	0.0240	0.0250	0.0260	0.0270	0.0280	0.0290
0.03	0.0300	0.0310	0.0320	0.0330	0.0340	0.0350	0.0360	0.0370	0.0380	0.0390
0.04	0.0400	0.0410	0.0420	0.0430	0.0440	0.0450	0.0460	0.0470	0.0480	0.0490
0.05	0.0500	0.0510	0.0520	0.0530	0.0541	0.0551	0.0561	0.0571	0.0581	0.0591
0.06	0.0601	0.0611	0.0621	0.0631	0.0641	0.0651	0.0661	0.0671	0.0681	0.0691
0.07	0.0701	0.0711	0.0721	0.0731	0.0741	0.0751	0.0761	0.0772	0.0782	0.0792
0.08	0.0802	0.0812	0.0822	0.0832	0.0842	0.0852	0.0862	0.0872	0.0882	0.0892
0.09	0.0902	0.0913	0.0923	0.0933	0.0943	0.0953	0.0963	0.0973	0.0983	0.0993
0.10	0.1003	0.1013	0.1024	0.1034	0.1044	0.1054	0.1064	0.1074	0.1084	0.1094
0.11	0.1104	0.1115	0.1125	0.1135	0.1145	0.1155	0.1165	0.1175	0.1186	0.1196
0.12	0.1206	0.1216	0.1226	0.1236	0.1246	0.1257	0.1267	0.1277	0.1287	0.1297
0.13	0.1307	0.1318	0.1328	0.1338	0.1348	0.1358	0.1368	0.1379	0.1389	0.1399
0.14	0.1409	0.1419	0.1430	0.1440	0.1450	0.1460	0.1471	0.1481	0.1491	0.1501
0.15	0.1511	0.1522	0.1532	0.1542	0.1552	0.1563	0.1573	0.1583	0.1593	0.1604
0.16	0.1614	0.1624	0.1634	0.1645	0.1655	0.1665	0.1676	0.1686	0.1696	0.1706
0.17	0.1717	0.1727	0.1737	0.1748	0.1758	0.1768	0.1779	0.1789	0.1799	0.1809
0.18	0.1820	0.1830	0.1841	0.1851	0.1861	0.1872	0.1882	0.1892	0.1903	0.1913
0.19	0.1923	0.1934	0.1944	0.1955	0.1965	0.1975	0.1986	0.1996	0.2007	0.2017
0.20	0.2027	0.2038	0.2048	0.2059	0.2069	0.2079	0.2090	0.2100	0.2111	0.2121
0.21	0.2132	0.2142	0.2153	0.2163	0.2174	0.2184	0.2195	0.2205	0.2216	0.2226
0.22	0.2237	0.2247	0.2258	0.2268	0.2279	0.2289	0.2300	0.2310	0.2321	0.2331
0.23	0.2342	0.2352	0.2363	0.2374	0.2384	0.2395	0.2405	0.2416	0.2427	0.2437
0.24	0.2448	0.2458	0.2469	0.2480	0.2490	0.2501	0.2512	0.2522	0.2533	0.2543
0.25	0.2554	0.2565	0.2575	0.2586	0.2597	0.2608	0.2618	0.2629	0.2640	0.2650
0.26	0.2661	0.2672	0.2683	0.2693	0.2704	0.2715	0.2726	0.2736	0.2747	0.2758
0.27	0.2769	0.2779	0.2790	0.2801	0.2812	0.2823	0.2833	0.2844	0.2855	0.2866
0.28	0.2877	0.2888	0.2899	0.2909	0.2920	0.2931	0.2942	0.2953	0.2964	0.2975
0.29	0.2986	0.2997	0.3008	0.3018	0.3029	0.3040	0.3051	0.3062	0.3073	0.3084
0.30	0.3095	0.3106	0.3117	0.3128	0.3139	0.3150	0.3161	0.3172	0.3183	0.3194
0.31	0.3205	0.3217	0.3228	0.3239	0.3250	0.3261	0.3272	0.3283	0.3294	0.3305
0.32	0.3316	0.3328	0.3339	0.3350	0.3361	0.3372	0.3383	0.3395	0.3406	0.3417
0.33	0.3428	0.3440	0.3451	0.3462	0.3473	0.3484	0.3496	0.3507	0.3518	0.3530
0.34	0.3541	0.3552	0.3564	0.3575	0.3586	0.3598	0.3609	0.3620	0.3632	0.3643
0.35	0.3654	0.3666	0.3677	0.3689	0.3700	0.3712	0.3723	0.3734	0.3746	0.3757
0.36	0.3769	0.3780	0.3792	0.3803	0.3815	0.3826	0.3838	0.3850	0.3861	0.3873
0.37	0.3884	0.3896	0.3907	0.3919	0.3931	0.3942	0.3954	0.3966	0.3977	0.3989
0.38	0.4001	0.4012	0.4024	0.4036	0.4047	0.4059	0.4071	0.4083	0.4094	0.4106
0.39	0.4118	0.4130	0.4142	0.4153	0.4165	0.4177	0.4189	0.4201	0.4213	0.4225
0.40	0.4236	0.4248	0.4260	0.4272	0.4284	0.4296	0.4308	0.4320	0.4332	0.4344
0.41	0.4356	0.4368	0.4380	0.4392	0.4404	0.4416	0.4428	0.4441	0.4453	0.4465
0.42	0.4477	0.4489	0.4501	0.4513	0.4526	0.4538	0.4550	0.4562	0.4574	0.4587
0.43	0.4599	0.4611	0.4624	0.4636	0.4648	0.4660	0.4673	0.4685	0.4698	0.4710
0.44	0.4722	0.4735	0.4747	0.4760	0.4772	0.4784	0.4797	0.4809	0.4822	0.4834
0.45	0.4847	0.4860	0.4872	0.4885	0.4897	0.4910	0.4922	0.4935	0.4948	0.4960
0.46	0.4973	0.4986	0.4999	0.5011	0.5024	0.5037	0.5049	0.5062	0.5075	0.5088
0.47	0.5101	0.5114	0.5126	0.5139	0.5152	0.5165	0.5178	0.5191	0.5204	0.5217
0.48	0.5230	0.5243	0.5256	0.5269	0.5282	0.5295	0.5308	0.5321	0.5334	0.5347
0.49	0.5361	0.5374	0.5387	0.5400	0.5413	0.5427	0.5440	0.5453	0.5466	0.5480

Table 11 – *continued*

r or ρ→	0.000	0.001	0.002	0.003	0.004	0.005	0.006	0.007	0.008	0.009
0.50	0.5493	0.5506	0.5520	0.5533	0.5547	0.5560	0.5573	0.5587	0.5600	0.5614
0.51	0.5627	0.5641	0.5654	0.5668	0.5682	0.5695	0.5709	0.5722	0.5736	0.5750
0.52	0.5763	0.5777	0.5791	0.5805	0.5818	0.5832	0.5846	0.5860	0.5874	0.5888
0.53	0.5901	0.5915	0.5929	0.5943	0.5957	0.5971	0.5985	0.5999	0.6013	0.6027
0.54	0.6042	0.6056	0.6070	0.6084	0.6098	0.6112	0.6127	0.6141	0.6155	0.6169
0.55	0.6184	0.6198	0.6213	0.6227	0.6241	0.6256	0.6270	0.6285	0.6299	0.6314
0.56	0.6328	0.6343	0.6358	0.6372	0.6387	0.6401	0.6416	0.6431	0.6446	0.6460
0.57	0.6475	0.6490	0.6505	0.6520	0.6535	0.6550	0.6565	0.6580	0.6595	0.6610
0.58	0.6625	0.6640	0.6655	0.6670	0.6685	0.6700	0.6716	0.6731	0.6746	0.6761
0.59	0.6777	0.6792	0.6807	0.6823	0.6838	0.6854	0.6869	0.6885	0.6900	0.6916
0.60	0.6931	0.6947	0.6963	0.6978	0.6994	0.7010	0.7026	0.7042	0.7057	0.7073
0.61	0.7089	0.7105	0.7121	0.7137	0.7153	0.7169	0.7185	0.7201	0.7218	0.7234
0.62	0.7250	0.7266	0.7283	0.7299	0.7315	0.7332	0.7348	0.7365	0.7381	0.7398
0.63	0.7414	0.7431	0.7447	0.7464	0.7481	0.7498	0.7514	0.7531	0.7548	0.7565
0.64	0.7582	0.7599	0.7616	0.7633	0.7650	0.7667	0.7684	0.7701	0.7718	0.7736
0.65	0.7753	0.7770	0.7788	0.7805	0.7823	0.7840	0.7858	0.7875	0.7893	0.7910
0.66	0.7928	0.7946	0.7964	0.7981	0.7999	0.8017	0.8035	0.8053	0.8071	0.8089
0.67	0.8107	0.8126	0.8144	0.8162	0.8180	0.8199	0.8217	0.8236	0.8254	0.8273
0.68	0.8291	0.8310	0.8328	0.8347	0.8366	0.8385	0.8404	0.8423	0.8441	0.8460
0.69	0.8480	0.8499	0.8518	0.8537	0.8556	0.8576	0.8595	0.8614	0.8634	0.8653
0.70	0.8673	0.8693	0.8712	0.8732	0.8752	0.8772	0.8792	0.8812	0.8832	0.8852
0.71	0.8872	0.8892	0.8912	0.8933	0.8953	0.8973	0.8994	0.9014	0.9035	0.9056
0.72	0.9076	0.9097	0.9118	0.9139	0.9160	0.9181	0.9202	0.9223	0.9245	0.9266
0.73	0.9287	0.9309	0.9330	0.9352	0.9373	0.9395	0.9417	0.9439	0.9461	0.9483
0.74	0.9505	0.9527	0.9549	0.9571	0.9594	0.9616	0.9639	0.9661	0.9684	0.9707
0.75	0.9730	0.9752	0.9775	0.9798	0.9822	0.9845	0.9868	0.9892	0.9915	0.9939
0.76	0.9962	0.9986	1.0010	1.0034	1.0058	1.0082	1.0106	1.0130	1.0154	1.0179
0.77	1.0203	1.0228	1.0253	1.0277	1.0302	1.0327	1.0352	1.0378	1.0403	1.0428
0.78	1.0454	1.0479	1.0505	1.0531	1.0557	1.0583	1.0609	1.0635	1.0661	1.0688
0.79	1.0714	1.0741	1.0768	1.0795	1.0822	1.0849	1.0876	1.0903	1.0931	1.0958
0.80	1.0986	1.1014	1.1042	1.1070	1.1098	1.1127	1.1155	1.1184	1.1212	1.1241
0.81	1.1270	1.1299	1.1329	1.1358	1.1388	1.1417	1.1447	1.1477	1.1507	1.1538
0.82	1.1568	1.1599	1.1630	1.1660	1.1692	1.1723	1.1754	1.1786	1.1817	1.1849
0.83	1.1881	1.1914	1.1946	1.1979	1.2011	1.2044	1.2077	1.2111	1.2144	1.2178
0.84	1.2212	1.2246	1.2280	1.2315	1.2349	1.2384	1.2419	1.2454	1.2490	1.2526
0.85	1.2562	1.2598	1.2634	1.2671	1.2707	1.2745	1.2782	1.2819	1.2857	1.2895
0.86	1.2933	1.2972	1.3011	1.3050	1.3089	1.3129	1.3169	1.3209	1.3249	1.3290
0.87	1.3331	1.3372	1.3414	1.3456	1.3498	1.3540	1.3583	1.3626	1.3670	1.3714
0.88	1.3758	1.3802	1.3847	1.3892	1.3938	1.3984	1.4030	1.4077	1.4124	1.4171
0.89	1.4219	1.4268	1.4316	1.4365	1.4415	1.4465	1.4516	1.4566	1.4618	1.4670
0.90	1.4722	1.4775	1.4828	1.4882	1.4937	1.4992	1.5047	1.5103	1.5160	1.5217
0.91	1.5275	1.5334	1.5393	1.5453	1.5513	1.5574	1.5636	1.5698	1.5762	1.5826
0.92	1.5890	1.5956	1.6022	1.6089	1.6157	1.6226	1.6296	1.6366	1.6438	1.6510
0.93	1.6584	1.6658	1.6734	1.6811	1.6888	1.6967	1.7047	1.7129	1.7211	1.7295
0.94	1.7380	1.7467	1.7555	1.7645	1.7736	1.7828	1.7923	1.8019	1.8117	1.8216
0.95	1.8318	1.8421	1.8527	1.8635	1.8745	1.8857	1.8972	1.9090	1.9210	1.9333
0.96	1.9459	1.9588	1.9721	1.9857	1.9996	2.0139	2.0287	2.0439	2.0595	2.0756
0.97	2.0923	2.1095	2.1273	2.1457	2.1649	2.1847	2.2054	2.2269	2.2494	2.2729
0.98	2.2976	2.3235	2.3507	2.3796	2.4101	2.4427	2.4774	2.5147	2.5550	2.5987
0.99	2.6467	2.6996	2.7587	2.8257	2.9031	2.9945	3.1063	3.2504	3.4534	3.8002

Table 12. Significance of rank (Spearman) correlation coefficient

Critical values of the coefficient $r_s = 1 - \left[6 \sum_{i=1}^{n} d_i^2 / n(n^2 - 1) \right]$, where $d = $ difference between ranks, for different values of $n = $ sample size and $\alpha = $ significance level (one tail). **Example:** If a random sample of 10 observations yields $r_s = 0.56$, the hypothesis that $\rho_s = 0$ in the population may be rejected at 5% significance level (one-tail test) as $0.56 > 0.5515 = r_s(\alpha = 0.05)$. When r_s is negative, ignore the sign and test as above. When ranks are tied, both observations are given the rank equal to the average of the two ranks, e.g. if two observations are ranked equal third, they are both given the rank of $3\frac{1}{2}$.

n \ α	.100	.050	.025	.010	.005	.001
4	.8000	.8000				
5	.7000	.8000	.9000	.9000		
6	.6000	.7714	.8286	.8857	.9429	
7	.5357	.6786	.7450	.8571	.8929	.9643
8	.5000	.6190	.7143	.8095	.8571	.9286
9	.4667	.5833	.6833	.7667	.8167	.9000
10	.4424	.5515	.6364	.7333	.7818	.8667
11	.4182	.5273	.6091	.7000	.7455	.8364
12	.3986	.4965	.5804	.6713	.7273	.8182
13	.3791	.4780	.5549	.6429	.6978	.7912
14	.3626	.4593	.5341	.6220	.6747	.7670
15	.3500	.4429	.5179	.6000	.6536	.7464
16	.3382	.4265	.5000	.5824	.6324	.7265
17	.3260	.4118	.4853	.5637	.6152	.7083
18	.3148	.3994	.4716	.5480	.5975	.6904
19	.3070	.3895	.4579	.5333	.5825	.6737
20	.2977	.3789	.4451	.5203	.5684	.6586
21	.2909	.3688	.4351	.5078	.5545	.6455
22	.2829	.3597	.4241	.4963	.5426	.6318
23	.2767	.3518	.4150	.4852	.5306	.6186
24	.2704	.3435	.4061	.4748	.5200	.6070
25	.2646	.3362	.3977	.4654	.5100	.5962
26	.2588	.3299	.3894	.4564	.5002	.5856
27	.2540	.3236	.3822	.4481	.4915	.5757
28	.2490	.3175	.3749	.4401	.4828	.5660
29	.2443	.3113	.3685	.4320	.4744	.5567
30	.2400	.3059	.3620	.4251	.4665	.5479

When $n > 30$, use Table 10 as an approximation.

The table was reproduced from W. J. Connover, *Practical Nonparametric Statistics*, Wiley, 1971; original source: G. J. Glasser and R. Winter, 'Critical values of the coefficient of rank correlation for testing the hypothesis of independence', *Biometrika*, Vol. 48, 1961, with permission of the authors and publishers.

Table 13. Significance of multiple correlation coefficient

Values of R^2 significant at 10%, 5% and 1% for different number of degrees of freedom, ν, and number of explanatory (independent) variables, k, where $\nu = n - k - 1$ and n = sample size. Example: In regression of Y on X and Z based on $n = 20$, $k = 2$, $\nu = 20 - 2 - 1 = 17$, and 5% value of $R^2 = 0.2970$, i.e. sample values of $R^2 > 0.2970$ are significantly different from zero at 5% level.

ν	$k = 1$ 10%	5%	1%	$k = 2$ 10%	5%	1%	$k = 3$ 10%	5%	1%	$k = 4$ 10%	5%	1%	$k = 5$ 10%	5%	1%
1	.9755	.9938	.9998	.9900	.9975	.9999	.9938	.9985	.9999	.9955	.9989	1.0000	.9965	.9991	1.0000
2	.8100	.9025	.9801	.9000	.9500	.9900	.9322	.9664	.9933	.9487	.9747	.9950	.9587	.9797	.9960
3	.6486	.7715	.9192	.7846	.8643	.9536	.8435	.9027	.9672	.8769	.9240	.9745	.8985	.9376	.9792
4	.5319	.6584	.8413	.8838	.7764	.9000	.7586	.8318	.9260	.8042	.8640	.9411	.8351	.8866	.9510
5	.4481	.5693	.7648	.6019	.6983	.8415	.6847	.7645	.8786	.7380	.8060	.9011	.7754	.8347	.9164
6	.3862	.4995	.6961	.5358	.6316	.7846	.6218	.7040	.8302	.6795	.7514	.8591	.7214	.7852	.8793
7	.3390	.4441	.6303	.4821	.5751	.7317	.5685	.6507	.7836	.6285	.7019	.8176	.6732	.7394	.8420
8	.3018	.3993	.5846	.4377	.5271	.6838	.5230	.6039	.7400	.5839	.6574	.7779	.6302	.6974	.8056
9	.2719	.3625	.5399	.4005	.4861	.6406	.4839	.5628	.6998	.5448	.6175	.7405	.5919	.6592	.7709
10	.2473	.3318	.5011	.3690	.4507	.6019	.4500	.5266	.6628	.5103	.5818	.7057	.5577	.6245	.7381
11	.2267	.3057	.4672	.3421	.4200	.5671	.4205	.4945	.6290	.4798	.5497	.6733	.5270	.5929	.7073
12	.2093	.2835	.4374	.3187	.3930	.5358	.3944	.4660	.5981	.4526	.5207	.6434	.4994	.5641	.6785
13	.1944	.2642	.4111	.2983	.3693	.5076	.3714	.4404	.5698	.4282	.4945	.6156	.4744	.5378	.6516
14	.1814	.2473	.3876	.2803	.3482	.4821	.3509	.4174	.5438	.4062	.4707	.5899	.4517	.5137	.6264
15	.1700	.2325	.3666	.2644	.3293	.4588	.3324	.3967	.5200	.3864	.4490	.5661	.4311	.4916	.6029
16	.1600	.2193	.3478	.2501	.3123	.4377	.3158	.3778	.4981	.3684	.4291	.5440	.4122	.4713	.5810
17	.1511	.2075	.3307	.2373	.2970	.4183	.3008	.3607	.4778	.3519	.4109	.5235	.3948	.4525	.5605
18	.1431	.1969	.3152	.2257	.2831	.4005	.2871	.3450	.4591	.3368	.3942	.5044	.3789	.4351	.5413
19	.1360	.1874	.3011	.2152	.2705	.3842	.2746	.3306	.4417	.3230	.3787	.4865	.3641	.4190	.5233
20	.1295	.1787	.2882	.2057	.2589	.3690	.2631	.3173	.4255	.3102	.3644	.4698	.3505	.4040	.5063
21	.1236	.1708	.2763	.1969	.2482	.3551	.2525	.3050	.4105	.2984	.3511	.4542	.3378	.3900	.4904
22	.1182	.1635	.2653	.1889	.2384	.3421	.2428	.2937	.3964	.2875	.3387	.4395	.3260	.3769	.4754
23	.1132	.1569	.2552	.1815	.2293	.3300	.2337	.2831	.3833	.2773	.3271	.4258	.3150	.3646	.4613
24	.1087	.1507	.2458	.1746	.2209	.3187	.2254	.2733	.3710	.2678	.3163	.4128	.3047	.3532	.4480
25	.1045	.1451	.2371	.1682	.2131	.3082	.2176	.2641	.3594	.2590	.3062	.4006	.2950	.3424	.4353
26	.1006	.1398	.2290	.1623	.2058	.2983	.2103	.2556	.3485	.2507	.2967	.3891	.2859	.3322	.4234
27	.0970	.1349	.2214	.1568	.1990	.2890	.2034	.2475	.3383	.2429	.2878	.3782	.2774	.3226	.4121
28	.0937	.1303	.2143	.1517	.1926	.2803	.1971	.2400	.3286	.2356	.2794	.3679	.2694	.3136	.4013
29	.0905	.1261	.2076	.1468	.1867	.2721	.1911	.2328	.3195	.2287	.2715	.3581	.2618	.3050	.3911
30	.0876	.1221	.2013	.1423	.1810	.2644	.1854	.2261	.3108	.2222	.2640	.3488	.2546	.2969	.3814
35	.0754	.1053	.1749	.1233	.1573	.2314	.1615	.1977	.2737	.1945	.2319	.3088	.2239	.2620	.3391
40	.0662	.0927	.1546	.1087	.1391	.2057	.1431	.1755	.2444	.1729	.2067	.2768	.1997	.2344	.3052
45	.0590	.0827	.1385	.0973	.1247	.1851	.1284	.1578	.2207	.1557	.1865	.2509	.1803	.2121	.2774
50	.0532	.0747	.1254	.0880	.1129	.1682	.1165	.1434	.2013	.1415	.1698	.2293	.1643	.1936	.2542
60	.0445	.0625	.1055	.0739	.0950	.1423	.0982	.1212	.1710	.1198	.1441	.1957	.1395	.1648	.2177
70	.0382	.0538	.0910	.0637	.0820	.1233	.0849	.1049	.1487	.1038	.1251	.1706	.1212	.1435	.1903
80	.0335	.0472	.0801	.0559	.0722	.1087	.0747	.0925	.1315	.0916	.1106	.1512	.1072	.1271	.1690
90	.0298	.0420	.0714	.0499	.0644	.0973	.0667	.0827	.1178	.0819	.0990	.1358	.0960	.1140	.1520
100	.0268	.0379	.0645	.0450	.0582	.0880	.0603	.0748	.1068	.0741	.0897	.1232	.0870	.1034	.1381
120	.0224	.0316	.0540	.0376	.0487	.0739	.0506	.0628	.0899	.0623	.0754	.1039	.0732	.0871	.1168
150	.0179	.0254	.0434	.0302	.0392	.0596	.0407	.0506	.0726	.0502	.0609	.0842	.0591	.0705	.0948
200	.0135	.0191	.0327	.0228	.0295	.0450	.0307	.0382	.0550	.0380	.0461	.0639	.0448	.0535	.0721
500	.0054	.0077	.0132	.0092	.0119	.0183	.0124	.0155	.0224	.0154	.0188	.0262	.0182	.0218	.0296
1000	.0027	.0038	.0066	.0046	.0060	.0092	.0062	.0078	.0113	.0077	.0094	.0132	.0092	.0110	.0150

Table 14. Von Neumann ratio

Critical values of $v = \sum_{i=2}^{n} (\bar{X}_i - X_{i-1})^2 / \sum_{i=1}^{n} (X_i - \bar{X})^2$, where $\bar{X} = \frac{1}{n} \sum_{i=1}^{n} X_i$, for different values of n = sample size and α = significance level (one tail). **Example**: If a random sample of $n = 10$ yields $v = 1.01$, the null hypothesis, H_0, that X_i are independently and normally distributed can be rejected at 5% significance level as $1.01 < 1.0621$ i.e. the test indicates positive autocorrelation. If sample $v > [4 - v(n, \alpha)]$, the test indicates negative autocorrelation.

n \ α	.050	.025	.010		n \ α	.050	.025	.010
5	0.8203	0.6645	0.5379		35	1.4589	1.3604	1.2490
6	0.8902	0.7213	0.5614		36	1.4661	1.3687	1.2585
7	0.9359	0.7795	0.6140		37	1.4730	1.3767	1.2677
8	0.9817	0.8247	0.6647		38	1.4796	1.3844	1.2766
9	1.0245	0.8697	0.7090		39	1.4860	1.3918	1.2851
10	1.0621	0.9111	0.7517		40	1.4921	1.3990	1.2934
11	1.0965	0.9486	0.7915		41	1.4980	1.4059	1.3014
12	1.1276	0.9829	0.8280		42	1.5038	1.4126	1.3091
13	1.1558	1.0143	0.8619		43	1.5093	1.4191	1.3166
14	1.1816	1.0432	0.8932		44	1.5147	1.4253	1.3238
15	1.2053	1.0697	0.9222		45	1.5198	1.4314	1.3308
16	1.2271	1.0943	0.9492		46	1.5249	1.4373	1.3376
17	1.2473	1.1171	0.9744		47	1.5297	1.4430	1.3442
18	1.2660	1.1383	0.9979		48	1.5345	1.4485	1.3506
19	1.2834	1.1581	1.0199		49	1.5390	1.4539	1.3568
20	1.2996	1.1766	1.0406		50	1.5435	1.4591	1.3629
21	1.3148	1.1940	1.0601		51	1.5478	1.4641	1.3687
22	1.3290	1.2103	1.0784		52	1.5520	1.4691	1.3745
23	1.3425	1.2257	1.0958		53	1.5561	1.4739	1.3800
24	1.3551	1.2403	1.1122		54	1.5601	1.4785	1.3854
25	1.3671	1.2540	1.1277		55	1.5640	1.4831	1.3907
26	1.3784	1.2671	1.1425		56	1.5678	1.4875	1.3959
27	1.3891	1.2795	1.1566		57	1.5714	1.4918	1.4009
28	1.3994	1.2913	1.1700		58	1.5750	1.4960	1.4058
29	1.4091	1.3025	1.1828		59	1.5785	1.5001	1.4106
30	1.4183	1.3132	1.1950		60	1.5819	1.5042	1.4152
31	1.4272	1.3235	1.2067					
32	1.4356	1.3333	1.2180					
33	1.4437	1.3427	1.2287					
34	1.4515	1.3517	1.2390					

Approximation: For $n > 60$, v is approximately normally distributed with $E(v) = 2$ and $\text{var}(v) = 4(n-2)/(n+1)(n-1)$ i.e. $v(n, \alpha) = 2 - Z_\alpha 2[(n-2)/(n+1)(n-1)]^{1/2}$ where Z is $N(0, 1)$ and $P(Z > Z_\alpha) = \alpha$.

The table was reproduced from J. Koerts and A. P. J. Abrahamse, *On the Theory and Applications of the General Linear Model*, Rotterdam University Press, 1969, with permission of the authors and publisher.

Table 15. Durbin–Watson *d*-statistic

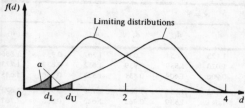

Limiting distributions

Critical values, lower (d_L) and upper (d_U), of the limiting distributions of d for different sample sizes (n), number of explanatory variables (k) and significance levels (α). **Example:** In regression of Y on X and Z (i.e. for $k = 2$) when $n = 20$ and $\alpha = 0.05$, $d_L = 1.100$ and $d_U = 1.537$. If sample $d < 1.100$ the hypothesis of no autocorrelation (i.e. $\rho = 0$) can be rejected; if $d > 1.537$, $\rho = 0$ cannot be rejected; if $1.100 < d < 1.537$ the test is inconclusive. For negative autocorrelation find $(4 - d)$ and test as above.

n	α	$k = 1$ d_L	d_U	$k = 2$ d_L	d_U	$k = 3$ d_L	d_U	$k = 4$ d_L	d_U	$k = 5$ d_L	d_U
10	.05	0.879	1.320	0.697	1.641	0.525	2.016	0.376	2.414	0.243	2.822
	.025	0.744	1.165	0.582	1.493	0.433	1.877	0.302	2.300	0.191	2.749
	.01	0.605	1.001	0.466	1.332	0.340	1.733	0.230	2.193	0.150	2.690
11	.05	0.927	1.324	0.758	1.604	0.595	1.928	0.444	2.283	0.315	2.645
	.025	0.793	1.173	0.640	1.456	0.495	1.791	0.366	2.158	0.253	2.545
	.01	0.653	1.010	0.519	1.297	0.396	1.641	0.286	2.029	0.193	2.453
12	.05	0.971	1.331	0.812	1.579	0.658	1.864	0.512	2.177	0.380	2.506
	.025	0.838	1.183	0.693	1.433	0.555	1.725	0.426	2.051	0.312	2.394
	.01	0.697	1.023	0.569	1.274	0.449	1.575	0.339	1.913	0.244	2.280
13	.05	1.010	1.340	0.861	1.562	0.715	1.816	0.574	2.094	0.444	2.390
	.025	0.878	1.196	0.742	1.418	0.609	1.677	0.484	1.966	0.369	2.276
	.01	0.738	1.038	0.616	1.261	0.499	1.526	0.391	1.826	0.294	2.150
14	.05	1.045	1.350	0.905	1.551	0.767	1.779	0.632	2.030	0.505	2.296
	.025	0.915	1.209	0.786	1.409	0.659	1.641	0.538	1.900	0.425	2.178
	.01	0.776	1.054	0.660	1.254	0.547	1.490	0.441	1.757	0.343	2.049
15	.05	1.077	1.361	0.946	1.543	0.814	1.750	0.685	1.977	0.562	2.220
	.025	0.949	1.222	0.827	1.405	0.706	1.614	0.589	1.848	0.478	2.099
	.01	0.811	1.070	0.700	1.252	0.591	1.464	0.488	1.704	0.391	1.967
16	.05	1.106	1.371	0.982	1.539	0.857	1.728	0.734	1.935	0.615	2.157
	.025	0.980	1.235	0.864	1.403	0.749	1.594	0.636	1.806	0.528	2.035
	.01	0.844	1.086	0.737	1.252	0.633	1.446	0.532	1.663	0.437	1.900
17	.05	1.133	1.381	1.015	1.536	0.897	1.710	0.779	1.900	0.664	2.104
	.025	1.009	1.249	0.898	1.403	0.788	1.578	0.680	1.773	0.575	1.983
	.01	0.874	1.102	0.772	1.255	0.672	1.432	0.574	1.630	0.480	1.847
18	.05	1.158	1.391	1.046	1.535	0.933	1.696	0.820	1.872	0.710	2.060
	.025	1.035	1.261	0.930	1.405	0.825	1.567	0.720	1.746	0.619	1.939
	.01	0.902	1.118	0.805	1.259	0.708	1.422	0.613	1.604	0.522	1.803
19	.05	1.180	1.401	1.074	1.536	0.967	1.685	0.859	1.848	0.752	2.023
	.025	1.060	1.274	0.960	1.407	0.859	1.558	0.758	1.723	0.660	1.902
	.01	0.928	1.132	0.835	1.265	0.742	1.415	0.650	1.584	0.561	1.767
20	.05	1.201	1.411	1.100	1.537	0.998	1.676	0.894	1.828	0.792	1.991
	.025	1.083	1.286	0.987	1.411	0.890	1.551	0.794	1.705	0.699	1.871
	.01	0.952	1.147	0.863	1.271	0.773	1.411	0.685	1.567	0.598	1.737
21	.05	1.221	1.420	1.125	1.538	1.026	1.669	1.927	1.812	0.829	1.964
	.025	1.104	1.297	1.013	1.415	0.920	1.546	0.827	1.690	0.735	1.845
	.01	0.975	1.161	0.890	1.277	0.803	1.408	0.718	1.554	0.633	1.712
22	.05	1.239	1.429	1.147	1.541	1.053	1.664	0.958	1.797	0.863	1.940
	.025	1.124	1.308	1.036	1.419	0.947	1.543	0.858	1.678	0.769	1.823
	.01	0.997	1.174	0.914	1.284	0.831	1.407	0.748	1.543	0.667	1.691
23	.05	1.257	1.437	1.168	1.543	1.078	1.660	0.986	1.785	0.895	1.920
	.025	1.143	1.319	1.059	1.424	0.973	1.541	0.887	1.668	0.801	1.804
	.01	1.018	1.187	0.938	1.291	0.858	1.407	0.777	1.535	0.698	1.673
24	.05	1.273	1.446	1.188	1.546	1.101	1.656	1.013	1.775	0.925	1.902
	.025	1.161	1.329	1.080	1.429	0.997	1.539	0.914	1.659	0.831	1.788
	.01	1.037	1.199	0.960	1.298	0.882	1.407	0.805	1.528	0.728	1.658

Table 15 – *continued*

n	α	k = 1 d_L	k = 1 d_U	k = 2 d_L	k = 2 d_U	k = 3 d_L	k = 3 d_U	k = 4 d_L	k = 4 d_U	k = 5 d_L	k = 5 d_U
25	.05	1.288	1.454	1.206	1.550	1.123	1.654	1.038	1.767	0.953	1.886
	.025	1.178	1.339	1.099	1.434	1.020	1.539	0.939	1.652	0.859	1.773
	.01	1.055	1.211	0.981	1.305	0.906	1.409	0.831	1.523	0.756	1.645
26	.05	1.302	1.461	1.224	1.553	1.143	1.652	1.062	1.759	0.979	1.873
	.025	1.193	1.349	1.118	1.439	1.041	1.539	0.963	1.646	0.886	1.761
	.01	1.072	1.222	1.001	1.312	0.928	1.411	0.855	1.518	0.783	1.635
27	.05	1.316	1.469	1.240	1.556	1.162	1.651	1.084	1.753	1.004	1.861
	.025	1.208	1.358	1.135	1.445	1.061	1.539	0.986	1.641	0.911	1.751
	.01	1.089	1.233	1.019	1.319	0.949	1.413	0.878	1.515	0.808	1.626
28	.05	1.328	1.476	1.255	1.560	1.181	1.650	1.104	1.747	1.028	1.850
	.025	1.223	1.367	1.152	1.450	1.080	1.540	1.008	1.638	0.935	1.742
	.01	1.104	1.244	1.037	1.325	0.969	1.415	0.900	1.513	0.832	1.618
29	.05	1.341	1.483	1.270	1.563	1.198	1.650	1.124	1.743	1.050	1.841
	.025	1.236	1.375	1.168	1.455	1.098	1.541	1.028	1.634	0.957	1.734
	.01	1.119	1.254	1.054	1.332	0.988	1.418	0.921	1.512	0.855	1.611
30	.05	1.352	1.489	1.284	1.567	1.214	1.650	1.143	1.739	1.071	1.833
	.025	1.249	1.383	1.183	1.460	1.116	1.543	1.047	1.632	0.979	1.727
	.01	1.133	1.263	1.070	1.339	1.006	1.421	0.941	1.511	0.877	1.606
32	.05	1.373	1.502	1.309	1.574	1.244	1.650	1.177	1.732	1.109	1.819
	.025	1.273	1.399	1.211	1.470	1.147	1.546	1.083	1.628	1.018	1.715
	.01	1.160	1.282	1.100	1.352	1.040	1.428	0.979	1.510	0.917	1.597
34	.05	1.393	1.514	1.333	1.580	1.271	1.652	1.208	1.728	1.144	1.808
	.025	1.295	1.413	1.236	1.479	1.176	1.550	1.116	1.626	1.054	1.707
	.01	1.184	1.299	1.128	1.364	1.070	1.435	1.012	1.511	0.954	1.591
36	.05	1.411	1.525	1.354	1.587	1.295	1.654	1.236	1.724	1.175	1.799
	.025	1.315	1.426	1.259	1.488	1.203	1.555	1.145	1.625	1.087	1.700
	.01	1.206	1.315	1.153	1.376	1.098	1.442	1.043	1.513	0.988	1.588
38	.05	1.427	1.535	1.373	1.594	1.318	1.656	1.261	1.722	1.204	1.792
	.025	1.333	1.439	1.280	1.497	1.227	1.560	1.172	1.626	1.117	1.695
	.01	1.227	1.330	1.176	1.388	1.124	1.449	1.072	1.515	1.019	1.585
40	.05	1.442	1.544	1.391	1.600	1.338	1.659	1.285	1.721	1.230	1.786
	.025	1.350	1.451	1.300	1.506	1.249	1.564	1.197	1.626	1.145	1.692
	.01	1.246	1.344	1.198	1.398	1.148	1.457	1.098	1.518	1.048	1.584
45	.05	1.475	1.566	1.430	1.615	1.383	1.666	1.336	1.720	1.287	1.776
	.025	1.388	1.477	1.343	1.525	1.298	1.577	1.251	1.630	1.205	1.687
	.01	1.288	1.376	1.245	1.423	1.201	1.474	1.156	1.528	1.111	1.584
50	.05	1.503	1.585	1.462	1.628	1.421	1.674	1.378	1.721	1.335	1.771
	.025	1.420	1.500	1.380	1.543	1.339	1.588	1.297	1.636	1.255	1.685
	.01	1.324	1.403	1.285	1.446	1.245	1.491	1.205	1.538	1.164	1.587
60	.05	1.549	1.616	1.514	1.652	1.480	1.689	1.444	1.727	1.408	1.767
	.025	1.471	1.538	1.438	1.573	1.404	1.610	1.369	1.649	1.334	1.688
	.01	1.383	1.449	1.350	1.484	1.317	1.520	1.283	1.558	1.249	1.598
70	.05	1.583	1.641	1.554	1.672	1.525	1.703	1.494	1.735	1.464	1.768
	.025	1.511	1.569	1.482	1.599	1.453	1.630	1.424	1.662	1.393	1.695
	.01	1.429	1.485	1.400	1.515	1.372	1.546	1.343	1.578	1.313	1.611
80	.05	1.611	1.662	1.586	1.688	1.560	1.715	1.534	1.743	1.507	1.772
	.025	1.544	1.594	1.518	1.620	1.493	1.647	1.467	1.674	1.441	1.703
	.01	1.466	1.515	1.441	1.541	1.416	1.568	1.390	1.595	1.364	1.624
90	.05	1.635	1.679	1.612	1.703	1.589	1.726	1.566	1.751	1.542	1.776
	.025	1.570	1.615	1.548	1.638	1.525	1.662	1.502	1.686	1.479	1.711
	.01	1.496	1.540	1.474	1.563	1.452	1.587	1.429	1.611	1.406	1.636
100	.05	1.654	1.694	1.634	1.715	1.613	1.736	1.592	1.758	1.571	1.780
	.025	1.593	1.633	1.673	1.654	1.552	1.675	1.532	1.696	1.511	1.719
	.01	1.522	1.562	1.503	1.583	1.482	1.604	1.462	1.625	1.441	1.647

Table 15 – *continued*

n	α	$k = 1$		$k = 2$		$k = 3$		$k = 4$		$k = 5$	
		d_L	d_U	d_L	d_U	d_L	d_U	d_L	d_U	d_L	d_U
150	.05	1.720	1.747	1.706	1.760	1.693	1.774	1.679	1.788	1.665	1.802
	.025	1.669	1.696	1.656	1.710	1.642	1.723	1.629	1.737	1.615	1.752
	.01	1.611	1.637	1.598	1.651	1.584	1.665	1.571	1.679	1.557	1.693
200	.05	1.758	1.779	1.748	1.789	1.738	1.799	1.728	1.809	1.718	1.820
	.025	1.715	1.735	1.704	1.745	1.694	1.755	1.684	1.765	1.674	1.776
	.01	1.664	1.684	1.654	1.694	1.644	1.704	1.633	1.714	1.623	1.725

The table was adapted from R. W. Farebrother: Durbin–Watson Tables, University of Manchester, 1978 (Mimeograph) with permission of the author.

Table 16.   Confidence intervals for median

$P(X_r < M < X_{n-r+1})$ where M = population median, n = sample size, and X_r and X_{n-r+1} are the rth and $(n-r+1)^{\text{th}}$ observations when they are arranged in ascending order of magnitude.   **Example:** If a random sample of $n = 6$ observations yields: 3, 5, 6, 7, 7, 9, and $r = 2$, $P(X_2 < M < X_5) = P(5 < M < 7) = 0.7813$.

n \ r	1	2	3	4	5	6	7	8	9	10	11	12
2	0.5000											
3	0.7500											
4	0.8750	0.3750										
5	0.9375	0.6250										
6	0.9687	0.7813	0.3125									
7	0.9844	0.8750	0.5468									
8	0.9922	0.9298	0.7110	0.2734								
9	0.9961	0.9610	0.8204	0.4922								
10	0.9980	0.9785	0.8907	0.6563	0.2461							
11	0.9990	0.9884	0.9346	0.7734	0.4512							
12	0.9995	0.9936	0.9614	0.8540	0.6124	0.2256						
13	0.9998	0.9966	0.9776	0.9078	0.7332	0.4190						
14	0.9999	0.9983	0.9871	0.9427	0.8205	0.5761	0.2095					
15	0.9999	0.9990	0.9926	0.9648	0.8815	0.6982	0.3928					
16	1.0000	0.9996	0.9960	0.9790	0.9234	0.7900	0.5456	0.1964				
17	1.0000	0.9998	0.9978	0.9874	0.9510	0.8566	0.6678	0.3710				
18	1.0000	0.9999	0.9987	0.9925	0.9691	0.9037	0.7621	0.5193	0.1855			
19	1.0000	1.0000	0.9994	0.9958	0.9810	0.9366	0.8330	0.6408	0.3524			
20	1.0000	1.0000	0.9996	0.9974	0.9882	0.9586	0.8846	0.7368	0.4966	0.1762		
21	1.0000	1.0000	0.9998	0.9985	0.9928	0.9734	0.9216	0.8108	0.6166	0.3364		
22	1.0000	1.0000	0.9999	0.9991	0.9957	0.9831	0.9475	0.8662	0.7137	0.4765	0.1682	
23	1.0000	1.0000	0.9999	0.9995	0.9974	0.9894	0.9653	0.9069	0.7900	0.5951	0.3224	
24	1.0000	1.0000	1.0000	0.9997	0.9985	0.9934	0.9773	0.9361	0.8484	0.6925	0.4587	0.1612
25	1.0000	1.0000	1.0000	0.9998	0.9991	0.9959	0.9854	0.9567	0.8922	0.7705	0.5756	0.3100

Approximation: When $n > 25$, for a desired confidence level $(1 - \alpha)$, the confidence interval is given by $X_r < M < X_{n-r+1}$, where r is the largest integer which does not exceed: $0.5 \, (n + 1 - Z_{\alpha/2}\sqrt{n})$, where Z is $N(0, 1)$ and where $P(Z > Z_{\alpha/2}) = \alpha/2$.   **Example:** For $n = 36$ and $\alpha = 0.05$, $0.5(36 + 1 - 1.96\sqrt{36}) = 12.62$ (using Table 5), i.e. $r = 12$ and $n - r + 1 = 36 - 12 + 1 = 25$, and thus $P(X_{12} < M < X_{25}) \geqslant 0.95$.

Table 17. Sign test

Probability that number of signs ($+$ or $-$, whichever is smaller) will occur X or less times in a random sample of n matched pairs. H_0: $P(X_A > X_B) = P(X_A < X_B) = \frac{1}{2}$, where X_A and X_B are the two scores of a matched pair. **Example**: If $n = 16$ matched pairs are observed, 12 showing differences in one direction ($+$) and 4 in the other ($-$), then $P(X \leqslant 4) = 0.0384$ and H_0 may be rejected at $\alpha = 0.0384$ level of significance (one tail test). A two tail test would reject H_0 at $2\alpha = 0.0768$ level.

n \ X	0	1	2	3	4	5	6	7	8	9	10	11	12
2	.2500	.7500											
3	.1250	.5000											
4	.0625	.3125	.6875										
5	.0313	.1875	.5000										
6	.0156	.1094	.3438	.6563									
7	.0078	.0625	.2266	.5000									
8	.0039	.0352	.1445	.3633	.6367								
9	.0020	.0195	.0898	.2539	.5000								
10	.0010	.0107	.0547	.1719	.3770	.6230							
11	.0005	.0059	.0327	.1133	.2744	.5000							
12	.0002	.0032	.0193	.0730	.1938	.3872	.6128						
13	.0001	.0017	.0112	.0461	.1334	.2905	.5000						
14	.0001	.0009	.0065	.0287	.0898	.2120	.3953	.6047					
15	.0000	.0005	.0037	.0176	.0592	.1509	.3036	.5000					
16	.0000	.0003	.0021	.0106	.0384	.1051	.2272	.4018	.5982				
17	.0000	.0001	.0012	.0064	.0245	.0717	.1662	.3145	.5000				
18	.0000	.0001	.0007	.0038	.0154	.0481	.1189	.2403	.4073	.5927			
19	.0000	.0000	.0004	.0022	.0096	.0318	.0835	.1796	.3238	.5000			
20	.0000	.0000	.0002	.0013	.0059	.0207	.0577	.1316	.2517	.4119	.5881		
21	.0000	.0000	.0001	.0007	.0036	.0133	.0392	.0946	.1917	.3318	.5000		
22	.0000	.0000	.0001	.0004	.0022	.0085	.0262	.0669	.1431	.2617	.4159	.5841	
23	.0000	.0000	.0000	.0002	.0013	.0053	.0173	.0466	.1050	.2024	.3388	.5000	
24	.0000	.0000	.0000	.0001	.0008	.0033	.0113	.0320	.0758	.1537	.2706	.4194	.5806
25	.0000	.0000	.0000	.0001	.0005	.0020	.0073	.0216	.0539	.1148	.2122	.3450	.5000

Approximation: For $n > 25$, $P(x \leqslant X) = P[Z \leqslant (2X + 1 - n)/\sqrt{n}]$ where Z is $N(0, 1)$. **Example**: For $n = 30$, $P(x \leqslant 10) = P[\{Z < 2(10) + 1 - 30\}/\sqrt{30}] = P(Z < -1.64) = 0.0505$, (using Table 5).

Table 18. Kolmogorov–Smirnov one-sample test

Critical values of D = maximum $|F_0(X) - S_n(X)|$, where $F_0(X)$ = expected (theoretical) cumulative frequency distribution $(\leqslant X)$ and $S_n(X)$ = observed cumulative frequency distribution $(\leqslant X)$ of a random sample of n observations. **Example:** For a sample of $n = 25$, observed values of $D \geqslant 0.26404$ are significant at $\alpha = 0.05$ level (two-tailed test). For a one-tailed test the sign of D has to be noted and α halved.

Sample size n	Level of significance for D					Sample size n	Level of significance for D				
	0.2	0.1	0.05	0.02	0.01		0.2	0.1	0.05	0.02	0.01
1	.90000	.95000	.97500	.99000	.99500	51	.14697	.16796	.18659	.20864	.22386
2	.68377	.77639	.84189	.90000	.92929	52	.14558	.16637	.18482	.20667	.22174
3	.56481	.63604	.70760	.78456	.82900	53	.14423	.16483	.18311	.20475	.21968
4	.49265	.56522	.62394	.68887	.73424	54	.14292	.16332	.18144	.20289	.21768
5	.44698	.50945	.56328	.62718	.66853	55	.14164	.16186	.17981	.20107	.21574
6	.41037	.46799	.51926	.57741	.61661	56	.14040	.16044	.17823	.19930	.21384
7	.38148	.43607	.48342	.53844	.57581	57	.13919	.15906	.17669	.19758	.21199
8	.35831	.40962	.45427	.50654	.54179	58	.13801	.15771	.17519	.19590	.21019
9	.33910	.38746	.43001	.47960	.51332	59	.13686	.15639	.17373	.19427	.20844
10	.32260	.36866	.40925	.45662	.48893	60	.13573	.15511	.17231	.19267	.20673
11	.30829	.35242	.39122	.43670	.46770	61	.13464	.15385	.17091	.19112	.20506
12	.29577	.33815	.37543	.41918	.44905	62	.13357	.15263	.16956	.18960	.20343
13	.28470	.32549	.36143	.40362	.43247	63	.13253	.15144	.16823	.18812	.20184
14	.27481	.31417	.34890	.38970	.41762	64	.13151	.15027	.16693	.18667	.20029
15	.26588	.30397	.33760	.37713	.40420	65	.13052	.14913	.16567	.18525	.19877
16	.25778	.29472	.32733	.36571	.39201	66	.12954	.14802	.16443	.18387	.19729
17	.25039	.28627	.31796	.35528	.38086	67	.12859	.14693	.16322	.18252	.19584
18	.24360	.27851	.30936	.34569	.37062	68	.12766	.14587	.16204	.18119	.19442
19	.23735	.27136	.30143	.33685	.36117	69	.12675	.14483	.16088	.17990	.19303
20	.23156	.26473	.29408	.32866	.35241	70	.12586	.14381	.15975	.17863	.19167
21	.22617	.25858	.28724	.32104	.34427	71	.12499	.14281	.15864	.17739	.19034
22	.22115	.25283	.28087	.31394	.33666	72	.12413	.14183	.15755	.17618	.18903
23	.21645	.24746	.27490	.30728	.32954	73	.12329	.14087	.15649	.17498	.18776
24	.21205	.24242	.26931	.30104	.32286	74	.12247	.13993	.15544	.17382	.18650
25	.20790	.23768	.26404	.29516	.31657	75	.12167	.13901	.15442	.17268	.18528
26	.20399	.23320	.25907	.28962	.31064	76	.12088	.13811	.15342	.17155	.18408
27	.20030	.22898	.25438	.28438	.30502	77	.12011	.13723	.15244	.17045	.18290
28	.19680	.22497	.24993	.27942	.29971	78	.11935	.13636	.15147	.16938	.18174
29	.19348	.22117	.24571	.27471	.29466	79	.11860	.13551	.15052	.16832	.18060
30	.19032	.21756	.24170	.27023	.28987	80	.11787	.13467	.14960	.16728	.17949
31	.18732	.21412	.23788	.26596	.28530	81	.11716	.13385	.14868	.16626	.17840
32	.18445	.21085	.23424	.26189	.28094	82	.11645	.13305	.14779	.16526	.17732
33	.18171	.20771	.23076	.25801	.27677	83	.11576	.13226	.14691	.16428	.17627
34	.17909	.20472	.22743	.25429	.27279	84	.11508	.13148	.14605	.16331	.17523
35	.17659	.20185	.22425	.25073	.26897	85	.11442	.13072	.14520	.16236	.17421
36	.17418	.19910	.22119	.24732	.26532	86	.11376	.12997	.14437	.16143	.17321
37	.17188	.19646	.21826	.24404	.26180	87	.11311	.12923	.14355	.16051	.17223
38	.16966	.19392	.21544	.24089	.25843	88	.11248	.12850	.14274	.15961	.17126
39	.16753	.19148	.21273	.23786	.25518	89	.11186	.12779	.14195	.15873	.17031
40	.16547	.18913	.21012	.23494	.25205	90	.11125	.12709	.14117	.15786	.16938
41	.16349	.18687	.20760	.23213	.24904	91	.11064	.12640	.14040	.15700	.16846
42	.16158	.18468	.20517	.22941	.24613	92	.11005	.12572	.13965	.15616	.16755
43	.15974	.18257	.20283	.22679	.24332	93	.10947	.12506	.13891	.15533	.16666
44	.15796	.18053	.20056	.22426	.24060	94	.10889	.12440	.13818	.15451	.16579
45	.15623	.17856	.19837	.22181	.23798	95	.10833	.12375	.13746	.15371	.16493
46	.15457	.17665	.19625	.21944	.23544	96	.10777	.12312	.13675	.15291	.16408
47	.15295	.17481	.19420	.21715	.23298	97	.10722	.12249	.13606	.15214	.16324
48	.15139	.17302	.19221	.21493	.23059	98	.10668	.12187	.13537	.15137	.16242
49	.14987	.17128	.19028	.21277	.22828	99	.10615	.12126	.13469	.15061	.16161
50	.14840	.16959	.18841	.21068	.22604	100	.10563	.12067	.13403	.14987	.16081

For $n > 100$, the two-tailed critical value $D_\alpha = \sqrt{-ln(\alpha/2)/2n}$.

For $\alpha = 0.05$ this is $1.358/\sqrt{n}$ and for $\alpha = 0.01$, $1.628/\sqrt{n}$.

The table was adapted from L. H. Miller, 'Table of percentage points of Kolmogorov statistics', *J. Amer. Statist. Assoc.*, Vol. 51 (1956), pp. 113–15, with permission of the author and publisher.

Table 19.   Kolmogorov–Smirnov two-sample test

Critical values of D = maximum $|S_1(X) - S_2(X)|$, where $S_1(X)$ and $S_2(X)$ are cumulative number of observations ($<X$) in sample 1 and 2 respectively, and where sample size $n_1 = n_2 = n$.   **Example:** In a two-tailed test, where $n = 27$ and $D > 10$, H_0 (that the samples are stochastically equal) may be rejected at $\alpha = 0.05$ level, i.e. a large enough D is evidence for rejection. In a one-tailed test the direction of the stochastic difference has to be predicted and the sign of D noted.

Sample size n	One-tailed test		Two-tailed test	
	0.05	0.01	0.05	0.01
3	3	∞	∞	∞
4	4	∞	4	∞
5	4	5	5	5
6	5	6	5	6
7	5	6	6	6
8	5	6	6	7
9	6	7	6	7
10	6	7	7	8
11	6	8	7	8
12	6	8	7	8
13	7	8	7	9
14	7	8	8	9
15	7	9	8	9
16	7	9	8	10
17	8	9	8	10
18	8	10	9	10
19	8	10	9	10
20	8	10	9	11
21	8	10	9	11
22	9	11	9	11
23	9	11	10	11
24	9	11	10	12
25	9	11	10	12
26	9	11	10	12
27	9	12	10	12
28	10	12	11	13
29	10	12	11	13
30	10	12	11	13

The one-tailed test was abridged from L. A. Goodman, 'Kolmogorov–Smirnov tests for psychological research', *Psychol. Bull.*, Vol. 51 (1954), table 3, p. 167, with permission of the author and publisher.

The two-tailed test was derived from F. J. Massey, Jr., 'The distribution of the maximum deviation between two sample cumulative step functions', *Ann. Math. Statist.*, Vol. 22 (1951), pp. 126–7, with permission of the author and publisher.

Table 20. Number of runs (Wald–Wolfowitz) test

Critical number of runs, $r(\alpha)$, in a sequence for different values of m_1 (number of outcomes of type A), m_2 (number of outcomes of type not A), and α (significant level) (main table). When $m_1 = m_2$ consult the other tables.   **Example**: A random sample of 20 articles has $m_1 = 12$ defectives (D) and $m_2 = 8$ non-defectives ($\bar{D}$), and contains $r = 6$ runs (a run being a sequence of Ds or $\bar{D}$s when the 20 articles are arranged in the order in which the sample is drawn, e.g. a sequence DD$\bar{D}$DDD has 3 runs). As the 5% lower tail critical value of r for $m_1 = 12$ and $m_2 = 8$ (found below the diagonal) is also $6 = r(0.05)$, the null-hypothesis that Ds and $\bar{D}$s occur randomly may be rejected at 5% significance level (one-tail test), but not at 1% level as $6 > 5 = r(0.01)$. The test suggests that like outcomes tend to follow each other, i.e. that there is positive autocorrelation. To test for negative autocorrelation, interchange m_1 and m_2, and refer to the portion of the table above the diagonal to find the critical value of runs in the upper tail.   **Example**: If $r \geqslant 15$ in the above sample, negative correlation would be indicated at 5% level of significance (one-tail test). For the Wald–Wolfowitz two-sample test, observations from both samples are combined and arranged in ascending or descending order, and the members of one sample are treated as As and of the other as not As.

m_1	α	m_2 2	4	6	8	10	12	14	16	18	20	Upper tail α
2	.005											.005
	.010											.010
	.025											.025
	.050											.050
4	.005											.005
	.010											.010
	.025			9								.025
	.050			9								.050
6	.005				13							.005
	.010		2		13							.010
	.025		2		12	13	13					.025
	.050		3		12	12	13	13				.050
8	.005		2	3		16	17	17				.005
	.010		2	3		15	16	17	17			.010
	.025		3	3		15	16	16	17	17	17	.025
	.050	2	3	4		14	15	16	16	16	17	.050
10	.005		2	3	4		19	19	20	21	21	.005
	.010		2	3	4		18	19	20	20	20	.010
	.025		3	4	5		17	18	19	19	20	.025
	.050	2	3	5	6		17	17	18	19	19	.050
12	.005		2	3	4	5		21	22	23	23	.005
	.010		3	4	5	6		21	22	22	23	.010
	.025	2	3	4	6	7		20	21	21	22	.025
	.050	2	4	5	6	7		19	20	21	21	.050
14	.005		2	4	5	6	7		24	25	25	.005
	.010		3	4	5	6	7		23	24	25	.010
	.025	2	3	5	6	7	8		22	23	24	.025
	.050	2	4	5	7	8	9		21	22	23	.050
16	.005		3	4	5	6	7	8		26	27	.005
	.010		3	4	6	7	8	9		26	26	.010
	.025	2	4	5	6	8	9	10		25	25	.025
	.050	2	4	6	7	8	10	11		24	25	.050
18	.005		3	4	6	7	8	9	10		29	.005
	.010		3	5	6	7	8	9	10		28	.010
	.025	2	4	5	7	8	9	10	11		27	.025
	.050	2	4	6	8	9	10	11	12		26	.050
20	.005		3	4	6	7	8	9	10	11		.005
	.010	2	3	5	6	8	9	10	11	12		.010
	.025	2	4	6	7	9	10	11	12	13		.025
	.050	2	4	6	8	9	11	12	13	14		.050

Table 20 – *continued*

Lower tail α	\(m_1 = m_2\) 4	5	6	7	8	9	10	11	12	13	14	15	16	17	18	19	20
.005			2	3	3	4	5	5	6	7	7	8	9	10	11	11	12
.010		2	2	3	4	4	5	6	7	7	8	9	10	10	11	12	13
.025		2	3	3	4	5	6	7	7	8	9	10	11	11	12	13	14
.050	2	3	3	4	5	6	6	7	8	9	10	11	11	12	13	14	15

Upper tail α	\(m_1 = m_2\) 4	5	6	7	8	9	10	11	12	13	14	15	16	17	18	19	20
.050	8	9	11	12	13	14	16	17	18	19	20	21	23	24	25	26	27
.025		10	11	13	14	15	16	17	19	20	21	22	23	25	26	27	28
.010		10	12	13	14	16	17	18	19	21	22	23	24	26	27	28	29
.005			12	13	15	16	17	19	20	21	23	24	25	26	27	29	30

Approximation: For $m_1 > 20$ or $m_2 > 20$, the distribution of r is approximately Normal with $E(r) = (2m_1 m_2 / m_1 + m_2) + 1$ and $\mathrm{var}(r) = 2m_1 m_2 (2m_1 m_2 - m_1 - m_2)/(m_1 + m_2)^2 (m_1 + m_2 - 1)$. When $m_1 = m_2$, $E(r) = m_1 + 1$ and $\mathrm{var}(r) = m_1(m_1 - 1)/(2m_1 - 1)$.

The tables were adapted from F. S. Swed and C. Eisenhart: 'Tables for testing randomness of grouping in a sequence of alternatives', *Annals of Mathematical Statistics*, Vol. 14 (1943), with permission of the authors and publisher.

Table 21. Wilcoxon matched-pairs signed-ranks test

Critical values of T = smaller sum of like-signed ranks (positive or negative) and their associated levels of significance. **Example:** If, say, $T = 2$ is the sum of the negative ranks when $n = 7$, H_0 (that there is no difference between the two groups) may be rejected at $\alpha = 0.05$ level of significance (two-tailed test). Similarly, H_0 may be rejected at $\alpha = 0.025$ level if it was predicted that the sum of negative ranks would be the smaller sum.

Number of matched-pairs n	Level of significance for one-tailed test, direction predicted			
	0.05	0.025	0.01	0.005
	Level of significance for two-tailed test, direction not predicted			
	0.10	0.05	0.02	0.01
5	1	—	—	—
6	2	1	—	—
7	4	2	0	—
8	6	4	2	0
9	8	6	3	2
10	11	8	5	3
11	14	11	7	5
12	17	14	10	7
13	21	17	13	10
14	26	21	16	13
15	30	25	20	16
16	36	30	24	19
17	41	35	28	23
18	47	40	33	28
19	54	46	38	32
20	60	52	43	37
21	68	59	49	43
22	75	66	56	49
23	83	73	62	55
24	92	81	69	61
25	101	90	77	68

For $n > 25$, the sum of the ranks, T, is approximately Normally distributed with zero mean and unit variance.

The table was adapted from F. Wilcoxon and R. A. Wilcox, *Some rapid approximate statistical procedures*, revised 1964, table 2, p. 28, Pearl River, New York: American Cyanamid Company, with permission of the authors and publisher.

Table 22. Mann–Whitney U-test (probabilities)

Probabilities that U is less or equal to an observed value of U when H_0 states that two samples come from populations which are stochastically equal. U = number of times a 'score' in the sample of size m precedes a 'score' in the sample of size n $(n \geqslant m)$ when all the $n + m$ 'scores' are jointly ranked.   Example: If the 'scores' in the sample with $m = 2$ observations are: 6 and 7 and the 'scores' in the sample with $n = 3$ observations are: 3, 5 and 9, then the joint ranking is: 3, 5, 6, 7 and 9 and $U = 0 + 0 + 2 = 2$ as there are no 'scores' from the first sample preceding scores 3 and 5 from the second sample, and two scores, i.e. 6 and 7, preceding 9. $P(U \leqslant 2) = 0.400$, and, therefore, H_0 cannot be rejected at $\alpha = 0.05$ level (one-tailed test). For a two-tailed test the probability has to be doubled. If U is larger than the values given in the table, change the direction of the one-tailed hypothesis, reverse the order in which the preceding 'scores' are counted and thus obtain $U' = nm - U$. Then test U' as above.

$n = 3$

U \ m	1	2	3
0	.250	.100	.050
1	.500	.200	.100
2	.750	.400	.200
3		.600	.350
4			.500
5			.650

$n = 4$

U \ m	1	2	3	4
0	.200	.067	.028	.014
1	.400	.133	.057	.029
2	.600	.267	.114	.057
3		.400	.200	.100
4		.600	.314	.171
5			.429	.243
6			.571	.343
7				.443
8				.557

$n = 5$

U \ m	1	2	3	4	5
0	.167	.047	.018	.008	.004
1	.333	.095	.036	.016	.008
2	.500	.190	.071	.032	.016
3	.667	.286	.125	.056	.028
4		.429	.196	.095	.048
5		.571	.286	.143	.075
6			.393	.206	.111
7			.500	.278	.155
8			.607	.365	.210
9				.452	.274
10				.548	.345
11					.421
12					.500
13					.579

$n = 6$

U \ m	1	2	3	4	5	6
0	.143	.036	.012	.005	.002	.001
1	.286	.071	.024	.010	.004	.002
2	.428	.143	.048	.019	.009	.004
3	.571	.214	.083	.033	.015	.008
4		.321	.131	.057	.026	.013
5		.429	.190	.086	.041	.021
6		.571	.274	.129	.063	.032
7			.357	.176	.089	.047
8			.452	.238	.123	.066
9			.548	.305	.165	.090
10				.381	.214	.120
11				.457	.268	.155
12				.545	.331	.197
13					.396	.242
14					.465	.294
15					.535	.350
16						.409
17						.469
18						.531

The table was reproduced from H. B. Mann and D. R. Whitney, 'On a test of whether one of two random variables is stochastically larger than the other', *Ann. Math. Statist.*, Vol. 18 (1947), pp. 52–4, with permission of the authors and publisher.

Table 22 – *continued*

$n = 7$

U \ m	1	2	3	4	5	6	7
0	.125	.028	.008	.003	.001	.001	.000
1	.250	.056	.017	.006	.003	.001	.001
2	.375	.111	.033	.012	.005	.002	.001
3	.500	.167	.058	.021	.009	.004	.002
4	.625	.250	.092	.036	.015	.007	.003
5		.333	.133	.055	.024	.011	.006
6		.444	.192	.082	.037	.017	.009
7		.556	.258	.115	.053	.026	.013
8			.333	.158	.074	.037	.019
9			.417	.206	.101	.051	.027
10			.500	.264	.134	.069	.036
11			.583	.324	.172	.090	.049
12				.394	.216	.117	.064
13				.464	.265	.147	.082
14				.538	.319	.183	.104
15					.378	.223	.130
16					.438	.267	.159
17					.500	.314	.191
18					.562	.365	.228
19						.418	.267
20						.473	.310
21						.527	.355
22							.402
23							.451
24							.500
25							.549

$n = 8$

U \ m	1	2	3	4	5	6	7	8	Normal z	Normal α
0	.111	.022	.006	.002	.001	.000	.000	.000	3.308	.001
1	.222	.044	.012	.004	.002	.001	.000	.000	3.203	.001
2	.333	.089	.024	.008	.003	.001	.001	.000	3.098	.001
3	.444	.133	.042	.014	.005	.002	.001	.001	2.993	.001
4	.556	.200	.067	.024	.009	.004	.002	.001	2.888	.002
5		.267	.097	.036	.015	.006	.003	.001	2.783	.003
6		.356	.139	.055	.023	.010	.005	.002	2.678	.004
7		.444	.188	.077	.033	.015	.007	.003	2.573	.005
8		.556	.248	.107	.047	.021	.010	.005	2.468	.007
9			.315	.141	.064	.030	.014	.007	2.363	.009
10			.387	.184	.085	.041	.020	.010	2.258	.012
11			.461	.230	.111	.054	.027	.014	2.153	.016
12			.539	.285	.142	.071	.036	.019	2.048	.020
13				.341	.177	.091	.047	.025	1.943	.026
14				.404	.217	.114	.060	.032	1.838	.033
15				.467	.262	.141	.076	.041	1.733	.041
16				.533	.311	.172	.095	.052	1.628	.052
17					.362	.207	.116	.065	1.523	.064
18					.416	.245	.140	.080	1.418	.078
19					.472	.286	.168	.097	1.313	.094
20					.528	.331	.198	.117	1.208	.113
21						.377	.232	.139	1.102	.135
22						.426	.268	.164	0.998	.159
23						.475	.306	.191	0.893	.185
24						.525	.347	.221	0.788	.215
25							.389	.253	0.683	.247
26							.433	.287	0.578	.282
27							.478	.323	0.473	.318
28							.522	.360	0.368	.356
29								.399	0.263	.396
30								.439	0.158	.437
31								.480	0.052	.481
32								.520		

Table 23. Mann–Whitney U-test (critical values)

Critical values of U for $m \leqslant 20$ and $9 \leqslant n \leqslant 20$ and their associated levels of significance (also see notes to Table 24).   **Example:** If, say, $m = 4$ and $n = 14$, H_0 may be rejected at $\alpha = 0.05$ level in a one-tailed test, and at $\alpha = 0.10$ level in a two-tailed test, when observed $U \leqslant 11$.

One-tailed test (0.05) with direction predicted
Two-tailed test (0.10) with direction not predicted

m \ n	9	10	11	12	13	14	15	16	17	18	19	20
2	1	1	1	2	2	2	3	3	3	4	4	4
3	3	4	5	5	6	7	7	8	9	9	10	11
4	6	7	8	9	10	11	12	14	15	16	17	18
5	9	11	12	13	15	16	18	19	20	22	23	25
6	12	14	16	17	19	21	23	25	26	28	30	32
7	15	17	19	21	24	26	28	30	33	35	37	39
8	18	20	23	26	28	31	33	36	39	41	44	47
9	21	24	27	30	33	36	39	42	45	48	51	54
10	24	27	31	34	37	41	44	48	51	55	58	62
11	27	31	34	38	42	46	50	54	57	61	65	69
12	30	34	38	42	47	51	55	60	64	68	72	77
13	33	37	42	47	51	56	61	65	70	75	80	84
14	36	41	46	51	56	61	66	71	77	82	87	92
15	39	44	50	55	61	66	72	77	83	88	94	100
16	42	48	54	60	65	71	77	83	89	95	101	107
17	45	51	57	64	70	77	83	89	96	102	109	115
18	48	55	61	68	75	82	88	95	102	109	116	123
19	51	58	65	72	80	87	94	101	109	116	123	130
20	54	62	69	77	84	92	100	107	115	123	130	138

One-tailed test (0.025) with direction predicted
Two-tailed test (0.05) with direction not predicted

m \ n	9	10	11	12	13	14	15	16	17	18	19	20
2	0	0	0	1	1	1	1	1	2	2	2	2
3	2	3	3	4	4	5	5	6	6	7	7	8
4	4	5	6	7	8	9	10	11	11	12	13	13
5	7	8	9	11	12	13	14	15	17	18	19	20
6	10	11	13	14	16	17	19	21	22	24	25	27
7	12	14	16	18	20	22	24	26	28	30	32	34
8	15	17	19	22	24	26	29	31	34	36	38	41
9	17	20	23	26	28	31	34	37	39	42	45	48
10	20	23	26	29	33	36	39	42	45	48	52	55
11	23	26	30	33	37	40	44	47	51	55	58	62
12	26	29	33	37	41	45	49	53	57	61	65	69
13	28	33	37	41	45	50	54	59	63	67	72	76
14	31	36	40	45	50	55	59	64	67	74	78	83
15	34	39	44	49	54	59	64	70	75	80	85	90
16	37	42	47	53	59	64	70	75	81	86	92	98
17	39	45	51	57	63	67	75	81	87	93	99	105
18	42	48	55	61	67	74	80	86	93	99	106	112
19	45	52	58	65	72	78	85	92	99	106	113	119
20	48	55	62	69	76	83	90	98	105	112	119	127

Table 23 – *continued*

One-tailed test (0.01) with direction predicted
Two-tailed test (0.02) with direction not predicted

m \ n	9	10	11	12	13	14	15	16	17	18	19	20
2					0	0	0	0	0	0	1	1
3	1	1	1	2	2	2	3	3	4	4	4	5
4	3	3	4	5	5	6	7	7	8	9	9	10
5	5	6	7	8	9	10	11	12	13	14	15	16
6	7	8	9	11	12	13	15	16	18	19	20	22
7	9	11	12	14	16	17	19	21	23	24	26	28
8	11	13	15	17	20	22	24	26	28	30	32	34
9	14	16	18	21	23	26	28	31	33	36	38	40
10	16	19	22	24	27	30	33	36	38	41	44	47
11	18	22	25	28	31	34	37	41	44	47	50	53
12	21	24	28	31	35	38	42	46	49	53	56	60
13	23	27	31	35	39	43	47	51	55	59	63	67
14	26	30	34	38	43	47	51	56	60	65	69	73
15	28	33	37	42	47	51	56	61	66	70	75	80
16	31	36	41	46	51	56	61	66	71	76	82	87
17	33	38	44	49	55	60	66	71	77	82	88	93
18	36	41	47	53	59	65	70	76	82	88	94	100
19	38	44	50	56	63	69	75	82	88	94	101	107
20	40	47	53	60	67	73	80	87	93	100	107	114

One-tailed test (0.001) with direction predicted
Two-tailed test (0.002) with direction not predicted

m \ n	9	10	11	12	13	14	15	16	17	18	19	20
4		0	0	0	1	1	1	2	2	3	3	3
5	1	1	2	2	3	3	4	5	5	6	7	7
6	2	3	4	4	5	6	7	8	9	10	11	12
7	3	5	6	7	8	9	10	11	13	14	15	16
8	5	6	8	9	11	12	14	15	17	18	20	21
9	7	8	10	12	14	15	17	19	21	23	25	26
10	8	10	12	14	17	19	21	23	25	27	29	32
11	10	12	15	17	20	22	24	27	29	32	34	37
12	12	14	17	20	23	25	28	31	34	37	40	42
13	14	17	20	23	26	29	32	35	38	42	45	48
14	15	19	22	25	29	32	36	39	43	46	50	54
15	17	21	24	28	32	36	40	43	47	51	55	59
16	19	23	27	31	35	39	43	48	52	56	60	65
17	21	25	29	34	38	43	47	52	57	61	66	70
18	23	27	32	37	42	46	51	56	61	66	71	76
19	25	29	34	40	45	50	55	60	66	71	77	82
20	26	32	37	42	48	54	59	65	70	76	82	88

The table was adapted from D. Aube, 'Extended tables for the Mann–Whitney Statistic', *Bulletin of the Institute of Educational Research*, Indiana University, Vol. 1, No. 2 (1953), tables 1, 3, 5 and 7, with the permission of the author and publisher.

Table 24. Kruskal–Wallis one-way analysis of variance by ranks

Probabilities that $H \geqslant$ an observed value of H, based on H_0 stating that all samples come from the same or identical populations with respect to averages. H is defined as:

$$H = \frac{12}{n(n+1)} \left[\sum_{i=1}^{k} \frac{R_i^2}{n_i} \right] - 3(n+1)$$

where k = number of samples, n_i = number of observations in ith sample, $n = \Sigma n_i$ = number of observations in all samples combined and R_i = sum of ranks in ith sample (column). All n observations are ranked jointly, the smallest is given rank 1, and the largest rank n. **Example:** If, say, $H \geqslant 6.7455$ when $n_1 = 4$, $n_2 = 3$ and $n_3 = 3$, H_0 may be rejected at $\alpha = 0.10$ level (one-tailed test).

n_1	n_2	n_3	H	P
2	1	1	2.7000	.500
2	2	1	3.6000	.200
2	2	2	4.5714	.067
			3.7143	.200
3	1	1	3.2000	.300
3	2	1	4.2857	.100
			3.8571	.133
3	2	2	5.3572	.029
			4.7143	.048
			4.5000	.067
			4.4643	.105
3	3	1	5.1429	.043
			4.5714	.100
			4.0000	.129
3	3	2	6.2500	.011
			5.3611	.032
			5.1389	.061
			4.5556	.100
			4.2500	.121
3	3	3	7.2000	.004
			6.4889	.011
			5.6889	.029
			5.6000	.050
			5.0667	.086
			4.6222	.100
4	1	1	3.5714	.200
4	2	1	4.8214	.057
			4.5000	.076
			4.0179	.114
4	2	2	6.0000	.014
			5.3333	.033
			5.1250	.052
			4.4583	.100
			4.1667	.105
4	3	1	5.8333	.021
			5.2083	.050
			5.0000	.057
			4.0556	.093
			3.8889	.129

n_1	n_2	n_3	H	P
4	3	2	6.4444	.008
			6.3000	.011
			5.4444	.046
			5.4000	.051
			4.5111	.098
			4.4444	.102
4	3	3	6.7455	.010
			6.7091	.013
			5.7909	.046
			5.7273	.050
			4.7091	.092
			4.7000	.101
4	4	1	6.6667	.010
			6.1667	.022
			4.9667	.048
			4.8667	.054
			4.1667	.082
			4.0667	.102
4	4	2	7.0364	.006
			6.8727	.011
			5.4545	.046
			5.2364	.052
			4.5545	.098
			4.4455	.103
4	4	3	7.1439	.010
			7.1364	.011
			5.5985	.049
			5.5758	.051
			4.5455	.099
			4.4773	.102
4	4	4	7.6538	.008
			7.5385	.011
			5.6923	.049
			5.6538	.054
			4.6539	.097
			4.5001	.104
5	1	1	3.8571	.143
5	2	1	5.2500	.036
			5.0000	.048
			4.4500	.071
			4.2000	.095
			4.0500	.119

n_1	n_2	n_3	H	P
5	2	2	6.5333	.008
			6.1333	.013
			5.1600	.034
			5.0400	.056
			4.3733	.090
			4.2933	.122
5	3	1	6.4000	.012
			4.9600	.048
			4.8711	.052
			4.0178	.095
			3.8400	.123
5	3	2	6.9091	.009
			6.8218	.010
			5.2509	.049
			5.1055	.052
			4.6509	.091
			4.4945	.101
5	3	3	7.0788	.009
			6.9818	.011
			5.6485	.049
			5.5152	.051
			4.5333	.097
			4.4121	.109
5	4	1	6.9545	.008
			6.8400	.011
			4.9855	.044
			4.8600	.056
			3.9873	.098
			3.9600	.102
5	4	2	7.2045	.009
			7.1182	.010
			5.2727	.049
			5.2682	.050
			4.5409	.098
			4.5182	.101
5	4	3	7.4449	.010
			7.3949	.011
			5.6564	.049
			5.6308	.050
			4.5487	.099
			4.5231	.103

n_1	n_2	n_3	H	P
5	4	4	7.7604	.009
			7.7440	.011
			5.6571	.049
			5.6176	.050
			4.6187	.100
			4.5527	.102
5	5	1	7.3091	.009
			6.8364	.011
			5.1273	.046
			4.9091	.053
			4.1091	.086
			4.0364	.105
5	5	2	7.3385	.010
			7.2692	.010
			5.3385	.047
			5.2462	.051
			4.6231	.097
			4.5077	.100
5	5	3	7.5780	.010
			7.5429	.010
			5.7055	.046
			5.6264	.051
			4.5451	.100
			4.5363	.102
5	5	4	7.8229	.010
			7.7914	.010
			5.6657	.049
			5.6429	.050
			4.5229	.099
			4.5200	.101
5	5	5	8.0000	.009
			7.9800	.010
			5.7800	.049
			5.6600	.051
			4.5600	.100
			4.5000	.102

When $k > 3$ and $n_i > 5$ for all i, H is distributed like χ^2 with $\nu = k - 1$ degrees of freedom and, therefore, probabilities associated with observed values of H may be found in Table 7.

The table was adapted from W. H. Kruskal and W. A. Wallis, 'Use of ranks in one-criterion variance analysis'. *J. Amer. Statist. Assoc.*, Vol. 47 (1952), table 6.1, pp. 614–17, with permission of the authors and publisher. The table contains the corrections given later by the authors in *J. Amer. Statist. Assoc.*, Vol. 48 (1953), p. 910.

(d) Miscellaneous

Table 25. Factorials and their logarithms

Factorial $n = n! = n(n-1)(n-2)\ldots 2 \times 1$.   **Example:** $5! = 5 \times 4 \times 3 \times 2 \times 1 = 120$ and $\log_{10}(5!) = 2.07918$. Note that $0! = 1$.

n	$n!$	$\log_{10}n!$
1	1	0.00000
2	2	0.30103
3	6	0.77815
4	24	1.38021
5	120	2.07918
6	720	2.85733
7	5 040	3.70243
8	40 320	4.60552
9	362 880	5.55976
10	3 628 800	6.55976
11	39 916 800	7.60116
12	479 001 600	8.68034
13	6 227 020 800	9.79428
14	87 178 291 200	10.94041
15	1 307 674 368 000	12.11650
16	20 922 789 888 000	13.32062
17	355 687 428 096 000	14.55107
18	6 402 373 705 728 000	15.80634
19	121 645 100 408 832 000	17.08509
20	2 432 902 008 176 640 000	18.38612

Table 26. Binomial coefficients

$$^nC_x = \binom{n}{x} = \frac{n!}{x!(n-x)!}.$$ **Example:** $^{15}C_4 = 1365$.

n	$\binom{n}{0}$	$\binom{n}{1}$	$\binom{n}{2}$	$\binom{n}{3}$	$\binom{n}{4}$	$\binom{n}{5}$	$\binom{n}{6}$	$\binom{n}{7}$	$\binom{n}{8}$	$\binom{n}{9}$	$\binom{n}{10}$
0	1										
1	1	1									
2	1	2	1								
3	1	3	3	1							
4	1	4	6	4	1						
5	1	5	10	10	5	1					
6	1	6	15	20	15	6	1				
7	1	7	21	35	35	21	7	1			
8	1	8	28	56	70	56	28	8	1		
9	1	9	36	84	126	126	84	36	9	1	
10	1	10	45	120	210	252	210	120	45	10	1
11	1	11	55	165	330	462	462	330	165	55	11
12	1	12	66	220	495	792	924	792	495	220	66
13	1	13	78	286	715	1287	1716	1716	1287	715	286
14	1	14	91	364	1001	2002	3003	3432	3003	2002	1001
15	1	15	105	455	1365	3003	5005	6435	6435	5005	3003
16	1	16	120	560	1820	4368	8008	11440	12870	11440	8008
17	1	17	136	680	2380	6188	12376	19448	24310	24310	19448
18	1	18	153	816	3060	8568	18564	31824	43758	48620	43758
19	1	19	171	969	3876	11628	27132	50388	75582	92378	92378
20	1	20	190	1140	4845	15504	38760	77520	125970	167960	184756

For $x > 10$ use the relation: $\binom{n}{x} = \binom{n}{n-x}$.   **Example:** $\binom{20}{14} = \binom{20}{6} = 38760$.

Table 27. Random digits

Random digits 0 to 9, which are 'blocked' for convenience, may be used in any systematic way; e.g. if a random sample of 5 is required from population consisting of 83 members, the first two columns may be used to identify the members of the population, i.e. numbers 01 to 83, and the selected numbers are: 29, 12, 02, 69 and 11. Numbers greater than 83 may be ignored. When the first two columns are exhausted, columns 3 and 4 may be used, etc.

29	32	95	99	57	98	08	36	97	08	65	30	47	22	00	38	60	10	01	10
12	11	80	16	17	01	03	97	59	73	74	98	73	65	85	59	74	66	37	58
87	58	22	25	55	35	72	79	28	15	69	17	42	98	72	05	47	12	40	99
02	92	42	87	57	53	53	34	55	75	83	64	09	10	19	33	29	57	62	98
69	28	63	73	98	45	61	10	43	20	08	10	43	16	81	17	62	99	09	16
11	95	68	77	86	91	76	11	63	34	15	08	35	39	37	12	74	15	00	10
06	43	41	02	13	65	23	94	48	88	88	87	03	90	77	68	98	09	17	22
68	55	98	08	39	59	85	46	66	13	42	90	86	13	29	12	38	48	27	54
41	01	06	65	10	29	29	91	86	24	45	59	04	88	17	68	31	01	91	13
46	75	71	76	88	04	42	94	41	42	39	79	14	46	13	49	37	18	28	08
80	14	13	43	24	47	61	47	42	24	24	82	12	23	54	81	33	18	96	89
30	56	60	77	80	33	67	68	31	67	73	23	45	30	55	81	51	87	68	58
53	50	41	02	98	49	97	32	43	55	75	33	51	20	99	64	76	20	80	98
84	14	75	87	37	58	51	94	06	73	27	94	23	76	77	81	72	90	45	41
08	27	89	33	87	52	24	57	50	22	22	76	60	05	79	86	58	83	88	41
97	08	50	16	41	67	40	56	13	12	68	67	36	22	08	55	76	86	45	67
97	08	37	42	48	95	90	48	34	88	19	66	38	94	64	95	07	78	23	86
70	15	04	10	34	95	57	63	75	82	88	74	28	24	66	99	52	65	36	98
06	38	31	17	38	24	98	52	67	04	95	54	89	79	45	28	05	18	60	17
63	87	79	25	86	56	74	17	45	32	53	62	09	04	86	65	87	48	82	02
17	00	56	31	14	18	56	97	91	78	85	82	06	24	88	49	17	68	51	50
17	76	35	38	19	24	47	21	09	43	09	72	02	64	66	06	78	21	70	41
57	77	32	13	60	37	68	66	11	23	30	62	97	71	02	20	13	22	00	40
35	86	97	84	91	77	73	03	37	77	50	24	54	51	40	20	66	16	34	84
72	68	64	77	89	72	77	67	45	72	25	56	78	69	72	63	86	52	07	43
91	01	78	50	50	91	99	15	36	02	74	42	55	33	19	88	35	17	58	37
70	37	55	94	53	05	78	53	23	29	15	57	70	30	88	63	20	12	64	38
11	06	17	48	24	57	50	76	81	77	30	12	92	27	19	32	63	70	97	80
60	37	89	98	61	05	51	89	47	28	34	83	98	44	66	96	84	64	64	92
37	41	11	09	04	84	38	51	91	49	23	78	53	95	40	17	73	23	04	70
28	97	38	27	97	54	95	94	54	79	93	88	00	82	39	61	93	78	07	88
14	29	17	18	84	03	10	62	15	70	01	15	06	30	97	79	55	98	79	39
81	70	53	83	20	25	26	56	55	56	33	58	74	21	76	94	24	80	12	50
08	20	90	25	43	22	81	74	51	76	53	39	59	35	34	46	55	54	73	50
61	95	25	85	66	34	76	39	98	88	45	57	64	11	17	06	43	35	27	09
64	58	31	05	45	77	25	20	02	09	36	87	63	01	10	08	01	19	19	06
75	49	97	87	79	31	66	57	89	56	56	97	71	43	65	62	36	77	50	87
66	95	10	78	42	24	91	82	74	29	00	53	44	70	18	23	48	09	90	99
85	37	61	48	07	99	13	01	16	94	37	31	28	96	59	77	62	24	95	84
06	87	15	09	48	31	18	66	87	11	19	71	67	20	93	92	02	96	15	65
11	15	95	59	69	81	75	75	88	69	95	12	75	69	18	10	60	35	31	47
03	64	44	33	46	16	02	28	14	33	61	57	28	33	96	47	49	86	85	83
68	89	57	51	94	84	09	80	37	90	52	99	85	52	49	66	63	69	11	31
43	13	09	12	00	65	69	54	11	00	20	94	22	93	90	16	82	64	27	46
42	68	71	56	74	17	71	63	80	81	02	41	49	27	92	44	44	13	45	21
12	55	09	80	30	50	34	96	31	71	19	21	79	42	17	57	04	04	19	00
88	84	87	74	01	39	99	02	75	76	61	88	97	89	06	97	15	70	26	27
49	27	92	08	87	65	12	32	27	96	11	26	30	88	48	89	29	73	50	47
46	51	54	92	06	44	85	83	14	78	68	83	33	17	03	10	99	10	17	34
34	96	78	90	18	41	44	69	10	30	48	98	32	76	12	81	29	83	02	87

Table 27 – *continued*

```
80  07  15  41  15    37  42  39  24  45    48  73  61  15  44    74  40  27  26  47
39  08  51  67  63    03  76  76  86  09    39  32  62  77  60    85  37  14  69  76
51  32  57  06  49    13  01  25  98  83    44  96  92  78  37    24  49  35  54  52
84  46  17  46  71    53  88  78  30  71    53  85  55  10  93    40  05  66  72  38
04  88  20  78  89    94  31  36  83  74    51  25  28  43  54    76  57  08  21  23

21  45  86  26  12    21  28  37  56  47    86  18  38  39  18    89  99  62  81  98
71  38  27  31  40    52  36  03  51  54    83  14  51  17  86    77  66  84  50  84
78  50  39  32  55    17  25  06  90  90    69  48  70  68  22    07  85  07  95  84
22  76  93  40  26    30  77  61  71  74    81  13  73  21  99    00  47  52  43  18
25  21  70  62  69    05  05  58  75  92    85  60  50  87  81    35  80  83  42  16

96  79  06  87  51    04  17  61  42  12    64  77  45  06  55    68  19  39  17  22
97  76  01  89  33    70  46  23  44  83    99  55  95  03  41    89  33  49  89  86
78  03  18  58  00    47  18  01  33  49    99  55  54  70  65    34  76  58  86  20
09  63  31  80  30    17  11  75  34  81    25  45  91  80  50    25  64  70  05  48
61  33  89  72  78    98  26  56  88  66    51  69  71  48  13    71  40  57  31  22

64  83  61  76  37    68  22  25  09  82    53  59  78  66  81    66  45  56  64  78
18  93  65  67  39    81  96  44  68  46    96  50  08  71  70    81  23  32  89  61
86  84  70  40  22    89  25  42  62  69    95  98  59  26  69    55  33  62  91  88
96  57  56  48  81    92  77  95  43  50    29  89  07  58  10    83  66  04  15  74
54  35  65  28  09    99  04  41  86  60    69  54  82  74  49    86  82  25  07  29

18  79  09  01  55    60  31  19  19  48    01  89  54  63  96    70  99  15  71  84
19  78  77  63  36    52  38  88  16  92    23  42  49  79  27    15  09  94  49  35
55  71  79  75  30    29  13  32  60  07    33  73  61  89  63    64  17  15  21  39
38  58  83  62  94    73  84  48  95  17    79  74  78  38  09    37  35  75  74  70
78  29  66  85  65    45  79  70  88  92    73  24  71  71  63    70  47  56  70  28

87  55  81  22  04    62  21  45  81  82    43  96  17  70  61    80  59  10  59  00
06  98  70  24  03    20  67  45  67  65    04  61  76  89  25    13  73  06  41  16
33  08  62  21  90    70  72  16  01  23    26  05  10  33  23    03  07  46  08
54  03  25  45  50    40  58  15  41  07    16  24  16  63  46    64  27  85  27  47
68  90  88  08  25    70  23  82  53  40    51  91  84  67  84    08  09  76  19  19

90  18  00  18  76    88  55  07  52  00    30  04  83  72  04    74  87  56  90  80
70  07  33  78  52    59  92  46  58  33    61  42  31  47  58    89  32  02  55  36
19  13  05  69  12    74  49  85  21  49    18  11  60  96  94    04  74  26  23  44
95  70  86  00  19    44  74  51  22  34    63  14  11  30  48    54  71  78  97  12
65  12  41  20  32    33  72  70  71  24    51  39  43  28  90    51  14  46  17  40

15  53  57  75  61    54  95  63  75  51    28  43  39  55  90    58  01  50  31  88
60  27  72  94  00    25  71  09  76  19    66  69  44  09  39    12  60  43  02  52
57  91  58  68  24    78  33  54  25  46    08  87  72  85  28    98  89  67  68  92
40  15  42  80  71    35  81  75  95  40    04  85  70  88  19    44  75  50  63  41
23  97  89  48  74    96  60  10  40  24    33  88  86  93  30    79  96  32  25  34

48  25  55  19  87    97  39  79  66  73    50  78  72  75  08    78  66  69  13  35
24  58  57  51  61    90  39  52  91  33    77  67  76  78  40    42  05  70  73  08
60  22  38  11  98    95  66  00  95  19    32  99  90  77  55    50  86  94  41  83
84  89  06  96  10    47  83  22  11  81    19  13  48  21  71    99  16  81  88  56
30  80  70  60  93    09  74  04  99  72    67  91  91  75  20    36  08  45  28  35

23  95  78  32  20    71  90  24  20  66    09  27  14  97  94    78  67  45  20  62
48  52  58  73  69    63  54  77  76  89    09  15  50  05  85    91  12  10  12  29
33  69  72  87  15    96  24  09  14  84    41  57  16  17  78    18  46  46  23  04
71  71  53  72  84    65  86  16  70  43    62  10  33  15  61    60  80  73  18  21
29  53  27  21  49    53  31  68  21  10    17  47  35  74  84    18  58  07  17  32

17  70  60  84  24    50  82  33  67  40    15  88  50  22  54    28  39  46  14  28
98  37  60  93  52    27  20  93  10  62    90  69  27  96  44    54  01  13  81  14
16  39  86  14  17    56  74  44  76  20    77  74  52  52  56    06  99  78  52  67
53  17  93  61  99    15  08  47  04  09    46  95  53  02  57    60  02  02  99  83
05  38  06  80  55    75  49  12  95  96    98  63  46  51  49    74  97  71  95  88
```

Table 28.   Random standardised Normal deviates

Random sample of numbers from Normal distribution with $\mu = 0$ and $\sigma = 1$ which can be used in any systematic way; e.g. to obtain a random sample of five, the first five numbers in the first row may be taken, i.e. -0.262, 1.560, 1.366, -0.222 and -0.063. If a random sample of five is required from a Normal distribution with $\mu = 10$ and $\sigma = 2$, say, the five numbers selected above (z) may be used again but must be transformed using the relationship $x = \sigma z + \mu$, i.e. $x_1 = 2(-0.262) + 10 = 9.476$, etc.

-0.262	1.560	1.366	-0.222	-0.063	-0.225	-0.094	0.280	-1.057	0.322
0.233	0.279	-2.806	1.493	-0.911	-1.002	-0.345	0.075	-1.472	1.760
-0.476	-0.806	0.546	1.428	-1.234	0.225	1.571	0.483	1.554	2.167
1.895	-0.559	1.690	0.791	0.142	0.568	-1.460	-1.555	-1.843	-0.544
2.353	1.590	2.182	-0.801	-0.217	0.066	-0.071	1.079	0.426	-0.517
0.028	-0.756	-0.170	0.171	0.617	-0.268	-0.390	-0.811	-0.183	-0.441
-0.619	-0.186	-0.971	0.559	1.775	-0.002	-0.621	-1.517	-0.410	-1.008
-0.779	-1.248	0.742	0.177	-0.232	0.702	-1.593	0.538	-0.007	-2.045
-0.269	0.856	-2.078	0.472	1.313	0.044	-0.369	0.183	0.733	-0.229
2.123	0.628	0.434	-0.018	1.271	0.174	-0.633	-0.012	-1.147	0.125
0.658	-0.899	0.822	-0.605	0.276	-1.425	-0.334	-1.032	-0.028	-0.787
0.394	-0.396	0.063	-0.990	-0.991	2.256	0.159	1.984	0.659	1.784
-0.302	0.944	-1.335	0.989	0.752	-0.510	0.442	-0.577	-0.114	0.129
-0.593	-1.112	0.616	0.696	0.780	1.682	1.021	-0.791	0.934	1.304
-1.655	1.664	1.102	1.585	1.088	-0.499	-1.577	-0.915	0.350	0.390
-1.014	0.980	0.077	0.945	1.016	1.848	2.643	0.963	0.670	1.678
1.721	1.166	-0.182	-0.259	-0.783	0.346	-0.741	0.023	-0.473	-0.161
0.201	0.207	-0.702	-0.236	1.100	1.460	0.776	-0.636	0.215	-1.502
-0.159	1.047	0.343	-0.752	-0.629	-0.668	-1.392	0.264	-0.810	0.836
-2.066	-1.648	1.103	-0.628	1.072	0.600	2.679	-0.583	1.704	-0.994
-0.439	-0.888	1.373	-0.802	0.041	-0.277	-0.904	0.760	-0.487	0.275
-0.674	-3.099	-1.221	-0.351	1.821	0.127	0.666	0.999	-0.016	0.452
-0.539	0.684	-0.128	-1.037	-0.276	0.196	-2.021	0.743	-0.818	1.134
-0.007	1.137	-0.089	-0.562	-1.008	-0.637	-0.901	-0.316	1.884	-0.846
1.274	-0.590	-0.335	1.555	-1.010	0.185	0.966	0.030	-0.244	-0.174
0.954	0.859	1.531	1.154	-2.578	-1.639	-0.249	-0.815	0.040	2.088
-0.588	1.693	-0.642	1.610	0.376	0.231	-0.482	-0.388	0.304	-1.578
-1.769	-0.381	-0.856	0.230	-0.159	0.322	-0.598	2.611	-1.599	-1.094
-1.186	-0.555	-0.319	-0.752	0.667	0.362	-0.611	-0.535	-0.604	0.252
1.354	-2.295	1.162	-2.210	0.126	-0.371	0.931	0.871	1.226	0.294
-0.690	-1.919	-2.066	0.715	-0.059	-1.536	-0.332	1.419	-1.477	-0.360
1.763	0.378	0.317	-0.589	-0.809	-1.665	0.709	2.375	0.081	1.800
0.292	0.595	0.963	-1.686	1.369	-1.379	0.789	-1.038	0.437	-1.615
0.407	0.281	-0.515	-0.002	1.787	-2.283	0.022	0.120	-0.741	0.053
-0.635	0.743	-0.141	0.173	-0.341	2.323	-1.863	-0.566	1.615	-0.210
0.694	1.178	-1.020	-0.531	0.219	0.932	-0.734	0.078	0.300	0.446
1.161	-0.212	0.211	0.347	-0.422	-0.280	1.811	-0.952	-0.308	1.569
2.075	-0.211	-1.026	1.136	-0.751	0.937	-1.560	-0.163	0.186	-1.156
1.046	-0.495	0.405	0.965	0.902	0.775	2.862	-0.179	-0.174	0.095
-0.111	-1.227	-0.475	0.988	0.747	-2.243	-0.481	0.278	-1.931	0.394
-0.760	0.440	1.332	0.660	1.621	2.075	0.066	0.085	1.548	-1.032
0.120	-0.559	0.462	-1.810	-0.172	-0.803	-0.489	0.111	-1.513	-0.326
-0.304	1.423	-0.403	0.560	0.921	-1.588	-1.194	-0.452	1.990	-0.710
-0.710	-0.136	1.192	-1.486	0.103	-1.881	0.837	-1.327	0.820	-1.882
1.913	-1.646	1.853	-1.737	0.356	-0.150	0.456	1.117	-1.028	-0.603
-0.012	-1.196	-0.117	0.798	0.574	-1.269	-0.036	1.327	-0.174	0.243
-1.614	0.448	-1.686	0.537	-0.047	1.993	0.485	1.099	-1.149	0.145
-1.058	0.498	0.226	0.863	-1.073	-1.148	1.422	-0.020	-0.020	-0.069
0.628	1.188	-0.652	-0.960	0.159	-0.795	0.623	1.106	0.863	-0.845
0.069	0.551	-0.610	1.477	-0.650	-0.253	-1.326	0.299	1.396	-0.321
-1.113	0.489	0.359	1.018	0.551	-0.529	0.071	-0.755	0.493	-0.959
0.669	-0.248	1.252	-0.396	0.076	1.403	0.058	0.946	-0.711	-0.189
-1.086	-0.008	-0.691	1.223	-0.589	0.955	0.508	0.676	1.513	-0.261
0.363	0.095	-0.841	-0.772	-0.315	0.823	1.514	0.267	0.494	-0.234
0.164	-0.905	0.669	0.687	0.837	0.199	-0.298	-2.013	-1.271	0.533
-0.604	-1.724	0.120	0.200	-0.303	1.536	-0.519	-0.478	-0.530	-0.812
-0.012	0.467	0.435	0.763	0.184	0.001	0.023	-0.182	-1.210	1.170
0.523	1.156	-0.010	0.639	-1.450	-1.101	0.071	0.520	0.923	1.744
0.195	1.624	0.316	-0.604	-0.573	0.282	0.797	-1.284	-2.068	-0.335
0.676	-0.328	-0.440	-0.831	0.826	0.507	-0.402	-0.560	0.333	1.137

Table 28 – *continued*

−1.227	−1.421	0.928	0.916	−0.930	0.159	0.530	1.137	−1.005	−0.148
1.072	−1.443	1.851	0.296	−0.805	0.474	−0.986	0.110	−1.281	−0.582
1.725	−0.076	−1.947	0.935	−0.222	0.027	−1.751	2.201	−1.416	−0.450
1.234	0.144	−1.104	0.620	−0.028	−0.080	0.062	0.292	−0.806	1.062
0.073	−1.481	−0.341	0.315	−0.720	1.686	−0.816	−0.425	−1.257	0.503
0.091	−0.239	0.166	−0.860	0.131	0.687	−0.944	−1.585	0.487	−3.242
0.171	1.816	0.084	−1.476	−0.028	−0.073	−1.065	−0.285	0.771	−0.510
−0.366	−0.630	0.515	0.147	−0.445	0.292	0.477	−0.690	−1.066	1.350
0.747	−1.466	−0.916	−0.313	−1.638	−1.427	−1.432	0.477	1.378	0.698
−2.076	0.055	−1.327	0.613	0.464	−1.589	−0.396	0.152	1.160	−0.041
−0.909	−0.240	0.207	−2.380	−0.127	−0.247	0.073	−1.067	−0.303	0.553
−0.191	0.692	−0.049	−1.281	0.843	−0.516	−0.473	−0.064	−0.058	0.695
−0.637	−1.506	−0.433	−0.252	−1.091	−0.393	0.098	−0.814	−1.952	−0.376
−0.585	−1.215	1.496	0.215	0.870	−0.677	0.887	−0.219	−0.808	2.165
1.336	−2.144	−0.332	−0.421	−0.649	−0.911	−0.593	−0.374	−0.555	−0.308
−0.483	−1.161	−0.914	0.188	−1.778	0.482	0.195	2.165	−0.681	−0.854
1.436	0.492	0.126	−1.793	−1.303	1.691	−0.844	−0.705	−0.262	−0.084
0.075	0.051	−0.689	0.440	−0.013	−0.284	−2.182	−0.425	−0.762	0.336
1.515	−0.790	−0.313	−0.342	−1.757	0.420	−0.548	−0.458	−0.232	−1.399
−0.926	1.020	−0.907	1.676	0.742	−1.523	−1.138	0.329	1.341	0.880
−0.791	2.030	0.953	−0.704	−0.030	2.294	1.010	−0.125	−0.293	−0.794
−1.011	−1.066	−2.273	0.306	−1.055	−0.233	−0.686	0.006	1.468	−0.465
1.788	−0.861	0.449	0.898	−1.471	−0.185	−0.584	0.785	−0.759	−0.569
1.517	1.092	1.095	−1.359	−0.961	1.239	−1.118	−1.988	−1.816	1.096
0.229	0.870	−1.943	−0.033	−0.709	−1.185	−0.442	−0.420	−0.334	−0.040
0.068	−0.584	0.279	0.149	−0.681	−0.021	0.460	−0.524	1.506	−1.442
0.003	−0.741	−0.215	−0.234	−0.819	−0.620	−0.005	−0.884	0.780	0.612
−0.026	2.155	−0.669	0.681	−0.176	−0.706	0.567	0.243	−0.887	−0.647
−0.181	−0.220	0.441	0.782	0.034	−0.798	−0.178	−0.909	−0.262	−0.465
−1.118	0.812	−0.161	−0.166	−0.485	0.632	0.101	−1.754	−1.791	0.463
−1.694	−0.563	0.298	−0.270	1.264	−1.792	−0.485	−0.933	0.308	0.650
0.787	0.016	1.012	0.419	0.180	3.001	1.297	−0.472	0.558	0.495
0.968	0.007	1.136	−0.259	2.315	0.839	0.022	2.469	0.775	0.266
−0.840	−0.713	−0.514	−1.634	−1.926	−0.435	0.598	1.240	1.088	0.298
0.716	1.153	0.638	0.391	0.742	−1.456	0.288	−0.634	−0.941	0.098
−0.387	0.894	−0.525	0.790	1.254	0.943	0.194	−0.421	0.115	0.683
0.405	2.851	0.354	0.564	1.564	1.536	1.825	−1.055	1.707	0.123
1.220	2.324	0.613	1.080	1.320	1.237	−2.213	−0.874	−2.041	−0.081
−0.941	0.719	0.002	−1.744	0.251	1.070	0.460	−1.598	0.656	−0.975
0.864	0.580	0.631	1.159	−0.982	−0.356	−0.023	−1.385	−2.075	+1.335

Table 29.   Unit Normal loss integral

Values of $L(z) = f(z) - z[1 - F(z)]$ where $f(z) = N(0, 1)$ and $F(z) = \int_{\infty}^{z} N(0,1)dt$.   **Example:** If $z = 2.06$, $L(z = 2.06) = 0.00722$.

When X is $N(\mu, \sigma^2)$, $z = |X - \mu|/\sigma$.

$z \rightarrow$ $\downarrow$	0.00	0.01	0.02	0.03	0.04	0.05	0.06	0.07	0.08	0.09
0.0	.39894	.39396	.38902	.38412	.37926	.37444	.36966	.36492	.36022	.35556
0.1	.35094	.34635	.34181	.33731	.33285	.32842	.32404	.31969	.31539	.31112
0.2	.30689	.30271	.29856	.29445	.29038	.28634	.28235	.27840	.27448	.27060
0.3	.26676	.26296	.25920	.25547	.25178	.24813	.24452	.24094	.23740	.23390
0.4	.23044	.22701	.22362	.22027	.21695	.21367	.21042	.20721	.20404	.20090
0.5	.19780	.19473	.19170	.18870	.18573	.18281	.17991	.17705	.17422	.17143
0.6	.16867	.16595	.16325	.16059	.15797	.15537	.15281	.15028	.14778	.14531
0.7	.14288	.14048	.13810	.13576	.13345	.13117	.12892	.12669	.12450	.12234
0.8	.12021	.11810	.11603	.11398	.11196	.10997	.10801	.10607	.10417	.10229
0.9	.10043	.09860	.09680	.09503	.09328	.09156	.08986	.08819	.08654	.08491
1.0	.08332	.08174	.08019	.07866	.07716	.07568	.07422	.07279	.07138	.06999
1.1	.06862	.06727	.06595	.06465	.06336	.06210	.06086	.05964	.05844	.05726
1.2	.05610	.05496	.05384	.05274	.05165	.05059	.04954	.04851	.04750	.04650
1.3	.04553	.04457	.04363	.04270	.04179	.04090	.04002	.03916	.03831	.03748
1.4	.03667	.03587	.03508	.03431	.03356	.03281	.03208	.03137	.03067	.02998
1.5	.02931	.02865	.02800	.02736	.02674	.02612	.02552	.02494	.02436	.02380
1.6	.02324	.02270	.02217	.02165	.02114	.02064	.02015	.01967	.01920	.01874
1.7	.01829	.01785	.01742	.01699	.01658	.01617	.01578	.01539	.01501	.01464
1.8	.01428	.01392	.01357	.01323	.01290	.01257	.01226	.01195	.01164	.01134
1.9	.01105	.01077	.01049	.01022	.00996	.00970	.00945	.00920	.00896	.00872
2.0	.00849	.00827	.00805	.00783	.00762	.00742	.00722	.00702	.00683	.00665
2.1	.00647	.00629	.00612	.00595	.00579	.00563	.00547	.00532	.00517	.00503
2.2	.00489	.00475	.00462	.00449	.00436	.00423	.00411	.00400	.00388	.00377
2.3	.00366	.00356	.00345	.00335	.00325	.00316	.00307	.00298	.00289	.00280
2.4	.00272	.00264	.00256	.00248	.00241	.00234	.00227	.00220	.00213	.00207
2.5	.00200	.00194	.00188	.00183	.00177	.00171	.00166	.00161	.00156	.00151
2.6	.00146	.00142	.00137	.00133	.00129	.00125	.00121	.00117	.00113	.00110
2.7	.00106	.00103	.00099	.00096	.00093	.00090	.00087	.00084	.00081	.00079
2.8	.00076	.00074	.00071	.00069	.00066	.00064	.00062	.00060	.00058	.00056
2.9	.00054	.00052	.00051	.00049	.00047	.00046	.00044	.00042	.00041	.00040
3.0	.00038	.00037	.00036	.00034	.00033	.00032	.00031	.00030	.00029	.00028
3.1	.00027	.00026	.00025	.00024	.00023	.00022	.00021	.00021	.00020	.00019
3.2	.00019	.00018	.00017	.00017	.00016	.00015	.00015	.00014	.00014	.00013
3.3	.00013	.00012	.00012	.00011	.00011	.00011	.00010	.00010	.00009	.00009
3.4	.00009	.00008	.00008	.00008	.00007	.00007	.00007	.00007	.00006	.00006
3.5	.00006	.00006	.00005	.00005	.00005	.00005	.00005	.00004	.00004	.00004
3.6	.00004	.00004	.00004	.00003	.00003	.00003	.00003	.00003	.00003	.00003
3.7	.00003	.00002	.00002	.00002	.00002	.00002	.00002	.00002	.00002	.00002
3.8	.00002	.00002	.00002	.00001	.00001	.00001	.00001	.00001	.00001	.00001
3.9	.00001	.00001	.00001	.00001	.00001	.00001	.00001	.00001	.00001	.00001

Table 30. Control charts for mean

Factors for construction of warning limits (5% of means outside the limits) and action limits (0.2% of means outside the limits).   **Example:** If a sample of size $n = 10$ is selected at random from a Normal population with mean $\mu = 100$ and standard deviation $\sigma = 5$, the warning limits for the sample mean $\bar{X}$ are: $\mu \pm W_\sigma \sigma = 100 \pm 0.6198 \times 5 = 100 \pm 3.099$, i.e. if samples are taken periodically, 95% of sample means should lie between 96.901 and 103.099. The corresponding action limits are: $\mu \pm a_\sigma \sigma = 100 \pm 0.9772 \times 5 = 100 \pm 4.886$. If long-run average sample range $\bar{R}$ for samples of size $n = 10$ is available, or if it is estimated from $\bar{R} = r\sigma = 3.0775 \times 5 = 15.3875$, the warning limits for $\bar{X}$ are: $\mu \pm W_R\bar{R} = 100 \pm 0.2014 \times 15.3875 = 100 \pm 3.099$, i.e the same as above. If average sample standard deviation (unadjusted) $\bar{S}$ for samples of size $n = 10$ is available, or if it is estimated from $\bar{S} = s\sigma = 0.9227 \times 5 = 4.6135$, the warning limits for $\bar{X}$ are: $\mu \pm W_S\bar{S} = 0.6717 \times 4.6135 = 100 \pm 3.099$, i.e. again the same as above. If $\bar{R}$ or $\bar{S}$ are available, but σ is not, an estimate of σ may be obtained from the relationships: $\sigma = (1/r)\bar{R}$ or $\sigma = (1/S)\bar{S}$.

n	W_R	a_R	W_S	a_S	W_σ	a_σ	r	$1/r$	s	$1/s$
2	1.2282	1.9365	2.4565	3.8730	1.3859	2.1851	1.1284	0.8862	0.5642	1.7725
3	0.6686	1.0541	1.5638	2.4656	1.1316	1.7841	1.6926	0.5908	0.7236	1.3820
4	0.4760	0.7505	1.2282	1.9365	0.9800	1.5451	2.0588	0.4857	0.7979	1.2533
5	0.3768	0.5942	1.0426	1.6438	0.8765	1.3820	2.3259	0.4299	0.8407	1.1894
6	0.3157	0.4978	0.9212	1.4524	0.8002	1.2616	2.5344	0.3946	0.8686	1.1512
7	0.2739	0.4319	0.8340	1.3150	0.7408	1.1680	2.7044	0.3698	0.8882	1.1259
8	0.2434	0.3837	0.7676	1.2103	0.6930	1.0926	2.8472	0.3512	0.9027	1.1078
9	0.2200	0.3468	0.7149	1.1272	0.6533	1.0301	2.9700	0.3367	0.9139	1.0942
10	0.2014	0.3175	0.6717	1.0590	0.6198	0.9772	3.0775	0.3249	0.9227	1.0837
11	0.1863	0.2937	0.6355	1.0019	0.5910	0.9317	3.1729	0.3152	0.9300	1.0753
12	0.1736	0.2738	0.6045	0.9531	0.5658	0.8921	3.2585	0.3069	0.9359	1.0684
13	0.1629	0.2569	0.5777	0.9108	0.5436	0.8571	3.3360	0.2998	0.9410	1.0627
14	0.1538	0.2424	0.5541	0.8737	0.5238	0.8259	3.4068	0.2935	0.9453	1.0579
15	0.1458	0.2298	0.5333	0.8408	0.5061	0.7979	3.4718	0.2880	0.9490	1.0537
16	0.1387	0.2187	0.5146	0.8113	0.4900	0.7726	3.5320	0.2831	0.9523	1.0501
17	0.1325	0.2089	0.4977	0.7847	0.4754	0.7495	3.5879	0.2787	0.9551	1.0470
18	0.1269	0.2001	0.4824	0.7606	0.4620	0.7284	3.6401	0.2747	0.9576	1.0442
19	0.1219	0.1922	0.4684	0.7386	0.4496	0.7089	3.6890	0.2711	0.9599	1.0418
20	0.1173	0.1850	0.4556	0.7183	0.4383	0.6910	3.7350	0.2677	0.9619	1.0396

The table was reproduced from H. R. Neave: *Statistics Tables*, George Allen and Unwin, 1978, Table 8.4, with permission of the author and publisher.

Table 31. Control charts for range and standard deviation

Factors for construction of warning limits (5% of sample values outside the limits) and action limits (0.2% of sample values outside the limits).   **Example:** If a sample of size $n = 8$ is selected at random from a Normal population with standard deviation $\sigma = 4$, the lower warning limit for the unadjusted sample standard deviation S is $W_{SL}\sigma = 0.5091 \times 4 = 2.0364$, and the upper $W_{SU}\sigma = 1.5673 \times 4 = 6.2692$, i.e. if samples are taken periodically, 95% of sample standard deviations should lie between 2.0364 and 6.2692. The lower action limit is $a_{SL}\sigma = 0.3030 \times 4 = 1.212$ and upper action limit $a_{SU}\sigma = 1.9316 \times 4 = 7.7264$. If long-run average sample range $\bar{R}$ for samples of size $n = 8$ is available or is estimated from $\bar{R} = r\sigma = 2.8472 \times 4 = 11.3888$ (r is found in Table 30), its lower limit is $W_{RL}\bar{R} = 0.4952 \times 11.3888 = 5.6397$, and upper warning limit $W_{RU}\bar{R} = 1.6173 \times 11.3888 = 18.4191$. The lower action limit is $a_{RL}\bar{R} = 0.2932 \times 11.3888 = 3.3392$ and the upper action limit by $a_{RU}\bar{R} = 2.0451 \times 11.3888 = 23.2912$. If $\bar{R}$ or $\bar{S}$ are available, but σ is not, an estimate of σ may be obtained from the relationships: $\sigma = (1/r)\bar{R}$ or $\sigma = (1/s)\bar{S}$, where $(1/r)$ and $(1/s)$ are given in Table 30.

n	a_{RL}	W_{RL}	W_{RU}	a_{RU}	a_{SL}	W_{SL}	W_{SU}	a_{SU}
2	0.0016	0.0393	2.8092	4.1241	0.0016	0.0393	2.8092	4.1241
3	0.0356	0.1791	2.1756	2.9916	0.0357	0.1795	2.1672	2.9657
4	0.0969	0.2888	1.9352	2.5787	0.0977	0.2911	1.9160	2.5274
5	0.1580	0.3653	1.8045	2.3577	0.1603	0.3702	1.7756	2.2858
6	0.2110	0.4206	1.7207	2.2172	0.2155	0.4285	1.6836	2.1288
7	0.2556	0.4624	1.6616	2.1187	0.2627	0.4734	1.6176	2.0166
8	0.2932	0.4952	1.6173	2.0451	0.3030	0.5091	1.5673	1.9316
9	0.3251	0.5218	1.5826	1.9875	0.3377	0.5385	1.5274	1.8643
10	0.3524	0.5438	1.5545	1.9410	0.3678	0.5632	1.4947	1.8094
11	0.3761	0.5624	1.5312	1.9024	0.3943	0.5842	1.4674	1.7636
12	0.3969	0.5783	1.5115	1.8697	0.4177	0.6025	1.4440	1.7246
13	0.4152	0.5922	1.4945	1.8417	0.4386	0.6185	1.4239	1.6909
14	0.4316	0.6044	1.4796	1.8172	0.4574	0.6328	1.4062	1.6613
15	0.4463	0.6153	1.4666	1.7957	0.4744	0.6455	1.3905	1.6352
16	0.4596	0.6250	1.4550	1.7765	0.4899	0.6570	1.3765	1.6119
17	0.4717	0.6338	1.4445	1.7592	0.5041	0.6674	1.3638	1.5909
18	0.4827	0.6417	1.4351	1.7437	0.5172	0.6769	1.3524	1.5719
19	0.4928	0.6490	1.4265	1.7295	0.5293	0.6857	1.3419	1.5546
20	0.5022	0.6557	1.4186	1.7165	0.5405	0.6937	1.3323	1.5388

The table was reproduced from H. R. Neave: *Statistics Tables*, George Allen and Unwin, 1978, Table 8.4, with permission of the author and publisher.

Section 2

Accounting tables

Notes on accounting tables

Table 32 *Amount of 1 at compound interest.* Let a given principal P (the present value of an amount of money) be invested at the rate of interest i (per period) and denote by S the compound amount of P at the end of n interest periods. Since P earns Pi in interest over the first interest period, it grows to $P + Pi = P(1 + i)$ at the end of that period. Similarly, at the end of the second interest period, the amount is $P(1 + i)(1 + i) = P(1 + i)^2$; at the end of the third interest period, the amount is $P(1 + i)^2(1 + i) = P(1 + i)^3$; and so on. These successive amounts form a geometric progression whose nth term is $S = P(1 + i)^n$.

Table 33 *Present value of 1 at compound interest.* Finding present values (or discounting as it is commonly called) is the reverse of compounding. The formula $S = P(1 + i)^n$, can be transformed into a present value formula. Dividing both sides by $(1 + i)^n$ we have:

$$P = \frac{S}{(1 + i)^n} = S(1 + i)^{-n}$$

Table 34 *Amount of annuity of 1 per period.* The amount of an annuity is defined as the value at the end of a specified number of periods of equal periodic (usually annual) payments (paid at the end of each period) and compounded at a fixed rate of interest per period. This is called an *ordinary* or *regular* annuity. Had the payment been made at the beginning of each period, the annuity would have been called an annuity *due* and each payment would have been shifted back one year. Table 34 refers to an *ordinary* annuity.

The annuity formula can be expressed algebraically, with S_n defined as the compound sum, R as the periodic payment, and n as the length of the annuity. Thus:

$$S_n = R(1 + i)^{n-1} + R(1 + i)^{n-2} + \cdots + R(1 + i)^1 + R(1 + i)^0$$
$$= R[(1 + i)^{n-1} + (1 + i)^{n-2} + \cdots + (1 + i)^1 + 1]$$
$$= R\left[\frac{(1 + i)^n - 1}{i}\right], \text{ (using the sum of the geometric progression)}.$$

This formula gives the amount of an annuity just after the nth payment has been made. The interest factor (the expression in [ ]) is usually denoted by $s_{n\,\daleth i}$ and read as s subscript n at rate i.

Table 35 *Present value of annuity of 1 per period.* The present value of an annuity is obtained by calculating present value of each of the equal payments and summing them. It can also be viewed as present value of the amount to which the annuity will accumulate. Defining the present value of an annuity of n years as A_n, we can express it algebraically as follows:

$$A_n = R(1 + i)^{-1} + R(1 + i)^{-2} + \cdots + R(1 + i)^{-n}$$
$$= R[(1 + i)^{-1} + (1 + i)^{-2} + \cdots + (1 + i)^{-n}]$$
$$= R\left[\frac{1 - (1 + i)^{-n}}{i}\right], \text{ (using the sum of the geometric progression)}.$$

This formula gives the present value of an annuity one period before the first payment is made. The interest factor (the expression in [ ]) is usually denoted by $a_{n\,\daleth i}$ and read as a subscript n at rate i.

Table 36 *Amount of 1 at compound interest (continuous compounding).* Using definitions and notation employed in note to Table 32, $S = P(1 + i)^n$, where $n =$ number of periods. Dividing a period into m sub-periods and compounding over the mn sub-periods gives $S = P\left(1 + \dfrac{i}{m}\right)^{mn}$. Defining $y = m/i$, $S = P\left(1 + \dfrac{1}{y}\right)^{yin} = P\left[\left(1 + \dfrac{1}{y}\right)^y\right]^{in}$. As m increases, y increases, and therefore $\left(1 + \dfrac{1}{y}\right)^y$ tends to e, and thus in the limit $S = Pe^{in} = Pe^x$ where $x = in$. Note that in the final expression interest is measured per period (not sub-period) and time in periods (not sub-periods).

Table 37 *Present value of 1 per period (continuous discounting).* When discounting is continuous, present value P of payment S made after n periods is Se^{-in} (see note to Table 36). If the period is subdivided into m sub-periods, each of length Δt, the payment per sub-period is S/m and its present value after mn sub-periods is $P = \dfrac{S}{m}e^{-\frac{i}{m}\,mn}$, as discount rate per sub-period is i/m. Summing such present values over the mn sub-periods (or rather integrating for as m increases Δt tends to dt in the limit), we have

$$P = \int_0^{mn} \frac{S}{m}e^{-\frac{i}{m}t}\,dt = \frac{S}{m}\left[-e^{-\frac{i}{m}t}\,\Big/\frac{i}{m}\right]_0^{mn} = \frac{S}{m}(1 - e^{-\frac{i}{m}\,mn})\Big/\frac{i}{m} = \frac{S}{m}mn(1 - e^{-\frac{i}{m}\,mn})\Big/\frac{i}{m}mn = Sn(1 - e^{-in})/in$$
$$= Sn(1 - e^{-x})/x \text{ where } x = in.$$

Note that in the final expression the discount rate is expressed per period (not sub-period) and time is measured in periods (not sub-periods).

Table 32. Amount of 1 at compound interest

$S = (1 + i)^n$ = value of 1 after n periods at compound interest i per period. **Example:** A sum of £1,000 deposited in a savings account which pays 4% interest compounded annually will grow in 5 years' time to:

$1000S = 1000(1.04)^5 = 1000(1.2167) = £1,216.70.$

i / n	$\frac{1}{4}$%	$\frac{1}{2}$%	$\frac{2}{3}$%	$\frac{3}{4}$%	1%	$1\frac{1}{2}$%	2%	$2\frac{1}{2}$%	3%	4%	5%	6%
1	1.0025	1.0050	1.0067	1.0075	1.0100	1.0150	1.0200	1.0250	1.0300	1.0400	1.0500	1.0600
2	1.0050	1.0100	1.0134	1.0151	1.0201	1.0302	1.0404	1.0506	1.0609	1.0816	1.1025	1.1236
3	1.0075	1.0151	1.0201	1.0227	1.0303	1.0457	1.0612	1.0769	1.0927	1.1249	1.1576	1.1910
4	1.0100	1.0202	1.0269	1.0303	1.0406	1.0614	1.0824	1.1038	1.1255	1.1699	1.2155	1.2625
5	1.0126	1.0253	1.0338	1.0381	1.0510	1.0773	1.1041	1.1314	1.1593	1.2167	1.2763	1.3382
6	1.0151	1.0304	1.0407	1.0459	1.0615	1.0934	1.1262	1.1597	1.1941	1.2653	1.3401	1.4185
7	1.0176	1.0355	1.0476	1.0537	1.0721	1.1098	1.1487	1.1887	1.2299	1.3159	1.4071	1.5036
8	1.0202	1.0407	1.0546	1.0616	1.0829	1.1265	1.1717	1.2184	1.2668	1.3686	1.4775	1.5938
9	1.0227	1.0459	1.0616	1.0696	1.0937	1.1434	1.1951	1.2489	1.3048	1.4233	1.5513	1.6895
10	1.0253	1.0511	1.0687	1.0776	1.1046	1.1605	1.2190	1.2801	1.3439	1.4802	1.6289	1.7908
11	1.0278	1.0564	1.0758	1.0857	1.1157	1.1779	1.2434	1.3121	1.3842	1.5395	1.7103	1.8983
12	1.0304	1.0617	1.0830	1.0938	1.1268	1.1956	1.2682	1.3449	1.4258	1.6010	1.7959	2.0122
13	1.0330	1.0670	1.0902	1.1020	1.1381	1.2136	1.2936	1.3785	1.4685	1.6651	1.8856	2.1329
14	1.0356	1.0723	1.0975	1.1103	1.1495	1.2318	1.3195	1.4130	1.5126	1.7317	1.9799	2.2609
15	1.0382	1.0777	1.1048	1.1186	1.1610	1.2502	1.3459	1.4483	1.5580	1.8009	2.0789	2.3966
16	1.0408	1.0831	1.1122	1.1270	1.1726	1.2690	1.3728	1.4845	1.6047	1.8730	2.1829	2.5404
17	1.0434	1.0885	1.1196	1.1354	1.1843	1.2880	1.4002	1.5216	1.6528	1.9479	2.2920	2.6928
18	1.0460	1.0939	1.1271	1.1440	1.1961	1.3073	1.4282	1.5597	1.7024	2.0258	2.4066	2.8543
19	1.0486	1.0994	1.1346	1.1525	1.2081	1.3270	1.4568	1.5987	1.7535	2.1068	2.5270	3.0256
20	1.0512	1.1049	1.1421	1.1612	1.2202	1.3469	1.4859	1.6386	1.8061	2.1911	2.6533	3.2071
21	1.0538	1.1104	1.1497	1.1699	1.2324	1.3671	1.5157	1.6796	1.8603	2.2788	2.7860	3.3996
22	1.0565	1.1160	1.1574	1.1787	1.2447	1.3876	1.5460	1.7216	1.9161	2.3699	2.9253	3.6035
23	1.0591	1.1216	1.1651	1.1875	1.2572	1.4084	1.5769	1.7646	1.9736	2.4647	3.0715	3.8197
24	1.0618	1.1272	1.1729	1.1964	1.2697	1.4295	1.6084	1.8087	2.0328	2.5633	3.2251	4.0489
25	1.0644	1.1328	1.1807	1.2054	1.2824	1.4509	1.6406	1.8539	2.0938	2.6658	3.3864	4.2919
30	1.0778	1.1614	1.2206	1.2513	1.3478	1.5631	1.8114	2.0976	2.4273	3.2434	4.3219	5.7435
35	1.0913	1.1907	1.2618	1.2989	1.4166	1.6839	1.9999	2.3732	2.8139	3.9461	5.5160	7.6861
40	1.1050	1.2208	1.3045	1.3483	1.4889	1.8140	2.2080	2.6851	3.2620	4.8010	7.0400	10.2857
45	1.1189	1.2516	1.3485	1.3997	1.5648	1.9542	2.4379	3.0379	3.7816	5.8412	8.9850	13.7646
50	1.1330	1.2832	1.3941	1.4530	1.6446	2.1052	2.6916	3.4371	4.3839	7.1067	11.4674	18.4202
75	1.2059	1.4536	1.6460	1.7514	2.1091	3.0546	4.4158	6.3722	9.1789	18.9453	38.8327	79.0569
100	1.2836	1.6467	1.9435	2.1111	2.7048	4.4320	7.2446	11.8137	19.2186	50.5049	131.5013	339.3021

Table 32 – *continued*

n	7%	8%	9%	10%	11%	12%	14%	16%	18%	20%	22%	24%
1	1.0700	1.0800	1.0900	1.1000	1.1100	1.1200	1.1400	1.1600	1.1800	1.2000	1.2200	1.2400
2	1.1449	1.1664	1.1881	1.2100	1.2321	1.2544	1.2996	1.3456	1.3924	1.4400	1.4884	1.5376
3	1.2250	1.2597	1.2950	1.3310	1.3676	1.4049	1.4815	1.5609	1.6430	1.7280	1.8158	1.9066
4	1.3108	1.3605	1.4116	1.4641	1.5181	1.5735	1.6890	1.8106	1.9388	2.0736	2.2153	2.3642
5	1.4026	1.4693	1.5386	1.6105	1.6851	1.7623	1.9254	2.1003	2.2878	2.4883	2.7027	2.9316
6	1.5007	1.5869	1.6771	1.7716	1.8704	1.9738	2.1950	2.4364	2.6996	2.9860	3.2973	3.6352
7	1.6058	1.7138	1.8280	1.9487	2.0762	2.2107	2.5023	2.8262	3.1855	3.5832	4.0227	4.5077
8	1.7182	1.8509	1.9926	2.1436	2.3045	2.4760	2.8526	3.2784	3.7589	4.2998	4.9077	5.5895
9	1.8385	1.9990	2.1719	2.3579	2.5580	2.7731	3.2519	3.8030	4.4355	5.1598	5.9874	6.9310
10	1.9672	2.1589	2.3674	2.5937	2.8394	3.1058	3.7072	4.4114	5.2338	6.1917	7.3046	8.5944
11	2.1049	2.3316	2.5804	2.8531	3.1518	3.4785	4.2262	5.1173	6.1759	7.4301	8.9117	10.6571
12	2.2522	2.5182	2.8127	3.1384	3.4985	3.8960	4.8179	5.9360	7.2876	8.9161	10.8722	13.2148
13	2.4098	2.7196	3.0658	3.4523	3.8833	4.3635	5.4924	6.8858	8.5994	10.6993	13.2641	16.3863
14	2.5785	2.9372	3.3417	3.7975	4.3104	4.8871	6.2613	7.9875	10.1472	12.8392	16.1822	20.3191
15	2.7590	3.1722	3.6425	4.1772	4.7846	5.4736	7.1379	9.2655	11.9737	15.4070	19.7423	25.1956
16	2.9522	3.4259	3.9703	4.5950	5.3109	6.1304	8.1372	10.7480	14.1290	18.4884	24.0856	31.2426
17	3.1588	3.7000	4.3276	5.0545	5.8951	6.8660	9.2765	12.4677	16.6722	22.1861	29.3844	38.7408
18	3.3799	3.9960	4.7171	5.5599	6.5436	7.6900	10.5752	14.4625	19.6733	26.6233	35.8490	48.0386
19	3.6165	4.3157	5.1417	6.1159	7.2633	8.6128	12.0557	16.7765	23.2144	31.9480	43.7358	59.5679
20	3.8697	4.6610	5.6044	6.7275	8.0623	9.6463	13.7435	19.4608	27.3930	38.3376	53.3576	73.8641
21	4.1406	5.0338	6.1088	7.4002	8.9492	10.8038	15.6676	22.5745	32.3238	46.0051	65.0963	91.5915
22	4.4304	5.4365	6.6586	8.1403	9.9336	12.1003	17.8610	26.1864	38.1421	55.2061	79.4175	113.5735
23	4.7405	5.8715	7.2579	8.9543	11.0263	13.5523	20.3616	30.3762	45.0076	66.2474	96.8894	140.8312
24	5.0724	6.3412	7.9111	9.8497	12.2392	15.1786	23.2122	35.2364	53.1090	79.4968	118.2050	174.6306
25	5.4274	6.8485	8.6231	10.8347	13.5855	17.0001	26.4619	40.8742	62.6686	95.3962	144.2101	216.5420
30	7.6123	10.0627	13.2677	17.4494	22.8923	29.9599	50.9502	85.8499	143.3706	237.3763	389.7579	634.8199
35	10.6766	14.7853	20.4140	28.1024	38.5749	52.7996	98.1002	180.3141	327.9973	590.6682	1053.4018	1861.0540
40	14.9745	21.7245	31.4094	45.2593	65.0009	93.0510	188.8835	378.7212	750.3783	1469.7716	2847.0378	5455.9126
45	21.0025	31.9204	48.3273	72.8905	109.5302	163.9876	363.6791	795.4438	1716.6839	3657.2620	7694.7122	15994.6902
50	29.4570	46.9016	74.3575	117.3909	184.5648	289.0022	700.2330	1670.7038	3927.3569	9100.4381	20796.5615	46890.4346
75	159.8760	321.2045	641.1909	1271.8954	2507.3988	4913.0558						
100	867.7163	2199.7613	5529.0408	13780.6123	34064.1753	83522.2657						

Table 33. Present value of 1 at compound interest

$V^n = (1+i)^{-n}$ = present value of 1 payable at the end of period n and discounted at compound interest i per period. Example:

Present value of £1,216.70 payable in 5 years' time discounted at 4% per annum is:

$1216.70(1.04)^{-5} = 1216.70(0.8219) = £1,000.$

n	¼%	½%	⅔%	¾%	1%	1½%	2%	2½%	3%	4%	5%	6%
1	.9975	.9950	.9934	.9926	.9901	.9852	.9804	.9756	.9709	.9615	.9524	.9434
2	.9950	.9901	.9868	.9852	.9803	.9707	.9612	.9518	.9426	.9246	.9070	.8900
3	.9925	.9851	.9803	.9778	.9706	.9563	.9423	.9286	.9151	.8890	.8638	.8396
4	.9901	.9802	.9738	.9706	.9610	.9422	.9238	.9060	.8885	.8548	.8227	.7921
5	.9876	.9754	.9673	.9633	.9515	.9283	.9057	.8839	.8626	.8219	.7835	.7473
6	.9851	.9705	.9609	.9562	.9420	.9145	.8880	.8623	.8375	.7903	.7462	.7050
7	.9827	.9657	.9546	.9490	.9327	.9010	.8706	.8413	.8131	.7599	.7107	.6651
8	.9802	.9609	.9482	.9420	.9235	.8877	.8535	.8207	.7894	.7307	.6768	.6274
9	.9778	.9561	.9419	.9350	.9143	.8746	.8368	.8007	.7664	.7026	.6446	.5919
10	.9753	.9513	.9357	.9280	.9053	.8617	.8203	.7812	.7441	.6756	.6139	.5584
11	.9729	.9466	.9295	.9211	.8963	.8489	.8043	.7621	.7224	.6496	.5847	.5268
12	.9705	.9419	.9234	.9142	.8874	.8364	.7885	.7436	.7014	.6246	.5568	.4970
13	.9681	.9372	.9172	.9074	.8787	.8240	.7730	.7254	.6810	.6006	.5303	.4688
14	.9656	.9326	.9112	.9007	.8700	.8118	.7579	.7077	.6611	.5775	.5051	.4423
15	.9632	.9279	.9051	.8940	.8613	.7999	.7430	.6905	.6419	.5553	.4810	.4173
16	.9608	.9233	.8991	.8873	.8528	.7880	.7284	.6736	.6232	.5339	.4581	.3936
17	.9584	.9187	.8932	.8807	.8444	.7764	.7142	.6572	.6050	.5134	.4363	.3714
18	.9561	.9141	.8873	.8742	.8360	.7649	.7002	.6412	.5874	.4936	.4155	.3503
19	.9537	.9096	.8814	.8676	.8277	.7536	.6864	.6255	.5703	.4746	.3957	.3305
20	.9513	.9051	.8756	.8612	.8195	.7425	.6730	.6103	.5537	.4564	.3769	.3118
21	.9489	.9006	.8698	.8548	.8114	.7315	.6598	.5954	.5375	.4388	.3589	.2942
22	.9466	.8961	.8640	.8484	.8034	.7207	.6468	.5809	.5219	.4220	.3418	.2775
23	.9442	.8916	.8583	.8421	.7954	.7100	.6342	.5667	.5067	.4057	.3256	.2618
24	.9418	.8872	.8526	.8358	.7876	.6995	.6217	.5529	.4919	.3901	.3101	.2470
25	.9395	.8828	.8469	.8296	.7798	.6892	.6095	.5394	.4776	.3751	.2953	.2330
30	.9278	.8610	.8193	.7992	.7419	.6398	.5521	.4767	.4120	.3083	.2314	.1741
35	.9163	.8398	.7925	.7699	.7059	.5939	.5000	.4214	.3554	.2534	.1813	.1301
40	.9050	.8191	.7666	.7416	.6717	.5513	.4529	.3724	.3066	.2083	.1420	.0972
45	.8937	.7990	.7415	.7145	.6391	.5117	.4102	.3292	.2644	.1712	.1113	.0727
50	.8826	.7793	.7173	.6883	.6080	.4750	.3715	.2909	.2281	.1407	.0872	.0543
75	.8292	.6879	.6075	.5710	.4741	.3274	.2265	.1569	.1089	.0528	.0258	.0126
100	.7790	.6073	.5145	.4737	.3697	.2256	.1380	.0846	.0520	.0198	.0076	.0029

Table 33 – *continued*

n	7%	8%	9%	10%	11%	12%	14%	16%	18%	20%	22%	24%
1	.9346	.9259	.9174	.9091	.9009	.8929	.8772	.8621	.8475	.8333	.8197	.8065
2	.8734	.8573	.8417	.8264	.8116	.7972	.7695	.7432	.7182	.6944	.6719	.6504
3	.8163	.7938	.7722	.7513	.7312	.7118	.6750	.6407	.6086	.5787	.5507	.5245
4	.7629	.7350	.7084	.6830	.6587	.6355	.5921	.5523	.5158	.4823	.4514	.4230
5	.7130	.6806	.6499	.6209	.5935	.5674	.5194	.4761	.4371	.4019	.3700	.3411
6	.6663	.6302	.5963	.5645	.5346	.5066	.4556	.4104	.3704	.3349	.3033	.2751
7	.6227	.5835	.5470	.5132	.4817	.4523	.3996	.3538	.3139	.2791	.2486	.2218
8	.5820	.5403	.5019	.4665	.4339	.4039	.3506	.3050	.2660	.2326	.2038	.1789
9	.5439	.5002	.4604	.4241	.3909	.3606	.3075	.2630	.2255	.1938	.1670	.1443
10	.5083	.4632	.4224	.3855	.3522	.3220	.2697	.2267	.1911	.1615	.1369	.1164
11	.4751	.4289	.3875	.3505	.3173	.2875	.2366	.1954	.1619	.1346	.1122	.0938
12	.4440	.3971	.3555	.3186	.2858	.2567	.2076	.1685	.1372	.1122	.0920	.0757
13	.4150	.3677	.3262	.2897	.2575	.2292	.1821	.1452	.1163	.0935	.0754	.0610
14	.3878	.3405	.2992	.2633	.2320	.2046	.1597	.1252	.0985	.0779	.0618	.0492
15	.3624	.3152	.2745	.2394	.2090	.1827	.1401	.1079	.0835	.0649	.0507	.0397
16	.3387	.2919	.2519	.2176	.1883	.1631	.1229	.0930	.0708	.0541	.0415	.0320
17	.3166	.2703	.2311	.1978	.1696	.1456	.1078	.0802	.0600	.0451	.0340	.0258
18	.2959	.2502	.2120	.1799	.1528	.1300	.0946	.0691	.0508	.0376	.0279	.0208
19	.2765	.2317	.1945	.1635	.1377	.1161	.0829	.0596	.0431	.0313	.0229	.0168
20	.2584	.2145	.1784	.1486	.1240	.1037	.0728	.0514	.0365	.0261	.0187	.0135
21	.2415	.1987	.1637	.1351	.1117	.0926	.0638	.0443	.0309	.0217	.0154	.0109
22	.2257	.1839	.1502	.1228	.1007	.0826	.0560	.0382	.0262	.0181	.0126	.0088
23	.2109	.1703	.1378	.1117	.0907	.0738	.0491	.0329	.0222	.0151	.0103	.0071
24	.1971	.1577	.1264	.1015	.0817	.0659	.0431	.0284	.0188	.0126	.0085	.0057
25	.1842	.1460	.1160	.0923	.0736	.0588	.0378	.0245	.0160	.0105	.0069	.0046
30	.1314	.0994	.0754	.0573	.0437	.0334	.0196	.0116	.0070	.0042	.0026	.0016
35	.0937	.0676	.0490	.0356	.0259	.0189	.0102	.0055	.0030	.0017	.0009	.0005
40	.0668	.0460	.0318	.0221	.0154	.0107	.0053	.0026	.0013	.0007	.0004	.0002
45	.0476	.0313	.0207	.0137	.0091	.0061	.0027	.0013	.0006	.0003	.0001	.0001
50	.0339	.0213	.0134	.0085	.0054	.0035	.0014	.0006	.0003	.0001	.0000	.0000
75	.0063	.0031	.0016	.0008	.0004	.0002	.0001	.0000	.0000	.0000	.0000	.0000
100	.0012	.0005	.0002	.0001	.0000	.0000	.0000	.0000	.0000	.0000	.0000	.0000

53

Table 34. Amount of annuity of 1 per period

$$s_{\overline{n}|i} = \frac{(1+i)^n - 1}{i} = \text{amount of an } \textit{ordinary} \text{ annuity of 1 per period, after } n \text{ periods, compounded at the rate of interest } i \text{ per period.}$$

Example: If £1,000 is invested at the end of each year for 5 years at compound interest of 4% per annum, the value of the annuity at the end of the 5th year will be:

$$1000 s_{\overline{5}|0.04} = 1000\left(\frac{1.04^5 - 1}{0.04}\right) = 1000(5.4163) = £5,416.30.$$

n	¼%	½%	¾%	1%	1½%	2%	2½%	3%	4%	5%	6%	7%
1	1.0000	1.0000	1.0000	1.0000	1.0000	1.0000	1.0000	1.0000	1.0000	1.0000	1.0000	1.0000
2	2.0025	2.0050	2.0075	2.0100	2.0150	2.0200	2.0250	2.0300	2.0400	2.0500	2.0600	2.0700
3	3.0075	3.0150	3.0226	3.0301	3.0452	3.0604	3.0756	3.0909	3.1216	3.1525	3.1836	3.2149
4	4.0150	4.0301	4.0452	4.0604	4.0909	4.1216	4.1525	4.1836	4.2465	4.3101	4.3746	4.4399
5	5.0251	5.0503	5.0756	5.1010	5.1523	5.2040	5.2563	5.3091	5.4163	5.5256	5.6371	5.7507
6	6.0376	6.0755	6.1136	6.1520	6.2296	6.3081	6.3877	6.4684	6.6330	6.8019	6.9753	7.1533
7	7.0527	7.1059	7.1595	7.2135	7.3230	7.4343	7.5474	7.6625	7.8983	8.1420	8.3938	8.6540
8	8.0704	8.1414	8.2132	8.2857	8.4328	8.5830	8.7361	8.8923	9.2142	9.5491	9.8975	10.2598
9	9.0905	9.1821	9.2748	9.3685	9.5593	9.7546	9.9545	10.1591	10.5828	11.0266	11.4913	11.9780
10	10.1133	10.2280	10.3443	10.4622	10.7027	10.9497	11.2034	11.4639	12.0061	12.5779	13.1808	13.8164
11	11.1385	11.2792	11.4219	11.5668	11.8633	12.1687	12.4835	12.8078	13.4864	14.2068	14.9716	15.7836
12	12.1664	12.3356	12.5076	12.6825	13.0412	13.4121	13.7956	14.1920	15.0258	15.9171	16.8699	17.8885
13	13.1968	13.3972	13.6014	13.8093	14.2368	14.6803	15.1404	15.6178	16.6268	17.7130	18.8821	20.1406
14	14.2298	14.4642	14.7034	14.9474	15.4504	15.9739	16.5190	17.0863	18.2919	19.5986	21.0151	22.5505
15	15.2654	15.5365	15.8137	16.0969	16.6821	17.2934	17.9319	18.5989	20.0236	21.5786	23.2760	25.1290
16	16.3035	16.6142	16.9323	17.2579	17.9324	18.6393	19.3802	20.1569	21.8245	23.6575	25.6725	27.8881
17	17.3443	17.6973	18.0593	18.4304	19.2014	20.0121	20.8647	21.7616	23.6975	25.8404	28.2129	30.8402
18	18.3876	18.7858	19.1947	19.6147	20.4894	21.4123	22.3863	23.4144	25.6454	28.1324	30.9057	33.9990
19	19.4336	19.8797	20.3387	20.8109	21.7967	22.8406	23.9460	25.1169	27.6712	30.5390	33.7600	37.3790
20	20.4822	20.9791	21.4912	22.0190	23.1237	24.2974	25.5447	26.8704	29.7781	33.0660	36.7856	40.9955
21	21.5334	22.0840	22.6524	23.2392	24.4705	25.7833	27.1833	28.6765	31.9692	35.7193	39.9927	44.8652
22	22.5872	23.1944	23.8823	24.4716	25.8376	27.2990	28.8629	30.5368	34.2480	38.5052	43.3923	49.0057
23	23.6437	24.3104	25.0010	25.7163	27.2251	28.8450	30.5844	32.4529	36.6179	41.4305	46.9958	53.4361
24	24.7028	25.4320	26.1885	26.9735	28.6335	30.4219	32.3490	34.4265	39.0826	44.5020	50.8156	58.1767
25	25.7646	26.5591	27.3849	28.2432	30.0630	32.0303	34.1578	36.4593	41.6459	47.7271	54.8645	63.2490
30	31.1133	32.2800	33.5029	34.7849	37.5387	40.5681	43.9027	47.5754	56.0849	66.4388	79.0582	94.4608
35	36.5292	38.1454	39.8538	41.6603	45.5921	49.9945	54.9282	60.4621	73.6522	90.3203	111.4348	138.2369
40	42.0132	44.1588	46.4465	48.8864	54.2679	60.4020	67.4026	75.4013	95.0255	120.7998	154.7620	199.6351
45	47.5661	50.3242	53.2901	56.4811	63.6142	71.8927	81.5161	92.7199	121.0294	159.7002	212.7435	285.7493
50	53.1887	56.6452	60.3943	64.4632	73.6828	84.5794	97.4843	112.7969	152.6671	209.3480	290.3359	406.5289
75	82.3792	90.7265	100.1833	110.9128	136.9728	170.7918	214.8883	272.6309	448.6314	756.6537	1300.9487	2269.6574
100	113.4500	129.3337	148.1445	170.4814	228.8030	312.2323	432.5487	607.2877	1237.6237	2610.0252	5638.3681	12381.6618

54

Table 34 – *continued*

n \ i	8%	9%	10%	11%	12%	14%	16%	18%	20%	22%	24%
1	1.0000	1.0000	1.0000	1.0000	1.0000	1.0000	1.0000	1.0000	1.0000	1.0000	1.0000
2	2.0800	2.0900	2.1000	2.1100	2.1200	2.1400	2.1600	2.1800	2.2000	2.2200	2.2400
3	3.2464	3.2781	3.3100	3.3421	3.3744	3.4396	3.5056	3.5724	3.6400	3.7084	3.7776
4	4.5061	4.5731	4.6410	4.7097	4.7793	4.9211	5.0665	5.2154	5.3680	5.5242	5.6842
5	5.8666	5.9847	6.1051	6.2278	6.3528	6.6101	6.8771	7.1542	7.4416	7.7396	8.0484
6	7.3359	7.5233	7.7156	7.9129	8.1152	8.5355	8.9775	9.4420	9.9299	10.4423	10.9801
7	8.9228	9.2004	9.4872	9.7833	10.0890	10.7305	11.4139	12.1415	12.9159	13.7396	14.6153
8	10.6366	11.0285	11.4359	11.8594	12.2997	13.2328	14.2401	15.3270	16.4991	17.7623	19.1229
9	12.4876	13.0210	13.5795	14.1640	14.7757	16.0853	17.5185	19.0859	20.7989	22.6700	24.7125
10	14.4866	15.1929	15.9374	16.7220	17.5487	19.3373	21.3215	23.5213	25.9587	28.6574	31.6434
11	16.6455	17.5603	18.5312	19.5614	20.6546	23.0445	25.7329	28.7551	32.1504	35.9620	40.2379
12	18.9771	20.1407	21.3843	22.7132	24.1331	27.2707	30.8502	34.9311	39.5805	44.8737	50.8950
13	21.4953	22.9534	24.5227	26.2116	28.0291	32.0887	36.7862	42.2187	48.4966	55.7459	64.1097
14	24.2149	26.0192	27.9750	30.0949	32.3926	37.5811	43.6720	50.8180	59.1959	69.0100	80.4961
15	27.1521	29.3609	31.7725	34.4054	37.2797	43.8424	51.6595	60.9653	72.0351	85.1922	100.8151
16	30.3243	33.0034	35.9497	39.1899	42.7533	50.9804	60.9250	72.9390	87.4421	104.9345	126.0108
17	33.7502	36.9737	40.5447	44.5008	48.8837	59.1176	71.6730	87.0680	105.9306	129.0201	157.2534
18	37.4502	41.3013	45.5992	50.3959	55.7497	68.3941	84.1407	103.7403	128.1167	158.4045	195.9942
19	41.4463	46.0185	51.1591	56.9395	63.4397	78.9692	98.6032	123.4135	154.7400	194.2535	244.0328
20	45.7620	51.1601	57.2750	64.2028	72.0524	91.0249	115.3797	146.6280	186.6880	237.9893	303.6006
21	50.4229	56.7645	64.0025	72.2651	81.6987	104.7684	134.8405	174.0210	225.0256	291.3469	377.4648
22	55.4568	62.8733	71.4027	81.2143	92.5026	120.4360	157.4150	206.3448	271.0307	356.4432	469.0563
23	60.8933	69.5319	79.5430	91.1479	104.6029	138.2970	183.6014	244.4868	326.2369	435.8607	582.6298
24	66.7648	76.7898	88.4973	102.1742	118.1552	158.6586	213.9776	289.4945	392.4842	532.7501	723.4610
25	73.1059	84.7009	98.3471	114.4133	133.3339	181.8708	249.2140	342.6035	471.9811	650.9551	898.0916
30	113.2832	136.3075	164.4940	199.0209	241.3327	356.7868	530.3117	790.9480	1181.8816	1767.0813	2640.9164
35	172.3168	215.7108	271.0244	341.5896	431.6635	693.5727	1120.7130	1816.6516	2948.3411	4783.6447	7750.2251
40	259.0565	337.8824	442.5926	581.8261	767.0914	1342.0251	2360.7572	4163.2130	7343.8578	12936.5353	22728.8026
45	386.5056	525.8587	718.9048	986.6386	1358.2300	2590.5648	4965.2739	9531.5771	18281.3099	34971.4191	66640.3758
50	573.7702	815.0836	1163.9085	1668.7712	2400.0182	4994.5213	10435.6488	21813.0937	45497.1907	94525.2793	195372.6443
75	4002.5566	7113.2321	12708.9537	22785.4434	40933.7987						
100	27484.5157	61422.6754	137796.1235	309665.2298	696010.5474						

Table 35. Present value of annuity of 1 per period

$a_{\overline{n}|i} = \dfrac{1-(1+i)^{-n}}{i}$ = present value of an ordinary annuity of 1 per period, after n periods, discounted at compound rate of interest of i per period. Example: Present value of 5 annual payments of £1,000 each (paid at the end of each year) and discounted by the compound rate of interest of 4% per annum is:

$$1000a_{\overline{5}|0.04} = 1000\left(\frac{1-1.04^{-5}}{0.04}\right) = 1000(4.4518) = £4,451.80.$$

n	$\tfrac{1}{4}\%$	$\tfrac{1}{2}\%$	$\tfrac{3}{4}\%$	1%	$1\tfrac{1}{2}\%$	2%	$2\tfrac{1}{2}\%$	3%	4%	5%	6%
1	0.9975	0.9950	0.9926	0.9901	0.9852	0.9804	0.9756	0.9709	0.9615	0.9524	0.9434
2	1.9925	1.9851	1.9777	1.9704	1.9559	1.9416	1.9274	1.9135	1.8861	1.8594	1.8334
3	2.9851	2.9702	2.9556	2.9410	2.9122	2.8839	2.8560	2.8286	2.7751	2.7232	2.6730
4	3.9751	3.9505	3.9261	3.9020	3.8544	3.8077	3.7620	3.7171	3.6299	3.5460	3.4651
5	4.9627	4.9259	4.8894	4.8534	4.7826	4.7135	4.6458	4.5797	4.4518	4.3295	4.2124
6	5.9478	5.8964	5.8456	5.7955	5.6972	5.6014	5.5081	5.4172	5.2421	5.0757	4.9173
7	6.9305	6.8621	6.7946	6.7282	6.5982	6.4720	6.3494	6.2303	6.0021	5.7864	5.5824
8	7.9107	7.8230	7.7366	7.6517	7.4859	7.3255	7.1701	7.0197	6.7327	6.4632	6.2098
9	8.8885	8.7791	8.6716	8.5660	8.3605	8.1622	7.9709	7.7861	7.4353	7.1078	6.8017
10	9.8639	9.7304	9.5996	9.4713	9.2222	8.9826	8.7521	8.5302	8.1109	7.7217	7.3601
11	10.8368	10.6770	10.5207	10.3676	10.0711	9.7868	9.5142	9.2526	8.7605	8.3064	7.8869
12	11.8073	11.6189	11.4958	11.2551	10.9075	10.5753	10.2578	9.9540	9.3851	8.8633	8.3838
13	12.7753	12.5562	12.4130	12.1337	11.7315	11.3484	10.9832	10.6350	9.9856	9.3936	8.8527
14	13.7410	13.4887	13.2430	13.0037	12.5434	12.1062	11.6909	11.2961	10.5631	9.8986	9.2950
15	14.7042	14.4166	14.1370	13.8651	13.3432	12.8493	12.3814	11.9379	11.1184	10.3797	9.7122
16	15.6650	15.3399	15.1284	14.7179	14.1313	13.5777	13.0550	12.5611	11.6523	10.8378	10.1059
17	16.6235	16.2586	16.0216	15.5623	14.9076	14.2919	13.7122	13.1661	12.1657	11.2741	10.4773
18	17.5795	17.1728	16.9089	16.3983	15.6726	14.9920	14.3534	13.7535	12.6593	11.6896	10.8276
19	18.5332	18.0824	17.7903	17.2260	16.4262	15.6785	14.9789	14.3238	13.1339	12.0853	11.1581
20	19.4845	18.9874	18.6658	18.0456	17.1686	16.3514	15.5892	14.8775	13.5903	12.4622	11.4699
21	20.4334	19.8880	19.5356	18.8570	17.9001	17.0112	16.1845	15.4150	14.0292	12.8212	11.7641
22	21.3800	20.7841	20.2112	19.6604	18.6208	17.6580	16.7654	15.9369	14.4511	13.1630	12.0416
23	22.3241	21.6757	21.0533	20.4558	19.3309	18.2922	17.3321	16.4436	14.8568	13.4886	12.3034
24	23.2660	22.5629	21.8891	21.2434	20.0304	18.9139	17.8850	16.9355	15.2470	13.7986	12.5504
25	24.2055	23.4456	22.7188	22.0232	20.7196	19.5235	18.4244	17.4131	15.6221	14.0939	12.7834
30	28.8679	27.7941	26.7751	25.8077	24.0158	22.3965	20.9303	19.6004	17.2920	15.3725	13.7648
35	33.4724	32.0354	30.6827	29.4086	27.0756	24.9986	23.1452	21.4872	18.6646	16.3742	14.4982
40	38.0199	36.1722	34.4469	32.8347	29.9158	27.3555	25.1028	23.1148	19.7928	17.1591	15.0463
45	42.5109	40.2072	38.0732	36.0945	32.5523	29.4902	26.8330	24.5187	20.7200	17.7741	15.4558
50	46.9462	44.1428	41.5664	39.1961	34.9997	31.4236	28.3623	25.7298	21.4822	18.2559	15.7619
75	68.3108	62.4136	57.2027	52.5871	44.8416	38.6771	33.7227	29.7018	23.6804	19.4850	16.4558
100	88.3825	78.5426	70.1746	63.0289	51.6247	43.0984	36.6141	31.5989	24.5050	19.8479	16.6175

Table 35 – *continued*

n \ i	7%	8%	9%	10%	11%	12%	14%	16%	18%	20%	22%	24%
1	0.9346	0.9259	0.9174	0.9091	0.9009	0.8929	0.8772	0.8621	0.8475	0.8333	0.8197	0.8065
2	1.8080	1.7833	1.7591	1.7355	1.7125	1.6901	1.6467	1.6052	1.5656	1.5278	1.4915	1.4568
3	2.6243	2.5771	2.5313	2.4869	2.4437	2.4018	2.3216	2.2459	2.1743	2.1065	2.0422	1.9813
4	3.3872	3.3121	3.2397	3.1699	3.1024	3.0373	2.9137	2.7982	2.6901	2.5887	2.4936	2.4043
5	4.1002	3.9927	3.8897	3.7908	3.6959	3.6048	3.4331	3.2743	3.1272	2.9906	2.8636	2.7454
6	4.7665	4.6229	4.4859	4.3553	4.2305	4.1114	3.8887	3.6847	3.4976	3.3255	3.1669	3.0205
7	5.3893	5.2064	5.0330	4.8684	4.7122	4.5638	4.2883	4.0386	3.8115	3.6046	3.4155	3.2423
8	5.9713	5.7466	5.5348	5.3349	5.1461	4.9676	4.6389	4.3436	4.0776	3.8372	3.6193	3.4212
9	6.5152	6.2469	5.9952	5.7590	5.5370	5.3282	4.9464	4.6065	4.3030	4.0310	3.7863	3.5655
10	7.0236	6.7101	6.4177	6.1446	5.8892	5.6502	5.2161	4.8332	4.4941	4.1925	3.9232	3.6819
11	7.4987	7.1390	6.8052	6.4951	6.2065	5.9377	5.4527	5.0286	4.6560	4.3271	4.0354	3.7757
12	7.9427	7.5361	7.1607	6.8137	6.4924	6.1944	5.6603	5.1971	4.7932	4.4392	4.1274	3.8514
13	8.3577	7.9038	7.4869	7.1034	6.7499	6.4235	5.8424	5.3423	4.9095	4.5327	4.2028	3.9124
14	8.7455	8.2442	7.7862	7.3667	6.9819	6.6282	6.0021	5.4675	5.0081	4.6106	4.2646	3.9616
15	9.1079	8.5595	8.0607	7.6061	7.1909	6.8109	6.1422	5.5755	5.0916	4.6755	4.3152	4.0013
16	9.4466	8.8514	8.3126	7.8237	7.3792	6.9740	6.2651	5.6685	5.1624	4.7296	4.3567	4.0333
17	9.7632	9.1216	8.5436	8.0216	7.5488	7.1196	6.3729	5.7487	5.2223	4.7746	4.3908	4.0591
18	10.0591	9.3719	8.7556	8.2014	7.7016	7.2497	6.4674	5.8178	5.2732	4.8122	4.4187	4.0799
19	10.3356	9.6036	8.9501	8.3649	7.8393	7.3658	6.5504	5.8775	5.3162	4.8435	4.4415	4.0967
20	10.5940	9.8181	9.1285	8.5136	7.9633	7.4694	6.6231	5.9288	5.3527	4.8696	4.4603	4.1103
21	10.8355	10.0168	9.2922	8.6487	8.0751	7.5620	6.6870	5.9731	5.3837	4.8913	4.4756	4.1212
22	11.0612	10.2007	9.4424	8.7715	8.1757	7.6446	6.7429	6.0113	5.4099	4.9094	4.4882	4.1300
23	11.2722	10.3711	9.5802	8.8832	8.2664	7.7184	6.7921	6.0442	5.4321	4.9245	4.4985	4.1371
24	11.4693	10.5288	9.7066	8.9847	8.3481	7.7843	6.8351	6.0726	5.4509	4.9371	4.5070	4.1428
25	11.6536	10.6748	9.8226	9.0770	8.4217	7.8431	6.8729	6.0971	5.4669	4.9476	4.5139	4.1474
30	12.4090	11.2578	10.2737	9.4269	8.6938	8.0552	7.0027	6.1772	5.5168	4.9789	4.5338	4.1601
35	12.9477	11.6546	10.5668	9.6442	8.8552	8.1755	7.0700	6.2153	5.5386	4.9915	4.5411	4.1644
40	13.3317	11.9246	10.7574	9.7791	8.9511	8.2438	7.1050	6.2335	5.5482	4.9966	4.5439	4.1659
45	13.6055	12.1084	10.8812	9.8628	9.0079	8.2825	7.1232	6.2421	5.5523	4.9986	4.5449	4.1664
50	13.8007	12.2335	10.9617	9.9148	9.0417	8.3045	7.1327	6.2463	5.5541	4.9995	4.5452	4.1666
75	14.1964	12.4611	11.0938	9.9921	9.0873	8.3316	7.1425	6.2499	5.5555	5.0000	4.5455	4.1667
100	14.2693	12.4943	11.1091	9.9993	9.0906	8.3332	7.1428	6.2500	5.5556	5.0000	4.5455	4.1667

Table 36. Amount of 1 at compound interest (continuous compounding)

Value of e^X for different values of X. **Example:** £1000 earning 6% p.a. interest being compounded continuously, after six years will be worth $1000 \times e^{0.06 \times 6} = 1000e^{0.36} = 1000 \times 1.4333 = £1433.3$.

$X\rightarrow$ ↓	0.00	0.01	0.02	0.03	0.04	0.05	0.06	0.07	0.08	0.09
0.0	1.0000	1.0101	1.0202	1.0305	1.0408	1.0513	1.0618	1.0725	1.0833	1.0942
0.1	1.1052	1.1163	1.1275	1.1388	1.1503	1.1618	1.1735	1.1853	1.1972	1.2092
0.2	1.2214	1.2337	1.2461	1.2586	1.2712	1.2840	1.2969	1.3100	1.3231	1.3364
0.3	1.3499	1.3634	1.3771	1.3910	1.4049	1.4191	1.4333	1.4477	1.4623	1.4770
0.4	1.4918	1.5068	1.5220	1.5373	1.5527	1.5683	1.5841	1.6000	1.6161	1.6323
0.5	1.6487	1.6653	1.6820	1.6989	1.7160	1.7333	1.7507	1.7683	1.7860	1.8040
0.6	1.8221	1.8404	1.8589	1.8776	1.8965	1.9155	1.9348	1.9542	1.9739	1.9937
0.7	2.0138	2.0340	2.0544	2.0751	2.0959	2.1170	2.1383	2.1598	2.1815	2.2034
0.8	2.2255	2.2479	2.2705	2.2933	2.3164	2.3396	2.3632	2.3869	2.4109	2.4351
0.9	2.4596	2.4843	2.5093	2.5345	2.5600	2.5857	2.6117	2.6379	2.6645	2.6912
1.0	2.7183	2.7456	2.7732	2.8011	2.8292	2.8577	2.8864	2.9154	2.9447	2.9743
1.1	3.0042	3.0344	3.0649	3.0957	3.1268	3.1582	3.1899	3.2220	3.2544	3.2871
1.2	3.3201	3.3535	3.3872	3.4212	3.4556	3.4903	3.5254	3.5609	3.5966	3.5328
1.3	3.6693	3.7062	3.7434	3.7810	3.8190	3.8574	3.8962	3.9354	3.9749	4.0149
1.4	4.0552	4.0960	4.1371	4.1787	4.2207	4.2631	4.3060	4.3492	4.3929	4.4371
1.5	4.4817	4.5267	4.5722	4.6182	4.6646	4.7115	4.7588	4.8066	4.8550	4.9038
1.6	4.9530	5.0028	5.0531	5.1039	5.1552	5.2070	5.2593	5.3122	5.3656	5.4195
1.7	5.4739	5.5290	5.5845	5.6407	5.6973	5.7546	5.8124	5.8709	5.9299	5.9895
1.8	6.0497	6.1105	6.1719	6.2339	6.2965	6.3598	6.4237	6.4883	6.5535	6.6194
1.9	6.6859	6.7531	6.8210	6.8895	6.9588	7.0287	7.0993	7.1707	7.2427	7.3155
2.0	7.3891	7.4633	7.5383	7.6141	7.6906	7.7679	7.8460	7.9248	8.0045	8.0849
2.1	8.1662	8.2482	8.3311	8.4149	8.4994	8.5849	8.6711	8.7583	8.8463	8.9352
2.2	9.0250	9.1157	9.2073	9.2999	9.3933	9.4877	9.5831	9.6794	9.7767	9.8749
2.3	9.9742	10.074	10.176	10.278	10.381	10.486	10.591	10.697	10.805	10.914
2.4	11.023	11.134	11.246	11.359	11.473	11.588	11.705	11.822	11.941	12.061
2.5	12.183	12.305	12.429	12.554	12.680	12.807	12.936	13.066	13.197	13.330
2.6	13.464	13.599	13.736	13.874	14.013	14.154	14.296	14.440	14.585	14.732
2.7	14.880	15.029	15.180	15.333	15.487	15.643	15.800	15.959	16.119	16.281
2.8	16.445	16.610	16.777	16.945	17.116	17.288	17.462	17.637	17.814	17.993
2.9	18.174	18.357	18.541	18.728	18.916	19.106	19.298	19.492	19.688	19.886
3.0	20.086	20.287	20.491	20.697	20.905	21.115	21.328	21.542	21.758	21.977
3.1	22.198	22.421	22.646	22.874	23.104	23.336	23.571	23.808	24.047	24.288
3.2	24.533	24.779	25.028	25.280	25.534	25.790	26.050	26.311	26.576	26.843
3.3	27.113	27.385	27.660	27.938	28.219	28.503	28.789	29.079	29.371	29.666
3.4	29.964	30.265	30.569	30.877	31.187	31.500	31.817	32.137	32.460	32.786
3.5	33.115	33.448	33.784	34.124	34.467	34.813	35.163	35.517	35.874	36.234
3.6	36.598	36.966	37.338	37.713	38.092	38.475	38.861	39.252	39.646	40.045
3.7	40.447	40.854	41.264	41.679	42.098	42.521	42.948	43.380	43.816	44.256
3.8	44.701	45.150	45.604	46.063	46.526	46.993	47.465	47.942	48.424	48.911
3.9	49.402	49.899	50.400	50.907	51.419	51.935	52.457	52.985	53.517	54.055
4.0	54.598	55.147	55.701	56.261	56.826	57.398	57.974	58.557	59.146	59.740

Table 37. Present value of a flow of 1 per period (continous discounting)

Values of $(1 - e^{-X})/X$ for different values of X. **Example:** Present value of an annual payment of £1000, for 5 years paid and discounted continuously over time using discount rate of 9% p.a. is $1000 \times 5(1 - e^{-0.09 \times 5})/0.09 \times 5 = 5000(1 - e^{-0.45})/0.45 = 5000 \times 0.8053 = 4026.5$.

$X \rightarrow$ $\downarrow$	0.00	0.01	0.02	0.03	0.04	0.05	0.06	0.07	0.08	0.09
0.0	1.0000	0.9950	0.9901	0.9851	0.9803	0.9754	0.9706	0.9658	0.9610	0.9563
0.1	0.9516	0.9470	0.9423	0.9377	0.9332	0.9286	0.9241	0.9196	0.9152	0.9107
0.2	0.9063	0.9020	0.8976	0.8933	0.8891	0.8848	0.8806	0.8764	0.8722	0.8681
0.3	0.8639	0.8598	0.8558	0.8517	0.8477	0.8437	0.8398	0.8359	0.8319	0.8281
0.4	0.8242	0.8204	0.8166	0.8128	0.8090	0.8053	0.8016	0.7979	0.7942	0.7906
0.5	0.7869	0.7833	0.7798	0.7762	0.7727	0.7692	0.7657	0.7622	0.7588	0.7554
0.6	0.7520	0.7486	0.7453	0.7419	0.7386	0.7353	0.7320	0.7288	0.7256	0.7224
0.7	0.7192	0.7160	0.7128	0.7097	0.7066	0.7035	0.7004	0.6974	0.6944	0.6913
0.8	0.6883	0.6854	0.6824	0.6795	0.6765	0.6736	0.6707	0.6679	0.6650	0.6622
0.9	0.6594	0.6566	0.6538	0.6510	0.6455	0.6483	0.6428	0.6401	0.6374	0.6348
1.0	0.6321	0.6295	0.6269	0.6243	0.6217	0.6191	0.6166	0.6140	0.6115	0.6090
1.1	0.6065	0.6040	0.6015	0.5991	0.5966	0.5942	0.5918	0.5894	0.5871	0.5847
1.2	0.5823	0.5800	0.5777	0.5754	0.5731	0.5708	0.5685	0.5663	0.5640	0.5618
1.3	0.5596	0.5574	0.5552	0.5530	0.5509	0.5487	0.5466	0.5444	0.5423	0.5402
1.4	0.5381	0.5361	0.5340	0.5320	0.5299	0.5279	0.5259	0.5239	0.5219	0.5199
1.5	0.5179	0.5160	0.5140	0.5121	0.5101	0.5082	0.5063	0.5044	0.5025	0.5007
1.6	0.4988	0.4970	0.4951	0.4933	0.4915	0.4897	0.4879	0.4861	0.4843	0.4825
1.7	0.4808	0.4790	0.4773	0.4756	0.4738	0.4721	0.4704	0.4687	0.4671	0.4654
1.8	0.4637	0.4621	0.4604	0.4588	0.4572	0.4555	0.4539	0.4523	0.4507	0.4492
1.9	0.4476	0.4460	0.4445	0.4429	0.4414	0.4399	0.4383	0.4368	0.4353	0.4338
2.0	0.4323	0.4309	0.4294	0.4279	0.4265	0.4250	0.4236	0.4221	0.4207	0.4193
2.1	0.4179	0.4165	0.4151	0.4137	0.4123	0.4109	0.4096	0.4082	0.4069	0.4055
2.2	0.4042	0.4029	0.4015	0.4002	0.3989	0.3976	0.3963	0.3950	0.3937	0.3925
2.3	0.3912	0.3899	0.3887	0.3874	0.3862	0.3849	0.3837	0.3825	0.3813	0.3801
2.4	0.3789	0.3777	0.3765	0.3753	0.3741	0.3729	0.3718	0.3706	0.3695	0.3683
2.5	0.3672	0.3660	0.3649	0.3638	0.3627	0.3615	0.3604	0.3593	0.3582	0.3571
2.6	0.3560	0.3550	0.3539	0.3528	0.3518	0.3507	0.3496	0.3486	0.3476	0.3465
2.7	0.3455	0.3445	0.3434	0.3424	0.3414	0.3404	0.3394	0.3384	0.3374	0.3364
2.8	0.3354	0.3344	0.3335	0.3325	0.3315	0.3306	0.3296	0.3287	0.3277	0.3268
2.9	0.3259	0.3249	0.3240	0.3231	0.3222	0.3212	0.3203	0.3194	0.3185	0.3176
3.0	0.3167	0.3158	0.3150	0.3141	0.3132	0.3123	0.3115	0.3106	0.3098	0.3089
3.1	0.3080	0.3072	0.3064	0.3055	0.3047	0.3039	0.3030	0.3022	0.3014	0.3006
3.2	0.2998	0.2990	0.2982	0.2974	0.2966	0.2958	0.2950	0.2942	0.2934	0.2926
3.3	0.2919	0.2911	0.2903	0.2896	0.2888	0.2880	0.2873	0.2865	0.2858	0.2850
3.4	0.2843	0.2836	0.2828	0.2821	0.2814	0.2807	0.2799	0.2792	0.2785	0.2778
3.5	0.2771	0.2764	0.2757	0.2750	0.2743	0.2736	0.2729	0.2722	0.2715	0.2709
3.6	0.2702	0.2695	0.2688	0.2682	0.2675	0.2669	0.2662	0.2655	0.2649	0.2642
3.7	0.2636	0.2629	0.2623	0.2617	0.2610	0.2604	0.2598	0.2591	0.2585	0.2579
3.8	0.2573	0.2567	0.2560	0.2554	0.2548	0.2542	0.2536	0.2530	0.2524	0.2518
3.9	0.2512	0.2506	0.2500	0.2495	0.2489	0.2483	0.2477	0.2471	0.2466	0.2460
4.0	0.2454	0.2449	0.2443	0.2437	0.2432	0.2426	0.2421	0.2415	0.2410	0.2404

Section 3

Logarithmic tables

Notes on the use of Tables 38, 39 and 40

1. Logarithms. The logarithm of a positive number (x) consists of two parts, an integral part, called the characteristic, and the decimal part, called the mantissa, which is usually positive. For numbers greater than 1, the characteristic is one less than the number of digits to the left of the decimal point, e.g. characteristics of 858.3, 85.83 and 8.583 are 2, 1 and 0 respectively. For numbers between 0 and 1, the characteristic is negative, and is greater by one than the number of zeros that follow the decimal point, e.g. characteristics of 0.8583, 0.08583 and 0.008583 are $\bar{1}$, $\bar{2}$ and $\bar{3}$ respectively. To find the logarithm of a number consisting of four figures, e.g. log 858.3, find the first two digits (85) in the first column of Table 38, then move along to the right until the column headed by the third figure(8) is reached and read off the mantissa (93349). Add to this number the mean difference for 3 (the fourth figure of the number) which is 15, and the result is 93364. As the characteristic of 858.3 is 2, log 858.3=2.93364. Similarly, log 0.8583=$\bar{1}$.93364. To find the logarithm of a five figure number, e.g. log 858.38, interpolate linearly between the mean difference for 3 (15) and 4 (20), i.e. (8/10)(20−15)=4, and, therefore, log 858.38=2.93368.

2. Antilogarithms. The number (x) corresponding to a given logarithm of x (i.e. its antilogarithm) may be found from Table 39. To find antilog 2.93364, say, ignore the characteristic, and find antilog 0.9336 = 85823. Linear interpolation between the mean difference for 6 (119) and 7 (139) gives (4/10)(139 − 119) = 8, and, therefore, antilog 0.93364 = 85831. Taking account of the characteristic, antilog 2.93364 = 858.31. Similarly, antilog $\bar{3}$.93364 = 0.0085831.

3. Multiplication. If x and y are two positive numbers, log xy = log x + log y, and, therefore, the product xy is equal to the antilog of the sum of log x and log y, e.g. log (48.36 × 0.09861) = log 48.36 + log 0.09861 = 1.68449 + $\bar{2}$.99392 = 1.68449 + 0.99392 + $\bar{2}$ = 2.67841 + $\bar{2}$ = 0.67841, and, therefore, antilog 0.67841 = 4.7688, i.e., 48.36 × 0.09861 = 4.7688.

4. Division. If x and y are two positive numbers, log (x/y) = log x − log y, and, therefore, the quotient x/y is equal to the antilog of (log x − log y), e.g. log (34.72/0.08156) = log 34.72 − log 0.08156 = 1.54057 − $\bar{2}$.91148 = 1.54057 + 2 − 0.91148 = 3.54057 − 0.91148 = 2.62909 (when subtracting a logarithm the sign of the characteristic and the mantissa is changed), and, therefore, antilog 2.62909 = 425.69, i.e., 34.72/0.08156 = 425.69.

5. Powers and roots. Log x^n = n log x, and, therefore, x^n is equal to the antilog of (n log x), e.g. log 0.3671^3 = 3 log 0.3671 = 3($\bar{1}$.56479) = $\bar{3}$ + 1.69437 = $\bar{2}$.69437, and, therefore, antilog $\bar{2}$.69437 = 0.049473, i.e., 0.3671^3 = 0.049473.

Similarly, log $\sqrt[n]{x}$ = log $x^{1/n}$ = 1/n log x, and, therefore, $\sqrt[n]{x}$ is equal to the antilog of (1/n log x), e.g. log $\sqrt[3]{2375}$ = $\frac{1}{3}$ log 2375 = $\frac{1}{3}$(3.37568) = 1.12523, and, therefore, antilog 1.12523 = 13.342, i.e., $\sqrt[3]{2375}$ = 13.342. An adjustment is required when the characteristic is negative, e.g. log $\sqrt[3]{0.02375}$ = $\frac{1}{3}$ log 0.02375 = $\frac{1}{3}$($\bar{2}$.37568) = $\frac{1}{3}$($\bar{3}$ + 1.37568) = $\bar{1}$.45856, and, therefore, antilog $\bar{1}$.45856 = 0.28745, i.e., $\sqrt[3]{0.02375}$ = 0.28745.

6. Logarithms to base e. Table 40 gives the characteristic and the mantissa of logarithms to base e of numbers between 1 and 10, e.g. $\log_e$ 7.3462 = 1.99419 (i.e. $\log_e$ 7.346 = 1.99416, and the interpolation for the last figure (2) between the mean difference for 6 (82) and 7 (95) gives (2/10)(95 − 82) = 3).

To find the number (x) whose logarithm to base e is given (i.e. to find its antilogarithm), locate the logarithm in the body of the table and read off the number on the axes, e.g. if $\log_e x$ = 2.23688, the value in the body of the table closest to it is 2.23645 = $\log_e$ 9.36, and the difference between the two numbers is 43 indicating that the third decimal of x is 4, and, therefore, x = 9.364 = antilog 2.23688.

If x > 10 use the multiplication rule, e.g. $\log_e$ 873 = $\log_e$ 8.73 × 10^2 = $\log_e$ 8.73 + $\log_e$ 10^2. Log 8.73 can be found from Table 40 directly, and $\log_e 10^2$ = 4.60517 is given at the foot of Table 40. If x < 1 proceed similarly, e.g. $\log_e$ 0.0253 = $\log_e$ 2.53 × 10^{-2} = $\log_e$ 2.53 + $\log_e$ 10^{-2}, and $\log_e 10^{-2}$ = $\bar{5}$.39483 can be found at the foot of Table 40.

7. Switching the base of logarithms. To convert logarithms to base 10 to logarithms to base e, and vice versa, use the relationships: $\log_e x$ = $\log_e$ 10 . $\log_{10} x$ = 2.30258 $\log_{10} x$, and $\log_{10} x$ = $\log_{10} e$. $\log_e x$ = 0.43429 $\log_e x$.

Table 38.   Logarithms (base 10)

x→ ↓	0	1	2	3	4	5	6	7	8	9	Mean differences 1	2	3	4	5	6	7	8	9
10	00000	00432	00860	01284	01703						43	85	128	170	212	255	297	339	382
						02119	02531	02938	03342	03743	41	81	122	162	203	243	283	324	364
11	04139	04532	04922	05308	05690						39	77	116	155	193	232	271	309	348
						06070	06446	06819	07188	07555	37	74	111	148	185	222	259	296	333
12	07918	08279	08636	08991	09342						36	71	107	142	178	213	249	284	319
						09691	10037	10380	10721	11059	34	68	102	137	171	205	239	273	307
13	11394	11727	12057	12385	12710						33	66	99	131	164	197	230	262	295
						13033	13354	13672	13988	14301	32	63	95	127	158	190	221	253	284
14	14613	14922	15229	15534	15836						31	61	92	122	153	183	214	244	274
						16137	16435	16732	17026	17319	30	59	89	118	147	177	206	236	265
15	17609	17898	18184	18469	18752						29	57	86	114	143	171	200	228	256
						19033	19312	19590	19866	20140	28	55	83	111	138	166	193	221	248
16	20412	20683	20952	21219	21484						27	54	80	107	134	161	187	214	241
						21748	22011	22272	22531	22789	26	52	78	104	130	156	182	208	233
17	23045	23300	23553	23805	24055						25	50	76	101	126	151	176	202	227
						24304	24551	24797	25042	25285	25	49	74	98	123	147	171	196	220
18	25527	25768	26007	26245	26482						24	48	72	95	119	143	167	190	214
						26717	26951	27184	27416	27646	23	46	70	93	116	139	162	185	209
19	27875	28103	28330	28556	28780						23	45	68	90	113	136	158	181	203
						29003	29226	29447	29667	29885	22	44	66	88	110	132	154	176	198
20	30103	30320	30535	30750	30963	31175	31387	31597	31806	32015	21	42	64	85	106	127	148	170	191
21	32222	32428	32634	32838	33041	33244	33445	33646	33846	34044	20	40	61	81	101	121	142	162	182
22	34242	34439	34635	34830	35025	35218	35411	35603	35793	35984	19	39	58	77	97	116	135	155	174
23	36173	36361	36549	36736	36922	37107	37291	37475	37658	37840	19	37	56	74	93	111	129	148	166
24	38021	38202	38382	38561	38739	38917	39094	39270	39445	39620	18	36	53	71	89	106	124	142	160
25	39794	39967	40140	40312	40483	40654	40824	40993	41162	41330	17	34	51	68	85	102	119	136	153
26	41497	41664	41830	41996	42160	42325	42488	42651	42813	42975	16	33	49	66	82	98	115	131	148
27	43136	43297	43457	43616	43775	43933	44091	44248	44404	44560	16	32	47	63	79	95	111	126	142
28	44716	44871	45025	45179	45332	45484	45637	45788	45939	46090	15	31	46	61	76	92	107	122	137
29	46240	46389	46538	46687	46835	46982	47129	47276	47422	47567	15	29	44	59	74	88	103	118	133
30	47712	47857	48001	48144	48287	48430	48572	48714	48855	48996	14	29	43	57	71	85	100	114	128
31	49136	49276	49415	49554	49693	49831	49969	50106	50243	50379	14	28	41	55	69	83	97	110	124
32	50515	50651	50786	50920	51055	51188	51322	51455	51587	51720	13	27	40	54	67	80	94	107	120
33	51851	51983	52114	52244	52375	52504	52634	52763	52892	53020	13	26	39	52	65	78	91	104	117
34	53148	53275	53403	53529	53656	53782	53908	54033	54158	54283	13	25	38	50	63	76	88	101	113
35	54407	54531	54654	54777	54900	55023	55145	55267	55388	55509	12	24	37	49	61	73	86	98	110
36	55630	55751	55871	55991	56110	56229	56348	56467	56585	56703	12	24	36	48	60	71	83	95	107
37	56820	56937	57054	57171	57287	57403	57519	57634	57749	57864	12	23	35	46	58	70	81	93	104
38	57978	58092	58206	58320	58433	58546	58659	58771	58883	58995	11	23	34	45	56	68	79	90	102
39	59106	59218	59329	59439	59550	59660	59770	59879	59988	60097	11	22	33	44	55	66	77	88	99
40	60206	60314	60423	60531	60638	60746	60853	60959	61066	61172	11	21	32	43	54	64	75	86	97
41	61278	61384	61490	61595	61700	61805	61909	62014	62118	62221	10	21	31	42	52	63	73	84	94
42	62325	62428	62531	62634	62737	62839	62941	63043	63144	63246	10	20	31	41	51	61	72	82	92
43	63347	63448	63548	63649	63749	63849	63949	64048	64147	64246	10	20	30	40	50	60	70	80	90
44	64345	64444	64542	64640	64738	64836	64933	65031	65128	65225	10	20	29	39	49	59	68	78	88
45	65321	65418	65514	65610	65706	65801	65896	65992	66087	66181	10	19	29	38	48	57	67	76	86
46	66276	66370	66464	66558	66652	66745	66839	66932	67025	67117	9	19	28	37	47	56	65	75	84
47	67210	67302	67394	67486	67578	67669	67761	67852	67943	68034	9	18	27	37	46	55	64	73	82
48	68124	68215	68305	68395	68485	68574	68664	68753	68842	68931	9	18	27	36	45	54	63	72	81
49	69020	69108	69197	69285	69373	69461	69548	69636	69723	69810	9	18	26	35	44	53	61	70	79
50	69897	69984	70070	70157	70243	70329	70415	70501	70586	70672	9	17	26	34	43	52	60	69	77
51	70757	70842	70927	71012	71096	71181	71265	71349	71433	71517	8	17	25	34	42	51	59	67	76
52	71600	71684	71767	71850	71933	72016	72099	72181	72263	72346	8	17	25	33	41	50	58	66	74
53	72428	72509	72591	72673	72754	72835	72916	72997	73078	73159	8	16	24	32	41	49	57	65	73
54	73239	73320	73400	73480	73560	73640	73719	73799	73878	73957	8	16	24	32	40	48	56	64	72
55	74036	74115	74194	74273	74351	74429	74507	74586	74663	74741	8	16	23	31	39	47	55	63	70
56	74819	74896	74974	75051	75128	75205	75282	75358	75435	75511	8	15	23	31	38	46	54	62	69
57	75587	75664	75740	75815	75891	75967	76042	76118	76193	76268	8	15	23	30	38	45	53	60	68
58	76343	76418	76492	76567	76641	76716	76790	76864	76938	77012	7	15	22	30	37	45	52	59	67
59	77085	77159	77232	77305	77379	77452	77525	77597	77670	77743	7	15	22	29	37	44	51	58	66

Table 38 – *continued*

x→	0	1	2	3	4	5	6	7	8	9	Mean differences 1	2	3	4	5	6	7	8	9
60	77815	77887	77960	78032	78104	78176	78247	78319	78390	78462	7	14	22	29	36	43	50	57	65
61	78533	78604	78675	78746	78817	78888	78958	79029	79099	79169	7	14	21	28	35	42	49	57	64
62	79239	79309	79379	79449	79518	79588	79657	79727	79796	79865	7	14	21	28	35	42	49	57	64
63	79934	80003	80072	80140	80209	80277	80346	80414	80482	80550	7	14	21	28	35	42	49	56	63
64	80618	80686	80754	80821	80889	80956	81023	81090	81158	81224	7	13	20	27	34	40	47	54	61
65	81291	81358	81425	81491	81558	81624	81690	81757	81823	81889	7	13	20	27	33	40	46	53	60
66	81954	82020	82086	82151	82217	82282	82347	82413	82478	82543	7	13	20	26	33	39	46	52	59
67	82607	82672	82737	82802	82866	82930	82995	83059	83123	83187	6	13	19	26	32	39	45	51	58
68	83251	83315	83378	83442	83506	83569	83632	83696	83759	83822	6	13	19	25	32	38	44	51	57
69	83885	83948	84011	84073	84136	84198	84261	84323	84386	84448	6	13	19	25	31	38	44	50	56
70	84510	84572	84634	84696	84757	84819	84880	84942	85003	85065	6	12	18	25	31	37	43	49	55
71	85126	85187	85248	85309	85370	85431	85491	85552	85612	85673	6	12	18	24	30	36	43	49	55
72	85733	85794	85854	85914	85974	86034	86094	86153	86213	86273	6	12	18	24	30	36	42	48	54
73	86332	86392	86451	86510	86570	86629	86688	86747	86806	86864	6	12	18	24	30	35	41	47	53
74	86923	86982	87040	87099	87157	87216	87274	87332	87390	87448	6	12	17	23	29	35	41	47	52
75	87506	87564	87622	87679	87737	87795	87852	87910	87967	88024	6	12	17	23	29	35	40	46	52
76	88081	88138	88195	88252	88309	88366	88423	88480	88536	88593	6	11	17	23	28	34	40	45	51
77	88649	88705	88762	88818	88874	88930	88986	89042	89098	89154	6	11	17	22	28	34	39	45	50
78	89209	89265	89321	89376	89432	89487	89542	89597	89653	89708	6	11	17	22	28	33	39	44	50
79	89763	89818	89873	89927	89982	90037	90091	90146	90200	90255	5	11	16	22	27	33	38	44	49
80	90309	90363	90417	90472	90526	90580	90634	90687	90741	90795	5	11	16	22	27	32	38	43	49
81	90849	90902	90956	91009	91062	91116	91169	91222	91275	91328	5	11	16	21	27	32	37	43	48
82	91381	91434	91487	91540	91593	91645	91698	91751	91803	91855	5	11	16	21	26	32	37	42	47
83	91908	91960	92012	92065	92117	92169	92221	92273	92324	92376	5	10	16	21	26	31	36	42	47
84	92428	92480	92531	92583	92634	92686	92737	92788	92840	92891	5	10	15	21	26	31	36	41	46
85	92942	92993	93044	93095	93146	93197	93247	93298	93349	93399	5	10	15	20	25	30	36	41	46
86	93450	93500	93551	93601	93651	93702	93752	93802	93852	93902	5	10	15	20	25	30	35	40	45
87	93952	94002	94052	94101	94151	94201	94250	94300	94349	94399	5	10	15	20	25	30	35	40	45
88	94448	94498	94547	94596	94645	94694	94743	94792	94841	94890	5	10	15	20	25	29	34	39	44
89	94939	94988	95036	95085	95134	95182	95231	95279	95328	95376	5	10	15	19	24	29	34	39	44
90	95424	95472	95521	95569	95617	95665	95713	95761	95809	95856	5	10	14	19	24	29	34	38	43
91	95904	95952	95999	96047	96095	96142	96190	96237	96284	96332	5	9	14	19	24	28	33	38	43
92	96379	96426	96473	96520	96567	96614	96661	96708	96755	96802	5	9	14	19	23	28	33	38	42
93	96848	96895	96942	96988	97035	97081	97128	97174	97220	97267	5	9	14	19	23	28	33	37	42
94	97313	97359	97405	97451	97497	97543	97589	97635	97681	97727	5	9	14	18	23	28	32	37	41
95	97772	97818	97864	97909	97955	98000	98046	98091	98137	98182	5	9	14	18	23	27	32	36	41
96	98227	98272	98318	98363	98408	98453	98498	98543	98588	98632	5	9	14	18	23	27	32	36	41
97	98677	98722	98767	98811	98856	98900	98945	98989	99034	99078	4	9	13	18	22	27	31	36	40
98	99123	99167	99211	99255	99300	99344	99388	99432	99476	99520	4	9	13	18	22	26	31	35	40
99	99564	99607	99651	99695	99739	99782	99826	99870	99913	99957	4	9	13	17	22	26	31	35	39

Table 39. Antilogarithms (base 10)

log x	0	1	2	3	4	5	6	7	8	9	Mean differences 1	2	3	4	5	6	7	8	9
.00	10000	10023	10046	10069	10093	10116	10139	10162	10186	10209	2	5	7	9	12	14	16	19	21
.01	10233	10257	10280	10304	10328	10351	10375	10399	10423	10447	2	5	7	10	12	14	17	19	21
.02	10471	10495	10520	10544	10568	10593	10617	10641	10666	10691	2	5	7	10	12	15	17	20	22
.03	10715	10740	10765	10789	10814	10839	10864	10889	10914	10940	2	5	7	10	12	15	17	20	22
.04	10965	10990	11015	11041	11066	11092	11117	11143	11169	11194	3	5	8	10	13	15	18	20	23
.05	11220	11246	11272	11298	11324	11350	11376	11402	11429	11455	3	5	8	10	13	16	18	21	24
.06	11482	11508	11535	11561	11588	11614	11641	11668	11695	11722	3	5	8	11	13	16	19	21	24
.07	11749	11776	11803	11830	11858	11885	11912	11940	11967	11995	3	5	8	11	14	16	19	22	25
.08	12023	12050	12078	12106	12134	12162	12190	12218	12246	12274	3	6	8	11	14	17	20	22	25
.09	12303	12331	12359	12388	12417	12445	12474	12503	12531	12560	3	6	9	11	14	17	20	23	26
.10	12589	12618	12647	12677	12706	12735	12764	12794	12823	12853	3	6	9	12	15	18	21	23	26
.11	12882	12912	12942	12972	13002	13032	13062	13092	13122	13152	3	6	9	12	15	18	21	24	27
.12	13183	13213	13243	13274	13305	13335	13366	13397	13428	13459	3	6	9	12	15	18	21	25	28
.13	13490	13521	13552	13583	13614	13646	13677	13709	13740	13772	3	6	9	13	16	19	22	25	28
.14	13804	13836	13868	13900	13932	13964	13996	14028	14060	14093	3	6	10	13	16	19	22	26	29
.15	14125	14158	14191	14223	14256	14289	14322	14355	14388	14421	3	7	10	13	16	20	23	26	30
.16	14454	14488	14521	14555	14588	14622	14655	14689	14723	14757	3	7	10	13	17	20	24	27	30
.17	14791	14825	14859	14894	14928	14962	14997	15031	15066	15101	3	7	10	14	17	21	24	28	31
.18	15136	15171	15205	15241	15276	15311	15346	15382	15417	15453	4	7	11	14	18	21	25	28	32
.19	15488	15524	15560	15596	15631	15668	15704	15740	15776	15812	4	7	11	14	18	22	25	29	32
.20	15849	15885	15922	15959	15996	16032	16069	16106	16144	16181	4	7	11	15	18	22	26	30	33
.21	16218	16255	16293	16331	16368	16406	16444	16482	16520	16558	4	8	11	15	19	23	26	30	34
.22	16596	16634	16672	16711	16749	16788	16827	16866	16904	16943	4	8	12	15	19	23	27	31	35
.23	16982	17022	17061	17100	17140	17179	17219	17258	17298	17338	4	8	12	16	20	24	28	32	36
.24	17378	17418	17458	17498	17539	17579	17620	17660	17701	17742	4	8	12	16	20	24	28	32	36
.25	17783	17824	17865	17906	17947	17989	18030	18072	18113	18155	4	8	12	17	21	25	29	33	37
.26	18197	18239	18281	18323	18365	18408	18450	18493	18535	18578	4	8	13	17	21	25	30	34	38
.27	18621	18664	18707	18750	18793	18836	18880	18923	18967	19011	4	9	13	17	22	26	30	35	39
.28	19055	19099	19143	19187	19231	19275	19320	19364	19409	19454	4	9	13	18	22	27	31	35	40
.29	19498	19543	19588	19634	19679	19724	19770	19815	19861	19907	5	9	14	18	23	27	32	36	41
.30	19953	19999	20045	20091	20137	20184	20230	20277	20324	20370	5	9	14	19	23	28	33	37	42
.31	20417	20464	20512	20559	20606	20654	20701	20749	20797	20845	5	10	14	19	24	29	33	38	43
.32	20893	20941	20989	21038	21086	21135	21184	21232	21281	21330	5	10	15	19	24	29	34	39	44
.33	21380	21429	21478	21528	21577	21627	21677	21727	21777	21827	5	10	15	20	25	30	35	40	45
.34	21878	21928	21979	22029	22080	22131	22182	22233	22284	22336	5	10	15	20	25	31	36	41	46
.35	22387	22439	22491	22542	22594	22646	22699	22751	22803	22856	5	10	16	21	26	31	36	42	47
.36	22909	22961	23014	23067	23121	23174	23227	23281	23335	23388	5	11	16	21	27	32	37	43	48
.37	23442	23496	23550	23605	23659	23714	23768	23823	23878	23933	5	11	16	22	27	33	38	44	49
.38	23988	24044	24099	24155	24210	24266	24322	24378	24434	24491	6	11	17	22	28	34	39	45	50
.39	24547	24604	24660	24717	24774	24831	24889	24946	25003	25061	6	11	17	23	29	34	40	46	51
.40	25119	25177	25235	25293	25351	25410	25468	25527	25586	25645	6	12	18	23	29	35	41	47	53
.41	25704	25763	25823	25882	25942	26002	26062	26122	26182	26242	6	12	18	24	30	36	42	48	54
.42	26303	26363	26424	26485	26546	26607	26669	26730	26792	26853	6	12	18	24	31	37	43	49	55
.43	26915	26977	27040	27102	27164	27227	27290	27353	27416	27479	6	13	19	25	31	38	44	50	56
.44	27542	27606	27669	27733	27797	27861	27925	27990	28054	28119	6	13	19	26	32	38	45	51	58
.45	28184	28249	28314	28379	28445	28510	28576	28642	28708	28774	7	13	20	26	33	39	46	53	59
.46	28840	28907	28973	29040	29107	29174	29242	29309	29376	29444	7	13	20	27	34	40	47	54	60
.47	29512	29580	29648	29717	29785	29854	29923	29992	30061	30130	7	14	21	27	34	41	48	55	62
.48	30200	30269	30339	30409	30479	30549	30620	30690	30761	30832	7	14	21	28	35	42	49	56	63
.49	30903	30974	31046	31117	31189	31261	31333	31405	31477	31550	7	14	22	29	36	43	50	58	65
.50	31623	31696	31769	31842	31915	31989	32063	32137	32211	32285	7	15	22	29	37	44	52	59	66
.51	32359	32434	32509	32584	32659	32734	32810	32885	32961	33037	8	15	23	30	38	45	53	60	68
.52	33113	33189	33266	33343	33420	33497	33574	33651	33729	33806	8	15	23	31	39	46	54	62	69
.53	33884	33963	34041	34119	34198	34277	34356	34435	34514	34594	8	16	24	32	39	47	55	63	71
.54	34674	34754	34834	34914	34995	35075	35156	35237	35318	35400	8	16	24	32	40	48	57	65	73
.55	35481	35563	35645	35727	35810	35892	35975	36058	36141	36224	8	17	25	33	41	50	58	66	74
.56	36308	36392	36475	36559	36644	36728	36813	36898	36983	37068	8	17	25	34	42	51	59	68	76
.57	37154	37239	37325	37411	37497	37584	37670	37757	37844	37931	9	17	26	35	43	52	61	69	78
.58	38019	38107	38194	38282	38371	38459	38548	38637	38726	38815	9	18	27	35	44	53	62	71	80
.59	38905	38994	39084	39174	39264	39355	39446	39537	39628	39719	9	18	27	36	45	54	63	72	82

Table 39 – *continued*

log x	0	1	2	3	4	5	6	7	8	9	1	2	3	4	5	6	7	8	9
											Mean differences								
.60	39811	39902	39994	40087	40179	40272	40365	40458	40551	40644	9	19	28	37	46	56	65	74	83
.61	40738	40832	40926	41020	41115	41210	41305	41400	41495	41591	9	19	28	38	47	57	66	76	85
.62	41687	41783	41879	41976	42073	42170	42267	42364	42462	42560	10	19	29	39	49	58	68	78	87
.63	42658	42756	42855	42954	43053	43152	43251	43351	43451	43551	10	20	30	40	50	60	70	79	89
.64	43652	43752	43853	43954	44055	44157	44259	44361	44463	44566	10	20	30	41	51	61	71	81	91
.65	44668	44771	44875	44978	45082	45186	45290	45394	45499	45604	10	21	31	42	52	62	73	83	94
.66	45709	45814	45920	46026	46132	46238	46345	46452	46559	46666	11	21	32	43	53	64	75	85	96
.67	46774	46881	46989	47098	47206	47315	47424	47534	47643	47753	11	22	33	44	54	65	76	87	98
.68	47863	47973	48084	48195	48306	48417	48529	48641	48753	48865	11	22	33	45	56	67	78	89	100
.69	48978	49091	49204	49317	49431	49545	49659	49774	49888	50003	11	23	34	46	57	68	80	91	103
.70	50119	50234	50350	50466	50582	50699	50816	50933	51050	51168	12	23	35	47	58	70	82	93	105
.71	51286	51404	51523	51642	51761	51880	52000	52119	52240	52360	12	24	36	48	60	72	84	96	108
.72	52481	52602	52723	52845	52966	53088	53211	53333	53456	53580	12	24	37	49	61	73	86	98	110
.73	53703	53827	53951	54075	54200	54325	54450	54576	54702	54828	12	25	37	50	63	75	88	100	113
.74	54954	55081	55208	55335	55463	55590	55719	55847	55976	56105	13	26	38	51	64	77	90	102	115
.75	56234	56364	56494	56624	56754	56885	57016	57148	57280	57412	13	26	39	52	65	79	92	105	118
.76	57544	57677	57810	57943	58076	58210	58345	58479	58614	58749	13	27	40	54	67	80	94	107	121
.77	58884	59020	59156	59293	59429	59566	59704	59841	59979	60117	14	27	41	55	69	82	96	110	123
.78	60256	60395	60534	60674	60814	60954	61094	61235	61376	61518	14	28	42	56	70	84	98	112	126
.79	61660	61802	61944	62087	62230	62373	62517	62661	62806	62951	14	29	43	57	72	86	101	115	129
.80	63096	63241	63387	63433	63680	63826	63973	64121	64269	64417	15	29	44	59	73	88	103	118	132
.81	64565	64714	64863	65013	65163	65313	65464	65615	65766	65917	15	30	45	60	75	90	105	120	135
.82	66069	66222	66374	66527	66681	66834	66988	67143	67298	67453	15	31	46	62	77	92	108	123	138
.83	67608	67764	67920	68077	68234	68391	68549	68707	68865	69024	16	31	47	63	79	94	110	126	142
.84	69183	69343	69502	69663	69823	69984	70146	70307	70469	70632	16	32	48	64	81	97	113	129	145
.85	70795	70958	71121	71285	71450	71614	71779	71945	72111	72277	16	33	49	66	82	99	115	132	148
.86	72444	72611	72778	72946	73114	73282	73451	73621	73790	73961	17	34	51	67	84	101	118	135	152
.87	74131	74302	74473	74645	74817	74989	75162	75336	75509	75683	17	35	52	69	86	104	121	138	155
.88	75858	76033	76208	76384	76560	76736	76913	77090	77268	77446	18	35	53	71	88	106	124	141	159
.89	77625	77804	77983	78163	78343	78524	78705	78886	79068	79250	18	36	54	72	90	108	127	145	163
.90	79433	79616	79799	79983	80168	80353	80538	80724	80910	81096	18	37	55	74	92	111	129	148	167
.91	81283	81470	81658	81846	82035	82224	82414	82604	82794	82985	19	38	57	76	95	114	132	151	170
.92	83176	83368	83560	83753	83946	84140	84333	84528	84723	84918	19	39	58	77	97	116	136	155	174
.93	85114	85310	85507	85704	85901	86099	86298	86497	86696	86896	20	40	59	79	99	119	139	159	178
.94	87096	87297	87498	87700	87902	88105	88308	88512	88716	88920	20	41	61	81	101	122	142	162	183
.95	89125	89331	89536	89743	89950	90157	90365	90573	90782	90991	21	41	62	83	104	125	145	166	187
.96	91201	91411	91622	91833	92045	92257	92470	92683	92897	93111	21	42	64	85	106	127	149	170	191
.97	93325	93541	93756	93972	94189	94406	94624	94842	95060	95280	22	43	65	87	109	130	152	174	196
.98	95499	95719	95940	96161	96383	96605	96828	97051	97275	97499	22	44	67	89	111	133	156	178	200
.99	97724	97949	98175	98401	98628	98855	99083	99312	99541	99770	23	45	68	91	114	137	159	182	205

Table 40. Logarithms (base e)

$\frac{x\rightarrow}{\downarrow}$	0	1	2	3	4	5	6	7	8	9	Mean differences 1	2	3	4	5	6	7	8	9
1.0	0.00000	0.00995	0.01980	0.02956	0.03922	0.04879	0.05827	0.06766	0.07696	0.08618	96	191	287	382	478	573	668	763	858
1.1	0.09531	0.10436	0.11333	0.12222	0.13103	0.13976	0.14842	0.15700	0.16551	0.17395	87	175	262	349	436	523	610	697	783
1.2	0.18232	0.19062	0.19885	0.20701	0.21511	0.22314	0.23111	0.23902	0.24686	0.25464	80	161	241	321	401	481	561	641	721
1.3	0.26236	0.27003	0.27763	0.28518	0.29267	0.30010	0.30748	0.31481	0.32208	0.32930	74	149	223	297	371	445	519	593	667
1.4	0.33647	0.34359	0.35066	0.35767	0.36464	0.37156	0.37844	0.38526	0.39204	0.39878	69	138	207	277	346	415	483	552	621
1.5	0.40547	0.41211	0.41871	0.42527	0.43178	0.43825	0.44469	0.45108	0.45742	0.46373	65	129	194	259	323	388	452	517	581
1.6	0.47000	0.47623	0.48243	0.48858	0.49470	0.50078	0.50682	0.51282	0.51879	0.52473	61	122	182	243	304	364	425	485	546
1.7	0.53063	0.53649	0.54232	0.54812	0.55389	0.55962	0.56531	0.57098	0.57661	0.58222	57	115	172	229	286	343	400	458	515
1.8	0.58779	0.59333	0.59884	0.60432	0.60977	0.61519	0.62058	0.62594	0.63127	0.63658	54	108	163	217	271	325	379	433	487
1.9	0.64185	0.64710	0.65233	0.65752	0.66269	0.66783	0.67294	0.67803	0.68310	0.68813	51	103	154	205	257	308	359	411	462
2.0	0.69315	0.69813	0.70310	0.70804	0.71295	0.71784	0.72271	0.72755	0.73237	0.73716	49	98	147	195	244	293	342	391	439
2.1	0.74194	0.74669	0.75142	0.75612	0.76081	0.76547	0.77011	0.77473	0.77932	0.78390	47	93	140	186	233	279	326	372	419
2.2	0.78846	0.79299	0.79751	0.80200	0.80648	0.81093	0.81536	0.81978	0.82418	0.82855	45	89	134	178	223	267	311	356	400
2.3	0.83291	0.83725	0.84157	0.84587	0.85015	0.85442	0.85866	0.86289	0.86710	0.87129	43	85	128	170	213	256	298	341	383
2.4	0.87547	0.87963	0.88377	0.88789	0.89200	0.89609	0.90016	0.90422	0.90826	0.91228	41	82	123	163	204	245	286	327	367
2.5	0.91629	0.92028	0.92426	0.92822	0.93216	0.93609	0.94001	0.94391	0.94779	0.95166	39	79	118	157	196	236	275	314	353
2.6	0.95551	0.95935	0.96317	0.96698	0.97078	0.97456	0.97833	0.98208	0.98582	0.98954	38	76	113	151	189	227	264	302	340
2.7	0.99325	0.99695	1.00063	1.00430	1.00796	1.01160	1.01523	1.01885	1.02245	1.02604	36	73	109	146	182	218	255	291	327
2.8	1.02962	1.03318	1.03674	1.04028	1.04380	1.04732	1.05082	1.05431	1.05779	1.06126	35	70	105	141	176	211	246	281	316
2.9	1.06471	1.06815	1.07158	1.07500	1.07841	1.08181	1.08519	1.08856	1.09192	1.09527	34	68	102	136	170	204	237	271	305
3.0	1.09861	1.10194	1.10526	1.10856	1.11186	1.11514	1.11841	1.12168	1.12493	1.12817	33	66	98	131	164	197	230	262	295
3.1	1.13140	1.13462	1.13783	1.14103	1.14422	1.14740	1.15057	1.15373	1.15688	1.16002	32	64	95	127	159	191	222	254	286
3.2	1.16315	1.16627	1.16938	1.17248	1.17557	1.17865	1.18173	1.18479	1.18784	1.19089	31	62	92	123	154	185	216	246	277
3.3	1.19392	1.19695	1.19996	1.20297	1.20597	1.20896	1.21194	1.21491	1.21788	1.22083	30	60	90	120	149	179	209	239	269
3.4	1.22378	1.22671	1.22964	1.23256	1.23547	1.23837	1.24127	1.24415	1.24703	1.24990	29	58	87	116	145	174	203	232	261
3.5	1.25276	1.25562	1.25846	1.26130	1.26413	1.26695	1.26976	1.27257	1.27536	1.27815	28	56	85	113	141	169	197	225	254
3.6	1.28093	1.28371	1.28647	1.28923	1.29198	1.29473	1.29746	1.30019	1.30291	1.30563	27	55	82	110	137	164	192	219	247
3.7	1.30833	1.31103	1.31372	1.31641	1.31909	1.32176	1.32442	1.32708	1.32972	1.33237	27	53	80	107	133	160	187	213	240
3.8	1.33500	1.33763	1.34025	1.34286	1.34547	1.34807	1.35067	1.35325	1.35584	1.35841	26	52	78	104	130	156	182	208	234
3.9	1.36098	1.36354	1.36609	1.36864	1.37118	1.37372	1.37624	1.37877	1.38128	1.38379	25	51	76	101	127	152	177	203	228
4.0	1.38629	1.38879	1.39128	1.39377	1.39624	1.39872	1.40118	1.40364	1.40610	1.40854	25	49	74	99	124	148	173	198	222
4.1	1.41099	1.41342	1.41585	1.41828	1.42070	1.42311	1.42552	1.42792	1.43031	1.43270	24	48	72	96	121	145	169	193	217
4.2	1.43508	1.43746	1.43984	1.44220	1.44456	1.44692	1.44927	1.45161	1.45395	1.45629	24	47	71	94	118	141	165	188	212
4.3	1.45862	1.46094	1.46326	1.46557	1.46787	1.47018	1.47247	1.47476	1.47705	1.47933	23	46	69	92	115	138	161	184	207
4.4	1.48160	1.48387	1.48614	1.48840	1.49065	1.49290	1.49515	1.49739	1.49962	1.50185	22	45	67	90	112	135	157	180	202
4.5	1.50408	1.50630	1.50851	1.51072	1.51293	1.51513	1.51732	1.51951	1.52170	1.52388	22	44	66	88	110	132	154	176	198
4.6	1.52606	1.52823	1.53039	1.53256	1.53471	1.53687	1.53902	1.54116	1.54330	1.54543	22	43	65	86	108	129	151	172	194
4.7	1.54756	1.54969	1.55181	1.55393	1.55604	1.55814	1.56025	1.56235	1.56444	1.56653	21	42	63	84	105	126	147	168	190
4.8	1.56862	1.57070	1.57277	1.57485	1.57691	1.57898	1.58104	1.58309	1.58515	1.58719	21	41	62	83	103	124	144	165	186
4.9	1.58924	1.59127	1.59331	1.59534	1.59737	1.59939	1.60141	1.60342	1.60543	1.60744	20	40	61	81	101	121	141	162	182
5.0	1.60944	1.61144	1.61343	1.61542	1.61741	1.61939	1.62137	1.62334	1.62531	1.62728	20	40	59	79	99	119	139	158	178
5.1	1.62924	1.63120	1.63315	1.63511	1.63705	1.63900	1.64094	1.64287	1.64481	1.64673	19	39	58	78	97	117	136	155	175
5.2	1.64866	1.65058	1.65250	1.65441	1.65632	1.65823	1.66013	1.66203	1.66393	1.66582	19	38	57	76	95	114	133	152	171
5.3	1.66771	1.66959	1.67147	1.67335	1.67523	1.67710	1.67896	1.68083	1.68269	1.68455	19	37	56	75	94	112	131	150	168
5.4	1.68640	1.68825	1.69010	1.69194	1.69378	1.69562	1.69745	1.69928	1.70111	1.70293	18	37	55	73	92	110	128	147	165
5.5	1.70475	1.70656	1.70838	1.71019	1.71199	1.71380	1.71560	1.71740	1.71919	1.72098	18	36	54	72	90	108	126	144	162
5.6	1.72277	1.72455	1.72633	1.72811	1.72988	1.73166	1.73342	1.73519	1.73695	1.73871	18	35	53	71	89	106	124	142	159
5.7	1.74047	1.74222	1.74397	1.74572	1.74746	1.74920	1.75094	1.75267	1.75440	1.75613	17	35	52	70	87	104	122	139	157
5.8	1.75786	1.75958	1.76130	1.76302	1.76473	1.76644	1.76815	1.76985	1.77156	1.77326	17	34	51	68	86	103	120	137	154
5.9	1.77495	1.77665	1.77834	1.78002	1.78171	1.78339	1.78507	1.78675	1.78842	1.79009	17	34	50	67	84	101	118	134	151
6.0	1.79176	1.79342	1.79509	1.79675	1.79840	1.80006	1.80171	1.80336	1.80500	1.80665	17	33	50	66	83	99	116	132	149
6.1	1.80829	1.80993	1.81156	1.81319	1.81482	1.81645	1.81808	1.81970	1.82132	1.82294	16	33	49	65	81	98	114	130	146
6.2	1.82455	1.82616	1.82777	1.82938	1.83098	1.83258	1.83418	1.83578	1.83737	1.83896	16	32	48	64	80	96	112	128	144
6.3	1.84055	1.84214	1.84372	1.84530	1.84688	1.84845	1.85003	1.85160	1.85317	1.85473	16	32	47	63	79	95	110	126	142
6.4	1.85630	1.85786	1.85942	1.86097	1.86253	1.86408	1.86563	1.86718	1.86872	1.87026	16	31	47	62	78	93	109	124	140
6.5	1.87180	1.87334	1.87487	1.87641	1.87794	1.87947	1.88099	1.88251	1.88403	1.88555	15	31	46	61	76	92	107	122	137
6.6	1.88707	1.88858	1.89010	1.89160	1.89311	1.89462	1.89612	1.89762	1.89912	1.90061	15	30	45	60	75	90	105	120	135
6.7	1.90211	1.90360	1.90509	1.90658	1.90806	1.90954	1.91102	1.91250	1.91398	1.91545	15	30	44	59	74	89	104	119	133
6.8	1.91692	1.91839	1.91986	1.92132	1.92279	1.92425	1.92571	1.92716	1.92862	1.93007	15	29	44	58	73	88	102	117	131
6.9	1.93152	1.93297	1.93442	1.93586	1.93730	1.93874	1.94018	1.94162	1.94305	1.94448	14	29	43	58	72	86	101	115	130

Table 40 – *continued*

x→	0	1	2	3	4	5	6	7	8	9	|	1	2	3	4	5	6	7	8	9
											Mean differences									
7.0	1.94591	1.94734	1.94876	1.95019	1.95161	1.95303	1.95445	1.95586	1.95727	1.95869		14	28	43	57	71	85	99	113	128
7.1	1.96009	1.96150	1.96291	1.96431	1.96571	1.96711	1.96851	1.96991	1.97130	1.97269		14	28	42	56	70	84	98	112	126
7.2	1.97408	1.97547	1.97685	1.97824	1.97962	1.98100	1.98238	1.98376	1.98513	1.98650		14	28	41	55	69	83	97	110	124
7.3	1.98787	1.98924	1.99061	1.99198	1.99334	1.99470	1.99606	1.99742	1.99877	2.00013		14	27	41	54	68	82	95	109	122
7.4	2.00148	2.00283	2.00418	2.00353	2.00687	2.00821	2.00956	2.01089	2.01223	2.01357		13	27	40	54	67	81	94	107	121
7.5	2.01490	2.01624	2.01757	2.01890	2.02022	2.02155	2.02287	2.02419	2.02551	2.02683		13	27	40	53	66	79	93	106	119
7.6	2.02815	2.02946	2.03078	2.03209	2.03340	2.03471	2.03601	2.03732	2.03862	2.03992		13	26	39	52	65	78	92	105	118
7.7	2.04122	2.04252	2.04381	2.04511	2.04640	2.04769	2.04898	2.05027	2.05156	2.05284		13	26	39	52	65	77	90	103	116
7.8	2.05412	2.05540	2.05668	2.05796	2.05924	2.06051	2.06179	2.06306	2.06433	2.06560		13	25	38	51	64	76	89	102	115
7.9	2.06686	2.06813	2.06939	2.07065	2.07191	2.07317	2.07443	2.07568	2.07694	2.07819		13	25	38	50	63	75	88	101	113
8.0	2.07944	2.08069	2.08194	2.08318	2.08443	2.08567	2.08691	2.08815	2.08939	2.09063		12	25	37	50	62	75	87	99	112
8.1	2.09186	2.09310	2.09433	2.09556	2.09679	2.09802	2.09924	2.10047	2.10169	2.10291		12	25	37	49	61	74	86	98	110
8.2	2.10413	2.10535	2.10657	2.10779	2.10900	2.11021	2.11142	2.11263	2.11384	2.11505		12	24	36	49	61	73	85	97	109
8.3	2.11626	2.11746	2.11866	2.11986	2.12106	2.12226	2.12346	2.12465	2.12585	2.12704		12	24	36	48	60	72	84	96	108
8.4	2.12823	2.12942	2.13061	2.13180	2.13298	2.13417	2.13535	2.13653	2.13771	2.13889		12	24	36	47	59	71	83	95	107
8.5	2.14007	2.14124	2.14242	2.14359	2.14476	2.14593	2.14710	2.14827	2.14943	2.15060		12	23	35	47	58	70	82	94	105
8.6	1.15176	2.15292	2.15409	2.15524	2.15640	2.15756	2.15871	2.15987	2.16102	2.16217		12	23	35	46	58	69	81	92	104
8.7	2.16332	2.16447	2.16562	2.16677	2.16791	2.16905	2.17020	2.17134	2.17248	2.17361		11	23	34	46	57	69	80	91	103
8.8	2.17475	2.17589	2.17702	2.17816	2.17929	2.18042	2.18155	2.18267	2.18380	2.18493		11	23	34	45	57	68	79	90	102
8.9	2.18605	2.18717	2.18830	2.18942	2.19054	2.19165	2.19277	2.19389	2.19500	2.19611		11	22	34	45	56	67	78	89	101
9.0	2.19722	2.19834	2.19944	2.20055	2.20166	2.20276	2.20387	2.20497	2.20607	2.20717		11	22	33	44	55	66	77	88	99
9.1	2.20827	2.20937	2.21047	2.21157	2.21266	2.21375	2.21485	2.21594	2.21703	2.21812		11	22	33	44	55	66	77	87	98
9.2	2.21920	2.22029	2.22138	2.22246	2.22354	2.22462	2.22570	2.22678	2.22786	2.22894		11	22	32	43	54	65	76	86	97
9.3	2.23001	2.23109	2.23216	2.23324	2.23431	2.23538	2.23645	2.23751	2.23858	2.23965		11	21	32	43	53	64	75	86	96
9.4	2.24071	2.24177	2.24284	2.24390	2.24496	2.24601	2.24707	2.24813	2.24918	2.25024		11	21	32	42	53	64	74	85	95
9.5	2.25129	2.25234	2.25339	2.25444	2.25549	2.25654	2.25759	2.25863	2.25968	2.26072		10	21	31	42	52	63	73	84	94
9.6	2.26176	2.26280	2.26384	2.26488	2.26592	2.26696	2.26799	2.26903	2.27006	2.27109		10	21	31	41	52	62	73	83	93
9.7	2.27213	2.27316	2.27419	2.27521	2.27624	2.27727	2.27829	2.27932	2.28034	2.28136		10	21	31	41	51	62	72	82	92
9.8	2.28238	2.28340	2.28442	2.28544	2.28646	2.28747	2.28849	2.28950	2.29051	2.29152		10	20	30	41	51	61	71	81	91
9.9	2.29253	2.29354	2.29455	2.29556	2.29657	2.29757	2.29858	2.29958	2.30058	2.30158		10	20	30	40	50	60	70	80	90
10.0	2.30259																			

n	1	2	3	4	5	6	7	8	9
$\log_e 10^n$	2.30259	4.60517	6.90776	9.21034	11.51293	13.81551	16.11810	18.42068	20.72327

n	1	2	3	4	5	6	7	8	9
$\log_e 10^{-n}$	$\bar{3}.69741$	$\bar{5}.39483$	$\bar{7}.09224$	$\overline{10}.78966$	$\overline{12}.48707$	$\overline{14}.18449$	$\overline{17}.88190$	$\overline{19}.57932$	$\overline{21}.27673$

67